Studies in Jewish Civilization, Volume 12: Millennialism from the Hebrew Bible to the Present

Proceedings
of the Twelfth Annual Symposium
of the Philip M. and Ethel Klutznick
Chair in Jewish Civilization
October 10-11, 1999

Studies in Jewish Civilization,
Volume 12:
Millennialism from the Hebrew Bible
to the Present

Editors

Leonard J. Greenspoon
Ronald A. Simkins

The Klutznick Chair in Jewish Civilization

Center
for the Study
of Religion and Society

CREIGHTON
UNIVERSITY
PRESS

Distributed by the University of Nebraska Press

Library of Congress Cataloguing in Publication Data

Studies in Jewish Civilization, Volume 12: Millennialism from the Hebrew bible
   to the present/
   Leonard J. Greenspoon and Ronald A. Simkins, editors.
   p. c.m—(Studies in Jewish civilization, ISSN 1070-8510; 12)
   "Proceedings of the twelfth annual Symposium of the Philip M. and Ethel
   Klutznick Chair in Jewish Civilization, October 10-11, 1999" Half t.p.
   ISBN 1-881871-41-x (paper)
   1. Millennium—History, theology, criticism, interpretation, etc.
   Congresses. I. Greenspoon, Leonard J. (Leonard Jay), Simkins, Ronald A.
   II. Philip M. and Ethel Klutznick Chair in Jewish Civilization (12th : 1999:
   Creighton University) III. Series

EDITORIAL
Creighton University Press
2500 California Plaza
Omaha, NE 68178

MARKETING & DISTRIBUTION
University of Nebraska Press
233 North 8th Street
Lincoln, NE 68588-0255

Printed in the United States of America

Dedicated with love and gratitude
to our wives and daughters

Tammy, Kelsey, and Allison Simkins

Ellie, Gallit, and Talya Greenspoon

Table of Contents

Acknowledgments

The Twelfth Annual Klutznick Symposium, titled, "'The End of Days'?: Millennialism from the Hebrew Bible to the Present," took place on October 10 and 11, 1999. A year earlier, we had determined that this would be an especially appropriate topic for Fall 1999. Although Klutznick Symposia do not typically make timeliness a high priority in selecting topics—we like to think our choices are timeless!—the extraordinary attention paid to "the end of the world" by everyone from religious leaders to advertisers made the topic especially attractive. In like manner, the previous Symposium, coming as it did during the 50th anniversary year of the founding of the State of Israel, focused on "Visions of Israel from Biblical to Modern Times."

Each Klutznick Symposium continues to benefit from the concerted efforts of a number of talented individuals. For the second year in a row, I drew strength from the wise advice generously offered by Michael Linn at the Omaha Jewish Community Center, and from Ron Simkins, my Creighton colleague and director of the Creighton Center for the Study of Religion and Society.

I am especially grateful to my elder daughter Gallit, who, in a period when we were without support staff, graciously stepped in to provide spirited assistance that more than once saved the day. Editorial specialist Adrian Koesters, who came on board in December of 1999, took immediate and effective charge of the lengthy but generally smooth process through which the words of Symposium presenters ended up as chapters in this volume. Co-editor Ron Simkins and I, along with these authors, know well how large a debt we all owe to Ms. Koesters.

We are also indebted to generous individuals and organizations without whom the Symposium could not take place. To each and every one of you go our sincerest thanks and hopes that this volume fulfills the goals you had in mind when making your contribution to us:

Dorothy and Henry Riekes
The Ike and Roz Friedman Foundation
The Eve and Louis Wintroub Endowment
Dr. Jerome Bleicher
Jewish Educational and Library Services of the Omaha Jewish
   Federation (JELS)
The Henry Monsky Lodge of B'nai B'rith

The Creighton College of Arts & Sciences
The Creighton University Committee on Lectures, Films,
  and Concerts
The Norman & Bernice Harris Center for Judaic Studies
  at the University of Nebraska-Lincoln
Midwest Express Airlines.

From the vantage point of December 2001, all of the hoopla of 1999 millennial fever seems far distant, and perhaps even a bit frivolous. But it was real and represented deeply held concerns and, in some cases, fears. At this time in our personal and national histories, there is no concern more deeply held than family. With that in mind, Ron and I dedicate this volume to our wives and daughters.

Leonard J. Greenspoon, Chairholder
The Klutznick Chair in Jewish Civilization
Creighton University
December, 2001
ljgrn@creighton.edu

Editors' Introduction

Few, if any, of the participants in the Twelfth Annual Klutznick Symposium, held in the fall of 1999, entertained serious doubts that the world would continue, pretty much as it had, after January 1, 2000. More, perhaps, expressed (albeit in muted formulation) some concern about Y2K and related technological malfunctions.

But all involved, presenters and audience members alike—in addition to everyone else in the world!—had opinions, often strongly expressed ones, about the millennial expectations that were then filling the media and feeding the popular imagination. If there were ever an occasion to step back and survey a topic rationally and reasonably from a variety of perspectives, this was it. And, as has been the case in previous symposia, these invited scholars rose to the occasion.

Already in antiquity, clocking the progress (or lack of progress) in history was a human preoccupation. Whether looking backward to a golden age "at the beginning" or forward to a bright or bleak future, humans have sought to measure time in years, months, hours, minutes, and seconds (or their equivalents). Millennial thought, expressed as doomsday fear, often centers on the image of a clock winding down, ominously counting off the last few hours or minutes remaining until midnight—and destruction.

We have adopted a more hopeful image of the clock to frame this introduction. In this scenario the striking of each hour—and with it, the summary of another paper—adds something significant to our knowledge about "millennialism from the Hebrew Bible to the present."

In keeping with the focus of the Klutznick Symposia, appropriate attention is paid to this topic as it developed within Jewish contexts, but larger perspectives are by no means ignored. In their own words, drawn from their opening and concluding paragraphs, each presenter/author describes below their overall intent:

Twelve Noon: Catherine Wessinger

"It is vitally important, as we make the transition to the next temporal millennium, that we take this historical moment to understand the dynamics of millennialism, both peaceful and violent....Millennial religious movements and groups will always be with us even after we pass the year 2000 because millennialism expresses the uniquely human expectation of salvation from finitude....I hope that an enhanced public understanding of the dynamics related to millennialism will contribute to less millennial violence in the next temporal millennium."

One O'clock: W. Michael Ashcraft

"To include children in the study of millennial religions is to right a wrong, to compensate for their virtual neglect as subjects of scholarship....It was up to the children, inspired throughout their lives by the Theosophical anticipation of spiritual greatness in the dawning cycle, to find as adults their own ways to live out the new age....That they did so at all certainly reflects the power of millennial discourse to mold a lifetime."

Two O'clock: Yaakov Ariel

"The evangelical view of Jerusalem and its place in God's plans for humanity has determined their actual involvement with the city and fascination with it....Evangelical involvement with Jerusalem influenced the development and character of Jerusalem and left its mark on the social and cultural amalgam of the city....Messianic expectations are, in this case, more than mere hopes; they shape present realities and future developments."

Three O'clock: James D. Tabor

"Will the arrival of the year 2000, and the ushering in of the third millennium, turn out to be "business as usual"—with all the media hype and apocalyptic hysteria gradually fading away into the all-too-familiar flow of daily life? Or will that magical number, so full of symbolic, cultural, and religious meaning, end up signaling something far more significant—something cosmic in its implications?... At any rate, on this day, at this hour, I say to you all: 'Welcome to the new era.'"

Four O'clock: Seth Ward

"The recent arrival of the year 2000 and its attendant celebrations provide more than adequate occasion to examine how Muslims, Jews, and Christians have "numbered their days," in the hopes that this exercise will also contribute in a small way towards obtaining a "heart of wisdom"....The Jewish, Christian, and Muslim eras are often considered to date from a specific epochal event—and that is certainly how they are presented. But in each case we have found that there are arbitrary considerations which are more of a calendrical and ideological nature than simply chronological."

Five O'clock: Matthew Goff

"Christian conceptions of evil are shaped by a rich lore of legends....It is commonly held that in the end-time Antichrist will reign on earth....Where did Christianity get such ideas? Antichrist's precursors stem from the Jewish milieu out of which Christianity arose. Christianity adapted various Jewish traditions of a final adversary. From these Jewish traditions Christianity developed its own eschatological adversary who is Christ's opposite."

Six O'clock: Richard A. Freund

"The apocalyptic view of the world or "the end of days" concept in both the Hebrew Bible and rabbinic literature can be summarized as follows: it is defined by a goal which is at once the personal salvation of an individual and the cosmic salvation of the world....The dynamism provided by the apocalyptic tradition did encourage speculation and raise significant hope for many Jews in times of serious despair."

Seven O'clock: David E. Timmer

"In 1541, the Franciscan missionary friar Toribio de Benavento sent a treatise on the indigenous peoples of Mexico to his relative, the Duke of Benavente....He predicts that like Egypt, Mexico "will flower and will be filled with hermits and contemplative penitents" drawn from the ranks of the new Indian Christians....As so often in the history of hope, apocalyptic ideas carry within themselves the seeds of their own disappointment. Yet those seeds can often mature, in unexpected ways, to bear our hopes in more modest and enduring forms."

Eight O'clock: Dereck Daschke

"In 1913, a year prior to the First World War, Sigmund Freud stood in the Italian Alps with some friends who were deeply affected by a sense of the impermanence of things....Two years later, Freud reflected on the devastation brought on by the war....Freud understood that loss points not only to an ending, but towards a new beginning as well....The texts examined in this paper as well as apocalypses from the same period do not represent documents of complete and perfect mourning....These texts are concerned with the future and express it in terms of transformative ideals which draw both individuals and cultures out of the problematic past and into the real future."

Nine O'clock: Eugene V. Gallagher

"In the 1990s several groups often identified as "cults" or new religious movements used the biblical book of Revelation to give vividness, depth, and gravity to their own apocalyptic scenarios....Each developed a thoroughly eclectic and idiosyncratic system, but ties to the biblical apocalyptic tradition played an important role in each. Their experience lends support to the suspicion that for any millennial movement to succeed in a world influenced by the biblical tradition, it must develop a way of making that tradition distinctively its own."

Ten O'clock: Jerome F. Shapiro

"Cinema is the most eloquent contemporary voice or poetry for our most ancient narrative and symbolic traditions. Popular films about the bomb are the most recent manifestation of the apocalyptic narrative tradition....The essentials of Atomic Bomb Cinema have not changed; nor, in the eons that have passed, have the essentials of the apocalyptic imagination and the apocalyptic genre....Everywhere there is still suffering and oppression, and still a need for stories (in our time, moving pictures) that exhort us to survive, self-actualize, and repair or restore a fractured world."

Eleven O'clock: Brenda E. Brasher

"In Christian tradition, millennialism—the transformation of the world into a just and peaceful society—is a central component of the main story told about the end of time. In its definitive form, the story, which includes millennialism in its sweep, stretches throughout the biblical book of Revelation....The painful paradox of The *X-Files* is that, as an amalgam of New Age, New Thought, and noirish 50s paranoia embedded in a Christian subtext, it does function for many of its fans as a kind of popular culture "book" of Revelation."

Midnight: The End of Days?

At midnight on Monday October 11, 1999, the second, and last, day of the Twelfth Annual Klutznick Symposium came to an end. At midnight, December 31, 1999, the second millennium of the Common Era peacefully, if noisily, concluded. Or was it midnight, December 31, 2000?

Regardless, on January 1, the sun rose, and, thank God, it continues to do so.

Contributors

Yaakov Ariel

Department of Religious Studies
University of North Carolina, Chapel Hill
Chapel Hill, NC 27599-3225
yariel@email.unc.edu

W. Michael Ashcraft

Division of Social Science
Truman State University
Kirksville, MO 63501
washcraf@truman.edu

Brenda E. Brasher

Department of Religion
Mount Union College
Alliance, OH 44601
brashebe@muc.edu

Dereck Daschke

Division of Social Science
Truman State University
Kirksville, MO 63501
ddaschke@truman.edu

Richard A. Freund

Maurice Greenberg Center for Judaic Studies
University of Hartford
Hartford, CT 06117
freund@mail.hartford.edu

Eugene V. Gallagher

Department of Religious Studies
Connecticut College
New London, CT 06320-4196
evgal@conncoll.edu

Matthew Goff

Religious Studies Department
Yale University
New Haven, Connecticut 06511
matthew.goff@yale.edu

Jerome F. Shapiro   Faculty of Integrated Arts and Sciences
                                     Hiroshima University
                                     Higashi-Hiroshima: 739-8521
                                     jfs@hiroshima-u.ac.jp

James D. Tabor   Department of Religious Studies
                                     University of North Carolina-Charlotte
                                     Charlotte, NC 28223
                                     jdtabor@email.uncc.edu

David E. Timmer   Department of Philosophy and Religion
                                     Central College
                                     Pella, IA 50219
                                     TimmerD@central.edu

Seth Ward   495 South Jersey Street
                                     Denver, CO 80224
                                     sward@du.edu

Catherine Wessinger   Religious Studies Department
                                     Loyola University
                                     New Orleans, LA 70118
                                     wessing@loyno.edu

Studies in Jewish Civilization,
Volume 12:
Millennialismfrom the Hebrew Bible
to the Present

Proceedings
of the Twelfth Annual Symposium
of the Philip M. and Ethel Klutznick
Chair in Jewish Civilization
October 10-11, 1999

Understanding Peaceful and Violent Contemporary Millennial Movements

Catherine Wessinger

The religious patterns that are now termed "millennialism" are ancient, reaching back into biblical history and earlier. These religious patterns are expressions of an authentic human longing for "salvation", i.e., release from the limitations and suffering of the human condition. Millennialism is often stimulated by significant dates, such as the year 2000 in the Christian calendar, but millennial expectations continue to be expressed when there are no such dates to stimulate religious imaginations. In the contemporary world, however, the year 2000 has heightened millennial hopes and fears among the world's peoples who are not Christians, including Jews, Muslims, Buddhists, and even the purportedly secular Communists in the People's Republic of China. Millennialism is often benign and nonviolent, but it has also been associated with relatively small as well as massive episodes of violence. Therefore, it is vitally important, as we make the transition to the next temporal millennium, that we take this historical moment to understand the dynamics of millennialism, both peaceful and violent.[1]

Millennialism involves distinctive religious patterns. I have found the definition of "religion" as being "ultimate concern," to be functional. Robert D. Baird defines "ultimate concern" as being "the most important thing in the world" for a believer or a community of believers.[2] In millennial religions, the focus is on accomplishing salvation for a community of believers. I define "salvation" as being the desired "condition of permanent well-being."[3]

The term "millennialism" has been drawn from the Christian tradition, in which the New Testament book of Revelation predicts that the kingdom of God on earth will last one thousand years. Religious studies scholars have separated the term "millennialism" from the concept of a period of time lasting exactly one thousand years and use it to refer to common religious

1

patterns. Therefore, I define "millennialism" as the belief in an imminent transition to a collective salvation in which the elect will experience well-being, and the unpleasant limitations of the human condition will be eliminated. This collective salvation, which is millennialism's ultimate concern (the millennial goal), is often expected to be earthly, but heavenly millennial expectations are also possible. If the earthly millennial kingdom fails to appear, it is not unusual for millennialists to shift to expecting a heavenly millennial kingdom.

The two most common millennial patterns are what I call "catastrophic millennialism" and "progressive millennialism."[4] Of the two, catastrophic millennialism is the most ancient pattern. Catastrophic millennialism is belief in an imminent and cataclysmic transition to the millennial kingdom. It involves a pessimism about human beings and society. Because we are totally evil and corrupt, the old order must be swept away violently to make way for the perfect millennial kingdom. Catastrophic millennialism involves a radical dualistic worldview in which reality is seen in terms of Good battling Evil. This dualism readily translates into a sense of "us" versus "them." Many catastrophic millennialists wage their warfare spiritually using faith and prayer as their weapons, and they await divine intervention to destroy their enemies. However, some catastrophic millennialists arm themselves for self-defense during the expected tribulation; if they are attacked, they will defend themselves, as did the Branch Davidians.[5] Other catastrophic millennialists believe they are called by God to wage war against enemies to overthrow the current order and establish the millennial kingdom. This latter type of catastrophic millennialism is seen in the United States today in the violent actions of radical members of a contemporary Euro-American nativist movement,[6] who identify Jews as being the children of Satan and people of color as being animals, and who commit acts of violence against Jews, mixed race couples, homosexuals, abortion doctors and staff, and representatives of the federal government. The dominant religious view that informs this white supremacist nativist movement is a religion called Christian Identity.[7]

Progressive millennialism is a perspective that is optimistic about improvement in human nature and society. Progressive millennialism is the belief that the imminent transition to the collective salvation will occur without catastrophe. The progressive millennial belief is that humans working in accordance with a divine or superhuman plan will create the millennial kingdom. This is the millennial perspective being promoted by Pope John Paul II at the end of the 1990s, and his teaching is consistent with Vatican II's emphasis on a "preferential option for the poor."[8] Progressive millennialism is the perspective of the Protestant Social Gospel movement that seeks to create God's kingdom on earth by means of social work and reform. Within contemporary New Age thought there are strong themes of progressive movement into the Age of Aquarius, as a critical mass of human beings achieve personal spiritual transformation; however, some New Age teachers also stress themes of catastrophic changes occurring prior to the establishment of the New Age.

Catastrophic millennialism and progressive millennialism are not mutually exclusive. If individuals and groups experience hardship, oppression, and persecution, they will stress catastrophic millennial themes. Persecution is a strong promoter of catastrophic millennial expectations as seen in the history of Judaism. When individuals and groups experience some social acceptance and prosperity, the emphasis on imminent divine cataclysm to save the faithful and to punish their enemies subsides, and progressive themes are emphasized.

It would appear that progressive millennialism is not likely to promote violence, stressing as it does the interconnectedness and unity of humanity, but sometimes believers in progress take violent actions to speed up progress, thus becoming revolutionary progressive millennialists. Examples of revolutionary progressive millennial movements include the Nazis of Europe, the Maoists of China, and the Khmer Rouge of Cambodia.[9] Revolutionary progressive millennialists possess the same radical dualistic perspective as catastrophic millennialists, which has the effect of dehumanizing and demonizing those who are identified as enemies. Dehumanizing or demonizing groups of people makes it seem legitimate to kill them.

Often millennial movements will have a "nativist" orientation. A "nativist millennial movement" consists of people who feel under attack by a foreign, colonizing government that is destroying their traditional way of life and is removing them from their land. Nativists long for a return to an idealized past golden age. Numerous nativists have identified themselves with the oppressions and deliverance of the Israelites as described in the Christian Old Testament.[10] Thus, there have been self-identified "Israelites" in many parts of the world, including Africa, Latin America, and North America. Identity Christians in the United States today believe that non-Semitic white people are the true Israelites, given the promised land of America by Yahweh. Euro-Americans are of course not the original inhabitants of North America, but they regard themselves as such. Rural white Protestants, in particular, feel oppressed by federal bureaucracies that seize their property and remove them from their land, traditional way of life, and means of livelihood. Nativists often feel resentment toward ethnic groups perceived as benefitting from association with the dominant government and economic system, and they frequently direct violence against the hated ethnic group and seek to remove them from their privileged social positions. Members of the contemporary Euro-American nativist movement often believe that Jews are engaged in a global conspiracy aimed at the domination and eradication of Christians, who according to Christian Identity, can only be white. The Euro-American nativists believe that a Zionist Occupation Government (ZOG) controls American government, media, and economic institutions.[11]

Nativist millennial movements take on all the possible millennial permutations, peaceful and violent. Nativist millennialism can take the form of either catastrophic millennialism or progressive millennialism. Catastrophic nativist millennialists may either await divine intervention to remove their oppressors, or they may become terrorists and revolutionaries who fight to eliminate their perceived oppressors.

Leaders of millennial movements often possess "charisma," defined in religious studies as having access to an unseen source of authority that is considered to be divine or superhuman. This unseen source of authority may be God, angels, masters, ancestors, or, increasingly these days, extraterrestrials. Charisma is socially constructed, and an individual will not possess charisma unless other people believe his or her claim to have access to an unseen source of authority.

Both prophets and messiahs have charisma. A "prophet" is someone who is believed to receive revelation from a divine or superhuman source. A prophet is commonly regarded as speaking God's words. Some prophets will be perceived as messiahs, but not all prophets are messiahs.

I use the term "messiah" to refer to an individual who is believed to possess the power to create the millennial kingdom. A messiah is a prophet in the sense of receiving revelation, but a messiah is also a special individual empowered to create the millennial kingdom.

Catastrophic millennialism and progressive millennialism may or may not involve messianism. A messiah is not necessary in a millennial movement. For example, passages recorded in the Quran speak of an imminent "Day of Doom," on which the stars, the sun, and the moon will fall from the sky, the earth will quake, the graves will be opened and the dead resurrected, and everyone will be judged. All this will be done by Allah no messiah will be needed. Nonetheless, messianic expectations developed later in Islam, especially in the Shi'ite expectation of the twelfth imam, the mahdi. Some Sunni Muslims expect the second coming of Jesus Christ. Likewise, progressive millennial movements may or may not have their prophets and messiahs.[12]

Millennialists who become involved in violence are most often catastrophic millennialists. Catastrophic millennial groups that become involved in violence are not all alike. It is important to distinguish three types of violent catastrophic millennial groups.

First, there are the "assaulted millennial groups." They are assaulted by persons in mainstream society because the believers' religious views and actions are misunderstood, feared, and despised. The group is assaulted because it is mistakenly thought to be dangerous to society. The group might be assaulted by law enforcement agents or by civilians. Today, such a group is likely to be labeled "cult" or "sect," both of which have become highly pejorative terms. The Mormons in nineteenth-century America, the Lakota Sioux at Wounded Knee, and the Branch Davidians of Waco, Texas, are examples of assaulted millennial groups.[13]

Second, "fragile millennial groups" become involved in violence. Members of fragile millennial groups initiate violent acts to preserve their ultimate concern, which is endangered by stresses within the group combined with the experience of "cultural opposition"[14] from the media, government agencies, former members, and concerned family members. Often the leader is a significant source of the group's fragility. The violence of a fragile group may be directed inwardly, outwardly, or both. Jonestown (murders and suicides in 1978), the Solar Temple (murders and suicides in 1994, 1995, 1997), and Heaven's Gate (group suicide in 1997) were fragile millennial groups.[15]

Third, there are revolutionary millennial movements possessing ideologies or theologies that motivate believers to commit violent acts to overthrow the old order so as to create the millennial kingdom. Revolutionary millennialists believe their violence is mandated by a divine or superhuman plan. As discussed above, revolutionary millennial movements may either be progressive or catastrophic in their dominant orientations. When a revolutionary millennial movement is not socially dominant, as is the case with the contemporary Euro-American nativist movement, its most fervent believers resort to terrorism. Many participants in the Euro-American nativist movement, such as the Montana Freemen,[16] hope their actions will spark the "second American revolution," but so far the majority of Americans and even their colleagues in the diffuse Patriot movement have declined to join them in revolutionary violence. When a revolutionary millennial movement is socially dominant, the violence reaches a massive scale, as demonstrated by the Nazis, Maoists, and the Khmer Rouge.

Millennial religious movements and groups will always be with us even after we pass the year 2000 because millennialism expresses the uniquely human expectation of salvation from finitude. Millennialism expresses the most cherished hopes and most ingrained fears of humanity. Even millennialism's radical dualism and its tendency to scapegoat groups of people who are envied and feared are, unfortunately, all too human.

Millennial beliefs are strong motivators to action. Millennialism can motivate people to work to transform themselves, their families, and communities. Millennialism can motivate people to found new religions and nations. Millennialism can motivate people either to withdraw from what is seen as evil society or to attack it.

I hope that an enhanced public understanding of the dynamics related to millennialism will contribute to less millennial violence in the next temporal millennium. Jim Jones' sign hanging in the Jonestown pavillion quoted Santayana as saying, "Those who do not remember the past are condemned to repeat it."[17] As we stand on the edge of time marking one temporal millennium from the next, it is time that we begin to learn the lessons of history regarding millennialism.

NOTES

[1]See Catherine Wessinger, ed., *Millennialism, Persecution, and Violence: Historical Cases* (Syracuse: Syracuse University Press, 2000), and *How the Millennium Comes Violently: From Jonestown to Heaven's Gate* (New York: Seven Bridges, 2000).
[2]Robert D. Baird, *Category Formation and the History of Religions* (The Hague: Mouton, 1971).
[3]Catherine Wessinger, "Millennial Terms," <http://www.loyno.edu/~wessing>.
[4]See Catherine Wessinger, "Millennialism With and Without the Mayhem: Catastrophic and Progressive Expectations," in *Millennium, Messiahs, and Mayhem: Contemporary Apocalyptic Movements,* ed. Thomas Robbins and Susan J. Palmer (New York: Routledge, 1997), 47-59.
[5]Wessinger, *How the Millennium Comes Violently,* 56-119; Stuart A. Wright, ed., *Armageddon in Waco: Critical Perspectives on the Branch Davidian Conflict* (Chicago: University of Chicago Press, 1995); James D. Tabor and Eugene V. Gallagher, *Why Waco? Cults and the Battle for Religious Freedom in America*

(Berkeley: University of California Press, 1995).

[6]For discussions of the Euro-American nativist millennial movement, see Wessinger, *Millennialism, Persecution, and Violence* and Wessinger, *How the Millennium Comes Violently.*

[7]Wessinger, *How the Millennium Comes Violently,* 177-8; Michael Barkun, *Religion and the Racist Right: The Origins of the Christian Identity Movement* (rev. ed.; Chapel Hill: University of North Carolina Press, 1997).

[8]*Ad Gentes,* "Decree on the Mission Activity of the Church," Pope Pius VI, December 7, 1965.

[9]See the following chapters in Wessinger, *Millennialism, Persecution, and Violence*: Robert Ellwood, "Nazism as a Millennialist Movement," 241-60, Scott Lowe, "Western Millennial Ideology Goes East: The Taiping Revolution and Mao's Great Leap Forward," 220-40, Richard C. Salter, "Time, Authority, and Ethics in the Khmer Rouge: Elements of the Millennial Vision in the Year Zero," 281-98.

[10]For example, black South Africans who called themselves "Israelites" were massacred by South African police at Bulhoek in 1921. See Christine Steyn, "Millenarian Tragedies in South Africa: The Xhosa Cattle-Killing Movement and the Bulhoek Massacre," in *Millennialism, Persecution, and Violence: Historical Cases* (ed. C. Wessinger; Syracuse: Syracuse University Press, 2000), 185-202.

[11]See the following chapters in Wessinger, *Millennialism, Persecution, and Violence*: Catherine Wessinger, "The Interacting Dynamics of Millennial Beliefs, Persecution, and Violence," 12-14; Jeffrey Kaplan, "Real Paranoids Have Real Enemies: The Genesis of the ZOG Discourse in the American National Socialist Subculture," 299-322, Jean E. Rosenfeld, "The Justus Freemen Standoff: The Importance of the Analysis of Religion in Avoiding Violent Outcomes," 323-44. Also see Wessinger, *How the Millennium Comes Violently,* 158-217.

[12]Catherine Wessinger, *Annie Besant and Progressive Messianism* (Lewiston, NY: Edwin Mellen Press, 1988).

[13]See the following chapters in all in Wessinger, *Millennialism, Persecution, and Violence*: Grant Underwood, "Millennialism, Persecution, and Violence: The Mormons," 43-61, Michelene E. Pesantubbee, "From Vision to Violence: The Wounded Knee Massacre," 62-81, Eugene V. Gallagher, "'Theology Is Life and Death': David Koresh on Violence, Persecution, and the Millennium," 82-100. See also Wessinger, *How the Millennium Comes Violently,* 56-119.

[14]John R. Hall, "Public Narratives and the Apocalyptic Sect: From Jonestown to Mt. Carmel," in *Armageddon in Waco: Critical Perspectives on the Branch Davidian Conflict* (ed. S. Wright; Chicago: University of Chicago Press, 1995), 207.

[15]See the following chapters in all in Wessinger, *Millennialism, Persecution, and Violence*: Rebecca Moore, "'American as Cherry Pie': Peoples Temple and Violence in America," 121-37; Massimo Introvigne, "The Magic of Death: The Suicides of the Solar Temple," 138-57. See also Wessinger, *How the Millennium Comes*

Violently, 30-55, 218-52.

[16]Wessinger, *How the Millennium Comes Violently,* 158-217; Jean Rosenfeld, "The Justus Freemen Standoff: The Importance of Analysis of Religion in Avoiding Violent Outcomes," in Wessinger, *Millennialism, Persecution, and Violence,* 323-44.

[17]See photograph in Wessinger, *How the Millennium Comes Violently,* 14.

The Dawn of the New Cycle:
Millennial Hopes and Pedagogical Realities

W. Michael Ashcraft

In the introduction to a ground-breaking collection of studies titled *Children in New Religions,* Susan J. Palmer and Charlotte E. Hardman state that the "study of children in new religious movements is largely uncharted terrain with intriguing opportunities for future researchers."[1] Although their book is about religious movements from the late 1960s to the present, their statement is also true for children in alternative religious groups preceding the 1960s. A few studies do shed light on experiences of children and images of childhood associated with various alternative or communitarian religions in times past, such as the Mormons, the Shakers, the Jehovah's Witnesses, and the Hutterites. A spate of studies investigate children in Christian fundamentalist homes and schools. But much more could and should be done.[2]

This is especially true in millennial religious movements, where the values that adults cherish are often at odds with the prevailing attitudes and assumptions of the cultures in which they live. Those who study such movements, either contemporary or historical, should consider children and images of childhood for two reasons. First, children are valuable in and of themselves. Along with their parents and other adults, they are co-residents, co-participants, and co-beneficiaries of millennial communities and teachings. To include them in the study of millennial religions is to right a wrong, to compensate for their virtual neglect as subjects of scholarship.

Children are often overlooked in studies of millennial movements because they are typically not literate testifiers to their own experiences; that is, they leave behind few documents that researchers can read and interpret. Also, adults, not children, are the representatives empowered to speak for millennial groups. Children are kept in the background, safely tucked away in classrooms and nurseries. In addition, they are not there by choice, as adults usually are.

A second reason for focusing on children in millennial groups is that such study can show us how the original millennial ideology that inspired the formation of these groups alters as time passes. The children become torchbearers for millennial hope, but, as they grow to adulthood, they express this hope in ways that their parents cannot anticipate. To follow the maturation of children in millennial groups is to track changes in millennial expectation and belief.

Catherine Wessinger makes a useful distinction in types of millennial groups. She uses the phrase "progressive millennialism" to denote the millennial hope that a golden era will arrive through "human cooperation with a divine (or superhuman) will." In contrast to cataclysmic millennialists, who expect natural and supernatural events of gigantic proportions to rupture the normal flow of time, progressive millennialists believe that a utopian future will unfold as humanity works within sacred history to transform society.[3]

What happens when a progressive millennial group's founding generation passes its ideals on to the next generation? Theosophists who lived at Point Loma, or Lomaland, in California provide an interesting case study. The children who grew to adulthood there manifested the potential for innovation in millennial expectation that was inherent in Theosophy. This quality would not be evident if we considered only those adults who first advocated this particular brand of millennialism. However, when we take the children into account, we can see how Theosophical millennialism evolved.

The Theosophists of Lomaland were a group of late nineteenth-century middle-class enthusiasts who followed the teachings of Helena P. Blavatsky (1831-1891), founder of the Theosophical Society.[4] Blavatsky and subsequent Theosophical spokespersons said that all religions teach the same fundamental truth: the world is interconnected, all the parts working together in a harmonious whole. There is no God, in the Jewish or Christian sense, but a divine impulse in the very warp and woof of reality, which emanates as the manifest world through grand cycles of time lasting millions of years. Human beings are egos or souls, continually reincarnating lifetime after lifetime, and doing so in vast groups, or life waves, which travel through time together. As one made his or her way through these reincarnations, argued Blavatsky, one became more spiritually and morally mature, capable of greater selflessness and service to others. Some souls eventually reach a level of maturity that qualitatively marks them as adepts, advanced beyond their contemporaries in spiritual matters. Yet other souls are even more accomplished, transcending the limits of time and space to shepherd life waves through their cycles. These greater entities were called Masters. Blavatsky said that she was contacted by Masters throughout her life and given many teachings from them to dispense to others.[5]

In the Theosophical perspective, the individual was part of a grand cosmic drama, one that would eventually be proven by modern-day science, yet one that also preserved a sense of profound mystery and transcendence for many in Blavatsky's day. The world, said the Masters, is always more vast and complex than our feeble human minds dare imagine. At its heart, however, was a very simple and comforting idea: universal brotherhood. The natural tendency of the universe was to evolve toward greater harmony and cooperation. Likewise, in human society the future promised inevitable progress in eradicating social inequality and injustice as greater numbers of people drew upon their innate moral and spiritual abilities to fashion a utopia on earth.

Blavatsky's writings are an intriguing mix of Hinduism, Buddhism, evolutionism, and comparative religion. In the late nineteenth century she captured the imagination of many Europeans and Americans; indeed, she captivated them. Some were willing to act on this new vision of the world by moving their families to a remote location: Point Loma. Situated at the northern end of the peninsula west of San Diego, across San Diego Bay, these Theosophists established a community in the scrub brush and sand. When they arrived, they felt like latter-day Columbuses and Magellans, charting a new world and establishing an exciting future. And they called their community Lomaland.[6]

To understand how these people got from the writings of Blavatsky to California, we must briefly delve into Theosophical history. Blavatsky and Henry Steel Olcott (1832-1907)[7] founded the Theosophist Society in New York City in 1875. Three years later they journeyed to India, reportedly on the Masters' orders, to make important connections with Sinhalese Buddhists and Hindus on the Indian subcontinent. They left behind a fledgling organization that was finally taken over by one of the original members of the Society, William Q. Judge (1851-1896), an Irish immigrant and attorney.[8] He rebuilt the American Theosophical movement almost single-handedly. At the time of his death in 1896, six thousand Theosophists supported lodges in major urban areas and in several smaller cities across the United States. Most members were religiously liberal, but culturally conservative. They supported reformist causes that middle-class Americans from antebellum times to the late nineteenth century found appealing. They were the "status-inconsistent"; their outward lives seemed comfortable, even prosperous by the economic standards of the day, but on their inward journeys to spiritual wholeness they cried out for something more satisfying than the popular religious messages of their time.[9] Theosophy met this need, and many embraced it with the fervor of converts to newfound faith.

Judge's successor was a middle-class reformer turned Theosophist named Katherine Tingley (1847-1929).[10] She shifted the movement's focus to reform activities, especially those related to children. Under her direction, Theosophists expanded Theosophical Sunday Schools begun during the Judge period.[11] The curriculum of these groups borrowed from the pedagogical philosophies then transforming American education, especially at the kindergarten and early grade levels.[12] But their purpose was to socialize children in a particular way, helping them to understand universal brotherhood and their place in it. A simple song sung by several generations of Lomaland children expresses this sense of interconnectedness:
Happy little sunbeams
Darting through the blue,
Even little sunbeams
Have a work to do.
Shining at our brightest,
We with radiance clad,
Help to make the rainbow,
Make the great world glad.[13]

Tingley also operated a home for urban children during the summer of 1897 in Pleasant Valley, New Jersey, away from the crime, dirt, noise, and overcrowding of New York's street life. Like other child-saving measures, this one included the teaching of values such as thrift, cooperation, and honesty among the children[14]. It had a millennial basis as well. One Theosophical writer, reporting on the closing ceremony at the home, said that although this cycle had closed, another was opening. The force garnered in this cycle would help make the next cycle's wave even greater. One of the adult care givers at the home was so moved by her experience at the beginning of the next cycle that she announced at the closing ceremony "that she felt as though she could move the universe."[15]

These references to opening and closing cycles come from the writings of Blavatsky. She describes the life waves of reincarnated souls as passing through many phases. At the beginning of each cycle, these souls are in a relatively spiritual state. As the cycle progresses, they become more engrossed in matter. Toward the end of the cycle, they once again achieve spiritual form. Blavatsky believed that the bulk of humanity was currently at a point where the material and spiritual were balanced. But they were also living during the spiritual upswing of a related cycle.[16] A soul now born in human form, she said, "will find itself as free from matter and all its qualities as it was in the beginning; having gained in addition the experience and wisdom, the fruition of all its personal lives, without their evil and temptations."[17] Blavatsky was confident that these souls would gain the upper hand, morally speaking, because karma, the law of cause and effect, ultimately led to justice and greater compassion. As more and more souls did and thought more and greater good, they increased the chances of good prevailing at ever higher levels.[18]

Blavatsky used terms from Indian thought to identify phases within each cycle. Such terms originally appeared in epic and Puranic literature that described four ages within cosmic cycles. Each cycle began with an "age of truth," followed by an era when virtue diminished and death and labor entered the human realm. The third period of a cycle witnessed an increase in evil that culminated in the closing age, or Kali Yuga, a dark time of discord marked by the triumph of evil. Indian sources identified Kali Yuga with the present, asserting that it began in 3102 BCE, the traditional date of the wars described in the Indian epic, the *Mahabharata*.[19]

Blavatsky imposed this four-part scheme upon the cycles in Theosophical doctrine. She claimed that the world was currently in a Kali Yuga: "Of all past centuries [the nineteenth century] is the most smilingly cruel, wicked, immoral, boastful, and incongruous."[20] But the present was also the threshold of a better era: "We are in the very midst of the Egyptian darkness of Kali-Yuga, the 'Black Age,' the first 5,000 years of which, its dreary first cycle, is preparing to close on the world between 1897 or 1898."[21] During either of these years a new cycle would dawn. Blavatsky arrived at this date by calculating that the Kali Yuga, supposedly begun in 3102 BCE, would last 5000 years. Although it would continue for hundreds of thousands of years into the future, the turning point toward higher spiritual development was to occur near the close of the nineteenth century. Afterward, incarnating souls would display increasing spiritual wisdom and compassion, their altruistic actions having greater impact on one another than those in the ages immediately preceding our own.[22]

Blavatsky's millennial vision resembles the progressive millennialism described in Wessinger's work. For the Theosophists, time was cyclical rather than linear. As Wessinger notes, millennial movements can exist within frames of reference that conceive time cyclically. Many millennial movements in Buddhist, Taoist, and Hindu cultures, for example, also understand the universe cyclically. So did Annie Besant, the Theosophical leader who was the subject of Wessinger's earlier work.[23]

Those Theosophists who moved to Lomaland interpreted various events during 1897 and 1898 as evidence that a new cycle had dawned could be found in their own annual Theosophical convention in Chicago on February 18, 1898. At this meeting they elected Tingley as their leader and gave her autocratic control of the Theosophical Society and all its auxiliary organizations. In Tingley and this new order, the new cycle would have both a harbinger and embodiment, they believed.[24]

Shortly before this crucial convention, Tingley and an entourage of selected followers made a world tour, cultivating contacts among European Theosophists and starting new local groups of Theosophists wherever they went. During this tour, she also garnered support for her fondest hope and dream, Lomaland. She envisioned it as a nursery, where souls incarnated in the bodies of infants and children would be nourished, spiritually and morally as well as physically. The name of the institution founded there was the School for the Revival of the Lost Mysteries of Antiquity (SRLMA). The Theosophists who founded it assumed that their teachings would be continuous with those of the ancient Greek mystery schools, which taught the timeless truth of Theosophy by other names. But at Lomaland, children would also realize their higher selves, or true spiritual natures, through moral training and education in the classics of western civilization. Tingley proclaimed during the cornerstone-laying ceremony for the SRLMA that: Through this School & its branches the children of the race will be taught the laws of physical life & the laws of physical, moral & mental health. They will learn to live in harmony with nature. They will become compassionate lovers of all that breathes.[25]

When they first arrived at Lomaland,[26] Theosophists had the zeal, optimism, and energy typical of so many other religious believers who thought that they were witness to the dawning of a new age. Jan Shipps found similar characteristics in the earliest period of Mormon settlement in Utah. The early Mormons believed that they were suspended in time, the sacred and non-sacred meeting on earth in human community. Many previous patterns of daily life were either suspended or gave way to new patterns.[27]

And so it was at Lomaland in those early days. Work took place around the clock, rather than during segmented portions of the day.

Residents ate meals hastily so that they could return to their tasks. Meetings occurred at various times of night, and those in attendance dressed in simple white garments.[28] A speaker at an early conference held at Lomaland told his listeners: "We are the center of it all. The world is a point in space and we are the nucleus of that world. It is with us that the future of humanity rests."[29] The "center" he referred to was Lomaland. Residents believed that the beginning of the new cycle was most apparent there, "the dynamic centre of the spiritual life of the earth."[30]

The SRLMA never materialized as an institution. As the years passed, a series of educational efforts, called Raja Yoga schools, were the venues for the training and socialization of children. The term "Raja Yoga" comes from the Hindu classic, Patanjali's *Yoga Sutra*, written between 100 BCE and 500 CE. Patanjali described an advanced state of meditation dependent upon ethical behavior as well as mental and physical disciplines.[31] Theosophists read the *Yoga Sutra* avidly. Judge recommended Patanjali and the inner development of Raja Yoga to readers of his magazine, *The Path*. He transformed Patanjali's pithy sayings, which codified yogic practice, into a convenient westernized program of moral and spiritual development devoid of the metaphysical trappings of either Eastern or Western religious traditions. Raja Yoga assumed a timeless free-floating quality, detached from cultural or historical expression. In Judge's hands, the raja yoga of Patanjali became a means to higher moral sensitivity and deeper appreciation of one's inner psychological landscape.[32] Therefore, when Tingley and Lomalanders advertised the SRLMA, they asserted that its purpose was to:

revive a knowledge of the Sacred Mysteries of Antiquity by promoting the physical, mental, moral and spiritual education and welfare of the people of all countries.[33]

The Raja Yoga system developed as the population of Lomaland grew. Thirty-two children were present during the first year, 1900, mostly sons and daughters of adult residents at the site. The Raja Yoga schools eventually educated as many as 600-700 children (or more) during a period of over forty years. As time passed, Lomaland settled into daily routines for adults and Raja Yoga children alike. The millennial fervor of those first years was not forgotten, but receded into the background as Lomalanders toiled to meet the challenges of raising children and sustaining their community.[34]

Routinization of millennial life found expression in the Raja Yoga system of education. Teaching assignments were flexible and multiple:

most teachers taught several subjects and had responsibilities outside the classroom, such as leading groups of children on nature walks, directing them in gardening, and providing private tutorials. In the 1920s, if not before, older students assumed teaching and care giving responsibilities, while continuing their high school or college-level studies. The curriculum also changed. As adults with diverse skills and talents moved to Lomaland, the children benefitted from many different classroom opportunities. They learned classical and foreign languages, literature, history, and the arts. Instruction in the sciences was weakest, although several trained engineers living at Lomaland taught mathematics. The music program rapidly expanded. Most Raja Yoga children learned to play one or more musical instruments and sang in one or more choral groups.[35]

Although children's residences also changed as time passed, group living remained constant. Girls of the Raja Yoga School moved into dormitory rooms in the central building on the grounds, the Academy, in 1904. Boys lived in circular group homes, first erected as tents when Theosophists moved to Lomaland and later rendered permanent with the addition of wooden siding. These homes contained a central room for daily activities, with beds around the outer periphery. As the children grew to adulthood, they either became group home caretakers or, if married, lived in bungalows that dotted the Lomaland site.[36]

The children of the Raja Yoga educational system matured in a protected environment. A former resident compared it to raising flowers in a hothouse.[37] This protection was deliberate. Lomaland parents and educators believed that "a pure moral atmosphere" inspired the children to goodness and nobility.[38] These adults advocated an environment that shielded the children from "the usual external distractions," isolating them mentally and physically.[39] Most children rarely left the site, unless they were in a group or accompanied by an adult. They did not read newspapers or other materials from outside Lomaland. Instead, adults culled items of interest from the newspapers for them.[40]

Intensive activity also characterized the learning environment at Lomaland. Children had duties around the grounds: gardening, sweeping and cleaning, assisting adult residents, providing kitchen labor. Their efforts replayed the activity of urban children in the Pleasant Valley home and Intensive resembled the activity that child reformers believed was beneficial to urban children placed in rural settings. They also attended classes, played sports, and performed in musical and dramatic productions with adult residents.

Although much of their lives was scripted throughout each day, Lomaland children did have some unscheduled time. "When we played we played with abandon," one former Raja Yoga student fondly remembered.[41] Another recalled that her group leader, an orphan transferred as an infant from a Theosophical orphanage in Buffalo to Lomaland, and now grown to young adulthood, knew all the best places to play at Lomaland. Often she led her group of girls into a wooded area to play "Follow the Arrow." In this version of hide-and-seek, one group left small chalkboards marked with arrows along their trail. Twenty minutes later the other group followed the trail in search of the first. On other occasions their leader took them to a sand slide in one of the canyons leading from the Point Loma plateau to the seashore, where they spent many happy hours.[42]

The children observed daily silence in order to concentrate on their tasks and meditate on their moral progress without interruption. One former Raja Yoga student's memories typify those regarding silence. He recalled that they could not talk at meals, in class, even in their group homes.[43] But they did not observe total silence. Appointed times in the schedule permitted talking.

Certain behaviors resulted in isolation as a form of punishment. For example, boys caught masturbating, or accused of the same, lived apart from younger boys. In general, punishment consisted of reduced contact with peers. One child, who as an adult said that her behavior was more unruly than most others, recalled being kept in her room in the Academy, tied to the bed for days at a time after trying to run away with another girl. When her punishment period ended, she did not return to the girls in her group. Instead, an adult accompanied her throughout each day until she left Lomaland at age sixteen. Although hers was an unusual situation, the practice of isolating her from peers resembled incidents recalled by others.[44]

These measures suggest a dichotomy between purity and pollution implicit in the Point Loma social structure. The Theosophists of Lomaland interpreted their community as the center for the coming new cycle. To them, Lomaland was the world in microcosm. Sexual indiscretion and satisfaction of selfish desires reflected one's lower nature, which warred with the higher or permanent nature. This lower nature threatened the structure of the Lomaland environment, just as it threatened the order of the human community in the larger world. When these behaviors became manifest in the lives of the children, the adults interpreted them as dangerous. Danger required response, and in Point Loma's case, they responded by isolating the polluters.[45]

Theosophists hoped that a moral child would result from this educational environment. In an affidavit sworn in 1919, a Lomaland adult claimed that the Raja Yoga system instructed children in morality far more effectively than any other available educational philosophy. She had studied the methods of John Dewey and other educators. None satisfied her until she met Tingley. She appreciated Tingley's system because "its object was not merely to cure defects already marring the life, nor to apply remedies after moral disease had gained a foothold...but to prevent the defects of moral blight in the first place."[46]

Lomaland educators and parents believed that Raja Yoga strengthened the child "to resist temptation." As noted earlier, Lomaland Theosophists were consistent with many values of American public education in the nineteenth century in their hope that their children would internalize the moral standards provided for them in a group setting. The goal was "a sort of interior morality."[47] The motivation was not fear of punishment, but inward desire to behave correctly. This moral attitude resulted in "self-control, alertness, obedience, health, [and an] even temper."[48] The moral child felt no jealousy when another child received praise. He or she achieved goals without acknowledging the achievement. One writer called this demeanor "the Point Loma type of character," which appeared "chiefly among the children of the Raja Yoga School."[49]

Raja Yoga was progressive millennialism, Lomaland-style. The first generation of Lomalanders hoped that their children would seed the larger society with good deeds and moral intentions, acting as "a healthy nucleus of future humanity."[50] These new-cycle individuals would avoid the temptations of society with ease because they entered it with knowledge of their own innate divinity. In the far future, it was assumed, the souls they helped to mature in this present incarnation would transform the world, making universal brotherhood a daily fact of life for the millions who lived in the many cultures of the world.[51]

However, the initial generation of Lomalanders had few, if any, specific ideas about how their charges would affect society. They merely assumed that moral goodness and spiritual acuity would work themselves out in the lives of Lomaland children in whatever ways were best, trusting that karma would see to the triumph of good over evil in the long run. Here was both the promise and curse of Lomaland's progressive millennialism. Since the adults at Lomaland were not preparing either themselves or their children for a future cataclysmic threat to social and cosmic order, they had no focal point for future hopes. In other words, there was no specific goal for which they were training their children, and they could not accurately predict how their children would conceptualize and embody the new life within. Instead, they looked to an inchoate but brightening future in which their children would be moral and spiritual pathfinders.

Not surprisingly, Raja Yoga children who grew to adulthood expressed their moral and spiritual lessons in various ways. Several of them remained formally committed to Theosophy throughout their lives. The organization that inherited the Lomaland tradition is called the Theosophical Society of America, headquartered in Altadena, California. Their current president, Grace F. Knoche, was a Raja Yoga from birth. The Society holds public meetings, publishes Theosophical classics, and provides for many spiritual seekers a way station en route to deeper reflection and enlightenment.[52] Another group of Theosophists with strong ties to Lomaland is Point Loma Publications, a San Diego press run by former Raja Yoga children at Lomaland.[53] Many of the people associated with both of these groups are elderly, and their numbers dwindle with each passing year.

Among those who wholeheartedly embraced the Raja Yoga morality, some exhibited a didactic, confident attitude. Raja Yoga teachers tried to avoid producing priggish, self-righteous individuals, but the system sometimes encouraged these qualities. One Raja Yoga child, grown to young adulthood, published a scathing denunciation of young men who smoked cigarettes and drank alcohol, warning that their flirtation with these vices could lead to more serious transgression.[54] Another frowned upon snacks between meals and associated poor eating habits with moral corruption.[55] One former Raja Yoga student who later became a psychotherapist suggested that the children whom he knew in the post-Tingley period, who grew to young adulthood under the Raja Yoga system, were conformist: they avoided innovation or risks and obeyed authority without question.[56] A group of Raja Yoga students in their teens, who journeyed with Tingley to Europe in 1913, seemingly choreographed this ingrained conformity when they strolled one evening in a Bremerhaven park. They walked in groups of two or three, talking and laughing, forming a large circle. A young woman in the group later recalled: "For quite some time we walked around only one way, until we were nearly dizzy, until finally I decided I was tired of going that way, so turned around, and bumped into all the other groups, so they turned around too, and thought what a good idea it was." This conformist thesis is probably true to some extent, but should not be pushed too far. After all, the young woman who reversed the direction of the promenade was herself a lifelong Raja Yoga student. Her initiative was also a quality valued by her parents and teachers.[57]

Other Raja Yoga students left Theosophical life behind when they moved away from the Lomaland site. Many of them remained bitter and angry about some aspects of their Lomaland childhoods. One of the most negative portrayals included comments like, "I can say that from my fourth to my fifteenth year I never experienced real love. The love of childhood simply did not exist for me," and "We divided up the world between 'us' and 'them.' If you wanted to criticize someone else, the fault was in you."[58] Often the resentment felt by adults who grew up at Lomaland was directed toward specific adults who abused their power, subjecting children to humiliating and painful ordeals in the name of moral development. How frequently such abuse occurred is impossible to gauge based upon anecdotal evidence, but the leadership of the Lomaland community would certainly not have condoned the more extreme measures that some children reported years later.

Falling somewhere between acceptance and rejection of Raja Yoga ideology were individuals who selectively incorporated elements of the Theosophical world view held by Lomalanders. Their efforts help us to see how the millennial expectations of a new humanity among the first generation of Lomalanders developed in interesting ways. For example, Judith Tyberg was a Raja Yoga child from birth. Her diaries reveal that as a young woman she wanted desperately to be accepted by Tingley as a true "Raja Yoga." She taught small children in her early twenties, later studying Sanskrit and Hindu philosophy under Tingley's successor, a self-taught polymath named Gottfried de Purucker. In the 1940s, the Theosophical community at Lomaland moved to Covina, then outside of Los Angeles. In that same decade, they also struggled over leadership succession. Tyberg was among the losers in this conflict. She was ejected from the Theosophical Society and, as a free agent, made her way to India to study at Hindu University in Benaras from 1947 to 1949. While in India, she encountered the teachings of Aurobindo Ghose and had sessions with Aurobindo's consort, Mirra Alfassa (or the Mother), at Aurobindo's ashram in Pondicherry. Tyberg returned to the United States and established the East West Cultural Center in Los Angeles, which she directed until her death in 1980. Her eclectic acceptance of various Asian religious perspectives grew out of her Theosophical awareness of the truth in all religions. But she embraced Aurobindo in particular, whose optimistic vision of a future guided by the supermental, as the next stage in human evolution, resembles the progressive millennial hopes of the Lomalanders, who also foresaw advanced humanity evolving in the future.[59]

Other former Raja Yoga students who fall somewhere between extreme advocacy and complete rejection of the Lomaland heritage were Sven Hildor and Marguerite Lemke Barton, who met and married at Lomaland. As teenagers, they were actively involved in musical and theatrical performances, holiday celebrations, and other events in the life of the Lomaland community. As young adults, they helped to raise and educate younger Raja Yoga children. They left Lomaland in 1929 because they disagreed with some of the harsher measures taken by Tingley and other leaders in the running of the community. They earned bachelors degrees at the University of California, Los Angeles, then opened the Barton School in Topanga, California, in 1932.[60] One of their former Lomaland teachers admitted that the Bartons carried "out many of the ideals I have had about education." The Barton School replayed many of the Raja Yoga educational activities perfected at Lomaland, but also departed in significant ways from Raja Yoga life.

Their school had a "wholesome country atmosphere," with cows giving fresh whole milk, a garden providing vegetables, and fruit trees providing fresh fruit. Lomaland also had gardens and a fruit orchard. The curriculum also resembled that at Lomaland. Children took classes in mathematics, literature and languages, arts and crafts, and music. The Bartons emphasized learning about various world cultures, especially during World War II, when Dutch and British children and teachers joined the school. Here, too, they reflected Lomaland's international, multicultural outlook, although the variety of cultures rarely extended beyond Europe.[61]

But the Bartons departed from the rigors of Lomaland in cultivating freedom and innovation among individual children. Although a promotional pamphlet for the school claimed that the Bartons instilled Lomaland values in the children— "mental balance, self-control, fearlessness and altruism to the extent that the child's own higher nature is allowed to express itself"— these qualities flowered in children in different ways.[62] Absent from the rhetoric and pedagogy of the Barton School was the insistence so common at Lomaland of instilling a certain type of character. Instead, children could find themselves in the various activities of the school, from helping with farm chores to individual tutorials to hiking and camping in the hills around Topanga, north of Los Angeles.[63]

Each year the Bartons hosted a May Festival at the school, in which children dressed in traditional folk costumes of various cultures. An opening parade included the children leading farm animals. Next came songs and dance performances from different folk cultures. Each festival culminated in a feast of dishes from different lands. The festival in 1946, for example, featured sixty-seven children in the parade, and their performance included the last scene from Shakespeare's "Midsummer's Night Dream." Unlike the highly regulated performances and activities characteristic of Lomaland, these festivals varied from year to year. Spontaneous activity was encouraged, as the gaiety of the event absorbed all involved. Festival days usually ended in a session of telling tales, or simply conversing among friends, around a large bonfire.[64]

The Bartons closed the school in 1948, and began an organic farm elsewhere in California. But they always retained a profound appreciation for the ideals of Lomaland: respect for diverse cultures and religions, openness to the insights and beauty that the arts could reveal, belief in karma and reincarnation, and cultivation of personal moral qualities such as integrity, diligence, and compassion. In announcing the school's closing to alumni, Marguerite wrote:

The aim in applied education should be to bring the best and soundest in upbringing to the greatest number of children from modest circumstances...there should be simplicity, and the building of inner richness and strength.[65]

Many years after closing their school, Hildor still admired faithful Theosophists "who are everlastingly striving to keep alive and pass on to others the living teachings."[66]

We could extend the list of Lomaland children, like Tyberg and the Bartons, who were guided by the light of this Theosophical form of progressive millennialism to forge new paths into the future. The millennial hopes of the first Lomalanders were broad enough to allow for such experimentation. Perhaps the more open-minded among those early Lomalander pioneers would not have objected to the conclusions reached by Tyberg, the Bartons, and other true Raja Yogas. But certainly at the time that Lomaland was founded, notions of the coming cycle did not include Aurobindo or the Barton School or many other innovations that second and third generation Lomalanders formulated.

It was up to the children, inspired throughout their lives by the Theosophical anticipation of spiritual greatness in the dawning cycle, to find as adults their own ways to live out the new age. That they did so quietly, with decorum and order, probably reflects the late Victorian period in which they spent their earliest years. That they did so at all certainly reflects the power of millennial discourse to mold a lifetime.

ACKNOWLEDGMENTS: I am grateful to faculty colleagues at Truman State University who read this manuscript and offered suggestions. Thanks also to participants at the Twelfth Annual Klutznick Symposium, for their response to my presentation of an earlier version of this essay.

NOTES

[1] Susan J. Palmer and Charlotte E. Hardman, eds., "Introduction: Alternative Childhoods," in *Children in New Religions* (New Brunswick and London: Rutgers University Press, 1999), 1.

[2] Studies of children in historic alternative religions include M. Guy Bishop, "Preparing to 'Take the Kingdom': Childrearing Directives in Early Mormonism," *Journal of the Early Republic* 7 (Fall 1987): 275-290; M. Guy Bishop, "Sex Roles, Marriage, and Childrearing at Mormon Nauvoo," *Western Illinois Regional Studies* 11.2 (1988): 30-45; Elizabeth Bohlken-Zumpe, *Torches Extinguished: Memories of a Communal Bruderhof: Childhood in Paraguay, Europe and the USA* (Carrier Pigeon, 1997); Judith Graham, "The New Lebanon Shaker Children's Order," *Winterthur Portfolio* 26 (Winter 1991): 215-30; Susan Landa, "Children and Cults: A Practical Guide," *Journal of Family Law* 29 (1991): 591-634; Stephen Paterwic, "From Individual to Community: Becoming a Shaker at New Lebanon," *Communal Societies* 11 (1991): 18-33; Barbara G. Harrison, *Visions of Glory: A History and a Memory of Jehovah's Witnesses* (New York: Simon and Schuster, 1978); Ruth Baer Lambach, "Colony Girl: A Hutterite Childhood," in *Women in Spiritual and Communitarian Societies in the United States* (ed. W. Chmielewski et al.; Syracuse: Syracuse University Press, 1992), 241-55; Gertrude Enders Huntington, "Freedom and the Hutterite Communal Family Pattern," in *Proceedings of the 15th Conference on Mennonite Educational and Cultural Problems* (North Newton: Mennonite Press, 1965), 88-111. On Christian fundamentalism and children, see Nancy Ammerman, *Bible Believers: Fundamentalists in the Modern World* (New Brunswick and London: Rutgers University Press, 1987), 166-87; Coleen McDannell, "Creating the Christian Home: Home Schooling in Contemporary America," in *American Sacred Space* (ed. D. Chidester and E. Linenthal; Bloomington: Indiana University Press, 1995); Alan Peshkin, *God's Choice: The Total World of a Fundamentalist Christian School* (Chicago: University of Chicago Press, 1986); Susan Rose, "Christian Fundamentalism and Education in the United States," in *Fundamentalisms and Society: Reclaiming the Sciences, the Family, and Education,* vol. 2 (ed. M. Marty and R. S. Appleby; Chicago and

London: University of Chicago Press, 1993), 452-89; and Melinda Bollar Wagner, *God's Schools: Choice and Compromise in American Society* (New Brunswick: Rutgers University Press, 1990).

[3]Catherine Wessinger, "Millennialism With and Without Mayhem," in *Millennium, Messiahs, and Mayhem* (ed. T. Robbins and S. Palmer; London: Routledge, 1997), 51. See also her article in this volume.

[4]See Sylvia Cranston, *HPB: The Extraordinary Life and Influence of Helena Blavatsky, Founder of the Modern Theosophical Movement* (New York: Putnam's, 1993).

[5]Blavatsky's teachings are found in numerous sources. Her magnum opus was *The Secret Doctrine: The Synthesis of Science, Religion, and Philosophy*, 2 volumes (1888; reprint, Pasadena: Theosophical University Press, 1988). She conveniently summarized the information found here and in other books and articles in *The Key to Theosophy*, (abr. and ed. Joy Mills; Wheaton: Theosophical Publishing House, 1972). Unfortunately, few non-Theosophists have studied her writings in depth. But the beginning of a Theosophical historiography has been made with recent work published by non-Theosophical scholars. See chapter six of Diana Barsham, *The Trial of Woman: Feminism and the Occult Sciences in Victorian Literature and Society* (New York: New York University Press, 1997); Mark Bevir, "The West Turns Eastward: Madame Blavatsky and the Transformation of the Occult Tradition," *Journal of the American Academy of Religion* 62:3 (Fall 1994): 747-68; and Stephen Prothero, "Theosophy's Sinner/Saint: Recent Books on Madame Blavatsky," *Religious Studies Review* 23:3 (July 1997): 257-62.

[6]The definitive study of Point Loma is Emmett Greenwalt, *California Utopia: Point Loma: 1897-1942* (rev. ed.; San Diego: Point Loma Publications, 1978). See also William M. Ashcraft, "'The Dawn of the New Cycle': Point Loma Theosophists and American Culture, 1896-1929" (Ph.D. diss., University of Virginia, 1995).

[7]See Stephen Prothero, *The White Buddhist: The Asian Odyssey of Henry Steel Olcott* (Bloomington: Indiana University Press, 1996).

[8] No critical biography of Judge currently exists. However, useful information can be found in Grace F. Knoche, "William Q. Judge," *Sunrise* (Apr./May 1986): 157-60; and Sven Eek and Boris de Zirkoff, *William Quan Judge, 1851-1896: The Life of a Theosophical Pioneer and Some of His Most Outstanding Articles* (Wheaton: The Theosophical Publishing House, 1969).

[9]Bruce F. Campbell, *Ancient Wisdom Revived: A History of the Theosophical Movement* (Berkeley and Los Angeles: University of California Press, 1980), 111; Robert S. Ellwood, Jr., "Theosophy," in *America's Alternative Religions* (ed. T. Miller; Albany: State University of New York Press, 1995), 322.

[10]No critical biography of Tingley currently exists. However, useful information can be found in Rosemary Radford Ruether, "Radical Victorians: The Quest for an Alternative Culture," in *Women and Religion in America: Volume 3: 1900-1968* (ed.

R. R. Ruether and R. S. Keller; San Francisco: Harper and Row, 1986), 1-10; "Tingley, Katherine Augusta Westcott," in *Biographical Dictionary of American Cult and Sect Leaders,* ed. J. Gordon Melton (New York: Garland, 1986), 189-91; *Sunrise Special Issue: Katherine Tingley (1847-1929)* (Apr./May 1998); and Katherine Tingley, *The Gods Await* (2nd and rev. ed.; Pasadena: Theosophical University Press, 1992).

[11]Penny Waterstone, "Domesticating Universal Brotherhood: Feminine Values and the Construction of Utopia, Point Loma Homestead, 1897-1920" (Ph.D. diss., University of Arizona, 1995), 81, 218; W. Michael Ashcraft, "The Child, Theosophy, and Victorian American Culture at Point Loma," *Theosophical History* 7:2 (April 1998): 72-3.

[12]In this period in American history, the antebellum emphasis on moral development within a controlled environment that had characterized public schooling since the reforms of Horace Mann (see Barbara Finkelstein, "Perfecting Childhood: Horace Mann and the Origins of Public Education in the United States," *Biography* 13:1 [1990]: 6-20) was built upon by early childhood education specialists like Elizabeth Palmer Peabody and Susan Blow, who incorporated the methods and theories of German educator Friedrich Froebel; see Caroline Winterer, "Avoiding a 'Hothouse System of Education': Nineteenth-Century Early Childhood Education from the Infant Schools to the Kindergartens," *The History of Education Quarterly* 32:3 (Fall 1992): 289-314; Ann Taylor Allen, "'Let Us Live with Our Children': Kindergarten Movements in Germany and the United States, 1840-1914," *The History of Education Quarterly* 28:1 (Spring 1988): 23-48; and Norman Brosterman, *Inventing Kindergarten* (New York: Harry N. Abrams, 1997).

[13]"Happy Little Sunbeams," *Songs for Lotus-Circles* (Point Loma: Theosophical University Press, 1934).

[14]Many middle-class urban reformers were concerned about the health and welfare of urban poor children and constructed institutions in the cities for them or transported them to rural areas, where the more natural environment and farm labor supposedly provided a moral educational for these children. See LeRoy Ashley, *Saving the Waifs: Reformers and Dependent Children, 1890-1917* (Philadelphia: Temple University Press, 1984); Marilyn Irvin Holt, *The Orphan Trains: Placing Out in America* (Lincoln and London: The University of Nebraska Press, 1992); and Joseph M. Hawes, *Children in Urban Society: Juvenile Delinquency in Nineteenth-Century America* (New York: Oxford University Press, 1971).

[15]"Lotus Home. Pleasant Valley, N.J.— Closing Exercises," *New Century* 1 (30 Sept. 1897): 6.

[16]H. P. Blavatsky, "Esoteric Buddhism and The Secret Doctrine," *Lucifer* 3 (November 1888); reprinted in *H. P. Blavatsky: Collected Writings, 1888-1889* (ed. de Zirkoff; Adyar: The Theosophical Publishing House, 1964), 186; Blavatsky,

"Esoteric Buddhism," 1: 153, 182, 185-6, 233.

[17] Blavatsky, "Esoteric Buddhism," 180-1.

[18] Blavatsky, "Esoteric Buddhism," 186.

[19] Jonathan Z. Smith, "Ages of the World," in *The Encyclopedia of Religion* 1:132.

[20] H. P. Blavatsky, "Our Cycle and the Next," *Lucifer 4* (May 1889); reprinted in *Collected Writings 1889-90*, 200.

[21] Blavatsky, *Collected Writings, 1889-1890*, 418.

[22] H. P. Blavatsky, "The Kali Yuga—The Present Age," *Collected Writings*, 102; Blavatsky, "Esoteric Buddhism,"xliv-v; 2:70, 147n.

[23] Wessinger, "Millennialism With and Without Mayhem," 54; see also Catherine Wessinger, *Annie Besant and Progressive Messianism (1847-1933)* (Lewiston/ Queenston: Edwin Mellen, 1988). Wessinger's cataclysmic and progressive millennialisms replace the terms pre- and postmillenialism derived from Christian thought.

[24] E.S.B., "Impressions of the Convention," *New Century* 1 (April 2, 1898): 11; "The Fifteenth Anniversary of the Chicago Theosophical Convention," *Theosophical Path* 4 (April 1913): 299.

[25] Katherine Tingley, "Words Used at Ceremony of Laying of Corner Stone of S.R.L.M.A.," Archives, Theosophical Society Pasadena; hereafter ATSP; "Corner Stone Laid. Mystic Ceremonial by Theosophists on Point Loma," *San Diego Union*, 24 Feb. 1897.

[26] Iverson L. Harris in an interview with Robert Wright, "Reminiscences of Lomaland: Madame Tingley and the Theosophical Institute in San Diego," *Journal of San Diego History* 20 (Summer 1974): 12.

[27] Jan Shipps, *Mormonism: The Story of a New Religious Tradition* (Urbana and Chicago: University of Illinois Press, 1985), 109-13, 122-5.

[28] Amos C. McAlpin, "A Sweet-scented Letter from Balmy Point Loma," *New Century* 3 (March 3, 1900): 5; H.T.P., "A Letter from Point Loma, Cal.," *New Century* 3 (September 8, 1900): 3.

[29] "The Brotherhood. Proceedings of the Congress on Point Loma's Heights," *San Diego Union*, 15 April 1899.

[30] "To Universal Brotherhood Lodges Throughout the World, in Unity Congress Assembled," 1 April 1900, ATSP, 1.

[31] *How to Know God: The Yoga Aphorisms of Patanjali*, Swami Prabhavananda and Christopher Isherwood, trans. and commentary (Hollywood: Vedanta Press, 1981). See Gavin Flood, *An Introduction to Hinduism* (Cambridge and New York: Cambridge University Press, 1996), 96-7.

[32] See Ramatirtha, "Culture of Concentration (A Paper Read Before the Aryan Theosophical Society of New York)," *The Path* 3 (July 1888): 118-23; and Hadji Erinn, "The Stream of Thought and Queries," *The Path* 4 (September 1889): 186.

[33]Katherine Tingley, *Mysteries of the Heart Doctrine, Prepared by Katherine Tingley and Her Pupils* (Point Loma: Theosophical Publishing Co., 1902), 156.

[34]Ashcraft, "'The Dawn of the New Cycle,'" 78-9.

[35]Emmett Greenwalt, *California Utopia: Point Loma: 1897-1942* (rev. ed.; San Diego: Point Loma Publications, 1978), 100-109; Observer, "Loma-land News Notes," *New Century* 5 (March 30, 1902): 10.

[36]Staffan Kronberg, "Life at the Raja Yoga School from a Growing Boy's Point of View," 1913-1921, archive of Point Loma Publications; hereafter PLP. A rough drawing of a group home is in *Universal Brotherhood Path* 15 (August 1900): 291. One such home still stands, in a neighborhood near the Point Loma site. Reminiscences of life in both the group homes and the Academy building are ubiquitous in interviews, both those conducted by the author and those found in the Oral History Program, San Diego Historical Society; hereafter, SDHS.

[37]John Davidson, interview by Bob Wright, 5 August 1967, Oral History Program, SDHS, San Diego, CA.

[38]Affidavit signed by Point Loma parents, 1909, ATSP.

[39]Lydia Ross, "Tempting Counterfeits Vs. Reality," *Theosophical Path* 1 (August 1911): 128.

[40]Gertrude W. Van Pelt, M.D., "The Raja Yoga College," *Searchlight* 3 (January 13, 1911): 59.

[41]Ingrid Van Mater, interview with author, Altadena, CA, 18 June 1992.

[42]Isabel Kimble to author, 9 November 1992.

[43]Tom Amneus, interview with author, Glendale, CA, 23 September 1993.

[44]May Davidson Atherton, interview by Sylvia Arden, 11 November 1982, Oral History Program, SDHS, San Diego, CA.

[45]Mary Douglas, *Purity and Danger: An Analysis of the Concepts of Pollution and Taboo* (1966; reprint; London, Boston, and Henley: Routledge & Kegan Paul, 1984), 113.

[46]A Raja-Yoga Student, *Katherine Tingley's Raja-Yoga System of Education: Its Aims and Achievements* (Point Loma: Aryan Theosophical Press, 1922), 18.

[47]Gertrude Van Pelt, "The Raja Yoga Study of Children," *New Century* 5 (January 12, 1902): 14.

[48]Raja Yoga Teacher, "Need for Discipline in Education," *New Century Path* 9 (October 21, 1906): 8.

[49]Student, "The Point Loma Type of Character," *Century Path* 13 (June 19, 1910): 15.

[50]Adam Kadmon, "The Raja Yoga School: Its Work for the Future," *New Century* 5 (April 27, 1902): 9.

[51]Observer, "Some Observations," *New Century* 5 (August 3, 1902):10.

[52]During World War II, Theosophists moved from Point Loma to Covina, in the

Los Angeles area, under the guidance of Tingley's successor, Gottfried de Purucker (1874-1942). Eventually the headquarters of the Theosophical Society that is the organizational inheritor of the Point Loma Theosophical tradition was moved to Pasadena, and then to its current location in Altadena, California. This organization is usually referred to as the Theosophical Society Pasadena to distinguish it from the Theosophical Society in America, headquartered in Wheaton, Illinois. The Theosophical Society Pasadena publishes a monthly magazine, *Sunrise: Theosophic Perspectives*, publishes Theosophical literature through the Theosophical University Press, and maintains a web site at http:// user.aol.com/tstec/hmpage/tsintro.htm.

[53]When de Purucker died, no clear successor emerged to lead the Theosophical Society, and for a period of several years a council governed the Society. In the late 40s, internal divisions developed over leadership, and many loyal Theosophists left Covina and the Theosophical Society. Among the exiles were Iverson L. Harris, Jr. and Emmett and Carmen Small. These individuals had lived at Point Loma and Covina for most of their lives. They were committed to the teachings of Blavatsky, Judge, Tingley, and de Purucker. To further those teachings, they started a publishing house, Point Loma Publications, Inc., and a periodical, *The Eclectic Theosophist*. The latter has ceased publication, but the former still provides reprints of Theosophical texts and maintains a website at http://www.wisdomtraditions.com (see "Later Point Loma History (Added by the Publishers)," in Charles Ryan, *H.P. Blavatsky and the Theosophical Movement: A Brief Historical Sketch* (2nd ed.; San Diego: Point Loma Publications, Inc., 1975).

[54]A Raja Yoga Student, "What Theosophy Means to a Young Man," *Century Path* 13 (October 9, 1910): 8.

[55]I.L.H., Jr., "Theosophy in Practice: The Duality of Human Nature," *Theosophical Path* 12 (January 1917): 60-2.

[56]Patrick Clemeshaw, interview with author, Escondido, CA, 15 June 1992.

[57]Kate Hanson, "A Student's Diary of *International Peace Congress,* Sweden, 1913," ATSP.

[58]Katarina Johansson, "Interview with Dr. Walo von Greyertz on Swedish Radio: program 1, 17 February 1988" (trans. and summarized, H. Arnold Barton, 27 December 1996; copy sent to author by H. Arnold Barton).

[59]See Mandakini (Madaleine Shaw), "Jyotipriya (Dr. Judith M. Tyberg) May 16, 1902-October 3, 1980 II," *Mother India* 33:3 (March 1981): 157-62; Mandakini, "Jyotipriya III," *Mother India* 33:4 (April 24, 1981): 210-19. On Aurobindo, see Beatrice Bruteau, *Worthy is the World: The Hindu Philosophy of Sri Aurobindo* (Rutherford: Fairleigh Dickinson University Press, 1971); Peter Heehs, *Sri Aurobindo, A Brief Biography* (Delhi, New York: Oxford University Press, 1989); Robert McDermott, ed., *The Essential Aurobindo* (Great Barrington: Lindisfarne Press, 1987); and Georges Van Vrekhem, *Beyond the Human Species: The Life and*

Work of Sri Aurobindo and The Mother (St. Paul: Paragon House, 1997).
[60]H. Arnold Barton to author, 19 September 1992.
[61] *The Barton School Topanga, California* (nd.).
[62]*Ibid.*
[63]H. Arnold Barton, "Recollections of the Barton School in Topanga, 1932 - 1948" (1984, given to author by Barton); newsletters from Bartons to alumni, 27 July 1940, 14 Aug. 1941.
[64]Barton, "Recollections"; newsletter, 29 May 1946.
[65]Newsletter, 4 June 1948.
[66]Hildor Barton to Iverson Harris Jr., 1 March 1951, Alexandria West Archive/Point Loma Publications.

Where the End Times Begin:
Jerusalem and the Millennial Vision of Evangelical Christians

Yaakov Ariel

In the early 1970s, the evangelist Billy Graham produced a film on Israel titled *His Land*.[1] He dedicated much of the film to Jerusalem, which he presented not only as the place where Jesus suffered, was crucified, and was resurrected, but also as the place to which Jesus will return and where he will establish his thousand-year reign on Earth. Influenced by a messianic premillennialist understanding of history, which expects this era to end and the Messianic age to begin, evangelicals like Graham have viewed Jerusalem as more than just an earthly city; in their eyes, it is a place which holds global cosmic significance as the site of the expected apocalypse and as the future capital of God's kingdom on Earth.

The evangelical view of Jerusalem and its place in God's plans for humanity has determined their actual involvement with the city and fascination with it. It also has determined their understanding of the Jewish people and the State of Israel, as well as their beliefs regarding the Arab-Israeli conflict. Graham took a strong pro-Israeli stance in his film, viewing the Jewish return to Zion as part of the divine plan. The Jews, in his opinion, are preparing the way for the arrival of the Lord and the turning of Jerusalem into the world's capital.

JERUSALEM IN CHRISTIAN PREMILLENNIALIST BELIEF

The perception of Jerusalem as the locale of major eschatological events in Christian messianic visions dates back to the earliest days of Christianity. The belief in the imminent return of Jesus and in the establishment of his reign on Earth for a thousand years was a common tenet of faith in early Christianity.[2] By the fifth century, however, Western Christianity had become predominantly amillennial in its outlook, and Christian theologians had begun interpreting biblical passages with eschatological

31

overtones in symbolic terms.[3] Messianic movements emerged, nonetheless, throughout the Middle Ages, and the Reformation in the sixteenth century was accompanied by a strong wave of eschatological expectations, particularly among some of the more radical sects. Some of these groups anticipated the return of the Jews to the Holy Land and the rebuilding of Jerusalem for a Jewish capital as events preceding the messianic era.[4]

The English civil war of the seventeenth century took place in the context of a new wave of messianic hopes that stressed the role and place of the Jewish people in the events of the End Times.[5] In the early nineteenth century, there was a dramatic rise in messianic expectations among Protestants, especially in the English-speaking world. Those expecting the Second Coming of Jesus often interpreted events such as the French Revolution and the Napoleonic Wars as signs that the current era was ending and the predicted eschatological events had begun.[6] The new premillennialist ferment brought about a renewed interest in the Jews in evangelical circles, specifically in the prospect of their national restoration and eventual conversion.[7] In 1840, at the urging of Lord Ashley Cooper (later Seventh Earl of Shaftesbury, leader of the evangelical party in Britain, and an ardent premillennialist), the British foreign secretary Lord Palmerston ordered his ambassador in Constantinople to support the idea of a large-scale Jewish settlement in Palestine.[8]

It was in Britain in this atmosphere of intensified eschatological expectations that dispensationalism, which holds distinctive beliefs about the Second Coming of Jesus, was born. This school of thought was crystallized in the 1830s by John Nelson Darby (1800-1882) and the group he led, the Plymouth Brethren. Dispensationalists assert that human history is divided into a specific number of ages or eras. The last age is the millennium, the thousand-year reign of Christ on Earth, and the present era is believed to be the one immediately preceding that last age. God's plan for humanity in each successive age can be reconstructed from the biblical text.[9] One of the most characteristic components of dispensational pre-millennialism has been the belief in "the secret, any moment, rapture of the church." The arrival of Jesus, according to this scheme, will take place in two stages. The first one will occur when Jesus comes for His saints: the true believers will be "raptured," snatched from earth, and meet Jesus in heaven. Remaining with Jesus there for seven years (or three and a half years, according to some versions), they will be spared the turmoil and misery to be inflicted on those who remain on earth. For the latter, this period will be known as the Great Tribulation and will be marked by natural disasters, such as earthquakes, floods, and famine, as well as wars and murderous dictatorial regimes.[10]

For the Jews, this period will be known as "the time of Jacob's trouble." Against the traditional claim of Christianity to be the true Israel, dispensationalists recognize the Jewish people to be both the historical Israel and the object of the biblical prophecies foretelling a restored Davidic kingdom in the messianic age, with Jerusalem as the capital. Premillennialists have predicted that the Jews will return to their ancient homeland "in unbelief," i.e., without accepting Jesus as their Savior, and establish a political commonwealth there. Living in spiritual blindness, they will let themselves be ruled by an Anti-Christian impostor of the Messiah, and will rebuild the Temple on its historical site in Jerusalem, as well as reinstate the sacrificial rituals. During the Anti-Christ's reign of terror, many people will become believers in Jesus and will be martyred.[11]

With the arrival of Jesus and the true believers to the Mount of Olives, the Anti-Christ's rule will come to an end. Jesus will crush this Satanic ruler and his armies, and establish his millennial kingdom. Those Jews who survive the turmoil and terror will then accept Jesus as their Savior. During the millennial period, the righteous rule of Christ on Earth, all nations will live in their ancestral lands. The Jews will inhabit David's ancient kingdom, and Jerusalem will serve as the capital of the entire world. The Jews will be at Jesus' right hand, assisting him in administrating the earth, and will function as evangelists, spreading the knowledge of God among the nations of the earth.[12]

This view of the role of Jerusalem in the messianic age gained ground among American evangelicals in the decades following the Civil War (1861-1865). Conservative members of major denominations shaped by nineteenth century revivalism, such as Baptists, Presbyterians, Methodists, Congregationalists, and Disciples of Christ, accepted the new messianic hope.[13] The premillennialist belief in the Second Coming of Christ in its dispensationalist form became a major component of the world view of the conservative evangelical camp, often known as 'fundamentalist,' that developed in American Protestantism in those years. Conservatives objected to many developments that had taken place within American culture and religion. In particular, they objected to the rise of a new "modernist" trend within American Protestantism and to the willingness of modernists to accept what the conservatives perceived as dangerous and destructive teachings, such as the higher criticism of the Bible.[14] In reaction to the new trends, they emphasized what they considered to be the fundamental components of their religious tradition: the insistence on the inerrancy and authority of the Bible, the need to undergo a personal experience of conversion in order to be saved, and the expected arrival of the Messiah and his thousand year reign on earth.[15] Dispensationalism became the philosophy of history for these conservative Protestants. It reflected their interpretation of the world's situation and their understanding of their position as the faithful remnant within an apostate culture. It has also served to reassure them that they know the course of history and that whatever social, economic, political, or environmental developments take place, they will certainly survive the turmoil.[16]

Dispensationalism has also shaped the evangelical view of Jerusalem. Influenced by their messianic faith, evangelicals view Jerusalem not merely as a city of the past, of prophets and kings, as well as Jesus' place of teaching, suffering, execution, and resurrection; for them, it is also the city of the future, where the Anti-Christ will rule, the locale of Jesus' Second Coming, and the glorious capital of the prophesied messianic kingdom. They view developments that take place in that city as decisive for the advancement of the messianic age.[17] Throughout the nineteenth and twentieth centuries, evangelicals influenced by premillennialist teachings have watched the developments in the Land of Israel and in Jerusalem in particular with great interest, their journals regularly updating the adherents of premillennialism.[18] Many have traveled to see the city at first hand.

PREMILLENNIALIST TOURISTS, MISSIONARIES, AND SETTLERS

From the early nineteenth century, with the "rediscovery" of Palestine or the Holy Land, and throughout the twentieth century, evangelical premillennialists came to Jerusalem to tour the city. Their visits often encouraged them in their messianic hope and in their conviction that Jerusalem was destined for a special role in the End Times.[19]

One noted premillennialist visitor was William Blackstone. A lay Methodist, he was converted to the dispensationalist belief while a successful businessman in Chicago in the 1870s. He decided to dedicate himself to evangelism and the propagation of the premillennialist belief. His first book, *Jesus is Coming*, first published in 1878, was translated into 42 languages and enjoyed a circulation of over a million and a half copies.[20] In his book, Blackstone emphasized the centrality of the Jewish people and the Land of Israel for the events of the End Times. In 1889, he visited Jerusalem. He was deeply impressed by developments that had taken place in that city and was convinced that he had seen "signs of the time," indicating that this era was ending and that the great events of the End of Age were soon to occur. Following his visit to Jerusalem, Blackstone decided to take a more active role in promoting Jewish national restoration, which he perceived as a necessary precursor to the arrival of the Lord. In 1891, he organized a petition to President Benjamin Harrison, urging him to convene an international conference of the world powers that would decide to give Palestine back to the Jews.[21]

Another major figure among premillennialists who visited Jerusalem was Blackstone's friend Dwight L. Moody, the leading evangelist in America at the time.[22] In the 1870s, Moody adopted the messianic belief in the imminent arrival of Jesus and incorporated it into his evangelistic campaigns. Moody, like other dispensationalists, was not devoid of prejudices against Jews, such as viewing them as greedy and dishonest. However, he accepted the belief that the Jewish nation was again to resume its leading role in a restored Davidic kingdom.[23] In Spring 1892, Moody visited Jerusalem, where he preached a sermon on the role of the Jews in God's plans for humanity and contended that Christians had a special duty to evangelize Jews.[24] In his visit to the Mount of Olives on Easter, Moody, overwhelmed, claimed that he had never been so awe-inspired in his entire life.[25]

The approaches Blackstone and Moody advocated in relation to the Jews, Christian pro-Zionist activity and missions, would become the two main avenues for evangelical Christians to express their interest in the Jews as the people who were destined to play a leading role in bringing about the millennial kingdom. Blackstone and Moody also inspired other evangelical leaders to visit Jerusalem. Although at the end of the nineteenth century and the beginning of the twentieth century evangelical tours to the city were limited in scope, such visits grew considerably by the latter decades of the twentieth century. Much of the tourism to Israel from the Americas during the 1980s-1990s was composed of evangelical Christians whose interest in the country derives from their messianic biblical outlook.[26]

Conservative Protestants do not recognize, in principle, the concept of pilgrimage and holy sites, but their attitude toward Jerusalem demonstrates that, in practice, many do. In past decades, millions of evangelical Christians have visited such sites as the Mount of Olives or the Garden Tomb.[27] Evangelical Christians, like Roman Catholics, refer to Israel as the Holy Land and view Jerusalem as the jewel in its crown.[28]

Tours to Jerusalem and Israel are organized by evangelical churches or organizations, including missions, Bible schools, and Christian colleges.

Leading evangelists such as Oral Roberts, Pat Robertson, Jerry Falwell, and John Hagee have gone on visits, often leading groups of evangelical tourists. One noted visit was that of Jimmy Swaggart in 1987, a short time after a scandal erupted involving his private life. His trip to Jerusalem offered the evangelist a re-legitimization, signifying that whatever sins he had committed were forgiven and that he could resume his role as a leading evangelist.[29]

Conservative evangelicals have promoted, at times, their own holy sites in Jerusalem, unique to their segment of Christianity. For example, some do not accept the traditional Christian identification of Golgotha and Calvary with the Church of the Holy Sepulcher.[30] Acknowledging the Holy Sepulcher as Jesus' burial site would have meant joining in a church already divided among Roman Catholics, Greek Orthodox, Armenians, Copts, and Ethiopians, each operating according to their own traditions. Accordingly, they sought out their own site for Jesus' burial. Instead of the Holy Sepulcher, these evangelicals came to believe that Jesus was buried in a site that they have named the Garden Tomb, near the northern wall of the old city of Jerusalem, not far from the Damascus Gate. A noted British evangelical, General Charles "Chinese" Gordon identified this archaeological site in 1883 as Jesus' burial site.[31] He and other evangelicals noted that the Church of the Holy Sepulcher in the old city of Jerusalem was inside the city wall. Since it was forbidden for Jews to bury their dead inside city boundaries, it could not have been Jesus' burial site. They also pointed out that the hill on which the Garden Tomb is located resembled a skull [*golgolet*] and argued that this was Golgotha, where Jesus was crucified and buried in the family tomb of Joseph of Arimathea. The Garden Tomb has become one of the standard sites on the evangelical tour of the city.[32]

In addition to pilgrims and archeologists, Jerusalem has attracted, since the early nineteenth century, evangelical missionaries. Motivated by their messianic beliefs, evangelicals have perceived special merit in evangelizing in the city. The premillennialist messianic belief inspired not only hopes for the imminent national restoration of the Jews and the reestablishment of David's kingdom, with Jerusalem as the capital of the world, but hopes for the conversion of the Jews as well. The rise of premillennialist beliefs in England in the early nineteenth century and the spread of dispensationalism in America towards the latter decades of the nineteenth century gave rise to numerous missionary societies and organizations aimed at evangelizing "the chosen people."[33]

A number of British and American missionary societies, as well as German pietist and Scandinavian ones, sent missionaries to the city, which became, by the end of the century, the most evangelized spot on earth. In 1819, among the early Protestant evangelical missionaries who visited the city were Pliny Fisk and Levi Parsons of the American Board of Commissioners of Foreign Missions.[34] Inspired by their messianic vision, they considered their work as evangelists in Jerusalem as a special calling.[35] On the British side, the impetus to establish the joint Prussian British bishopric in Jerusalem came from the premillennialist messianic understanding of the importance of Jerusalem to Christendom.[36] Other missionary societies followed and the evangelical missionary endeavors persisted throughout the nineteenth century.[37]

In the latter part of the nineteenth century, the Christian and Missionary Alliance saw a strong calling for itself in the city. This missionary organization, which later became a mission-oriented denomination, had the ambition of spreading the Gospel throughout the world, but the Jerusalem mission was a high priority on the organization's early agenda.[38] For the founders of the Christian and Missionary Alliance, Jerusalem was not just another city in a far and distant land; spreading the Gospel among the Jews of Jerusalem was planting seeds among God's chosen nation, in the very place where the Messiah would arrive.

F. H. Senft, of the Christian and Missionary Alliance headquarters, visited Jerusalem in 1899. In a letter sent home and later published in the organization's magazine, he wrote, "We should bear in mind that the center of all true missionary work is Jerusalem."[39] In February 1893, Albert B. Simpson, the Alliance leader, visited Jerusalem on a world tour of Christian and Missionary Alliance posts. In addition to being a superintendent's inspection, the visit was something of a pilgrimage to the Holy City. Simpson was moved and overwhelmed when confronted with the sites he had read about for decades in the Bible. "Sweet Olivet, sweet Bethany, my heart shall oft remember thee," was one of a number of hymns he composed during that visit.[40]

The situation for the missions and other premillennialist Christians changed dramatically with the outbreak of World War I. The Ottoman Turks viewed British subjects residing in the city as enemies. In 1917, when the United States joined the war on the Entente side, the Turkish government became openly hostile toward all English-speaking missionaries and residents in the city. Even though the war damaged evangelical missionary enterprises in Jerusalem, evangelization efforts resumed when the war ended.

The period from 1918 through 1948 was one of prosperity and security for the Christian evangelical community in Jerusalem. The British, who governed the country, viewed it as their duty to protect Christian interests, including the free operation of missions.[41] A number of evangelical groups established themselves in the city during these favorable years of British rule, including the Southern Baptist church, the Church of God, the Church of the Nazarene, and missionary agencies such as the American Board of Missions to the Jews. British societies represented in the city before the Great War, such as the Church Missionary Society (CMS), resumed their activities with vigor. Circumstances again changed considerably in 1948, following the British evacuation of the country and the war between Arabs and Jews. Many evangelical missionaries left the country and, when the war ended, the city of Jerusalem was divided between Jordan and Israel. Nonetheless, the establishment of the State of Israel brought about a renewed interest in the prospect of Jewish conversions to Christianity.[42] The birth of a Jewish state gave many evangelical Christians a sense that the arrival of the Lord was imminent and that the messianic times were progressing according to prediction.[43] These new political realities strongly enhanced the desire to evangelize the Jews, especially those in their ancient capital to which the Messiah was soon to return. "Suddenly everybody seems to be 'called of God' to go to Jerusalem as a missionary!" wrote Joseph Cohn, the director of the American Board of Missions to the Jews, one of the largest missions to the Jews in America at the time.[44]

To the surprise of many and to the chagrin of Jewish Orthodox activists, the State of Israel decided to protect the missionary endeavor as part of maintaining the *status quo ante bellum* in religious matters, i.e., the legal situation in religious matters as its existed during the British period.[45] In so doing, the Israeli government sought, with some success, to reassure the Christian churches that a Jewish state did not work against their old freedoms and traditional privileges in the country. It did not wish to be blamed by foreign governments and churches, or by the foreign press, for restricting Christian liberties.

This does not mean to say that there were no anti-missionary sentiments in the city. In one extreme case in the early 1960s, when resentment against large and visible missionary activity was growing, the police were sent to break up anti-missionary demonstrations.[46] Antagonism by some Israelis did not, however, deter evangelicals from propagating the

Gospel in the city.

During the 1950s and '60s, Jerusalem was proportionately the most evangelized city on earth.[47] Hundreds of enthusiastic missionaries were evangelizing a population that, in the Israeli part of the city, grew during that period from 80,000 to 180,000. Evangelical missions in Jerusalem became part of the scenery. A representative of an American mission sent a report back home: "The number of missionaries stationed permanently and temporarily is relatively larger than in any other mission field in the world."[48]

Many of these evangelization efforts were directed toward the poor population of new Jewish immigrants from Middle Eastern and North African countries who settled in neighborhoods near the border with Jordan, such as Musrara, Bakaa, and Abu-Tor. The missionary presence helped to shape social activities in the city, and left its mark on the educational and medical infrastructure.[49]

Evangelical missionary work inspired by messianic expectations continued throughout the 1970s, '80s, and '90s. Evangelical missionary policy shifted from missionaries representing foreign societies to local congregations of Jewish converts assisted by missionary groups. Such communities as the Messianic Assembly, or Netivia, have been influenced strongly by evangelical theology, terminology, and morality — including premillennialist messianic hope, which has served to give the groups a sense of purpose and a notion that they are taking part in the fulfillment of prophecy.[50]

In addition to visitors or missionaries who came to the city to live, there were those convinced evangelicals who wished to witness with their own eyes the imminent arrival of the Messiah. In the late nineteenth century these included the founders of the American Colony, headed by Horatio and Anna Spafford. Following a series of personal tragedies, the Spaffords decided to leave Chicago for Jerusalem. "Jerusalem," Horatio Spafford wrote in his diary, "is where my Lord lived, suffered, and conquered, and I wish to learn how to live, suffer, and especially to conquer."[51] The American Colony introduced a number of medical and charitable, as well as economic, enterprises to the city and played an important role in the development of Jerusalem.[52]

Premillennialist evangelicals also built educational enterprises in the city, based on the idea that evangelical students and scholars should come to Jerusalem and became acquainted with the country at first hand. One such institution is the Institute for Holy Land Studies (IHLS). Its founder,

Douglas Young, a former dean of a conservative evangelical theological seminary in Minneapolis, established the IHLS in the 1950s as a place where evangelical students could come for a semester or a year, or could take a graduate degree in biblical studies. The concept of the school thus resembles that of Jewish institutions of higher learning in the city, and is based on the idea that Jerusalem should serve as a center of academic studies and research, a site of intellectual pilgrimage for Christian believers.[53]

In the latter decades of the twentieth century, psychotherapists in Jerusalem have noticed a phenomenon they have labeled "the Jerusalem Syndrome."[54] This syndrome occurs among people of conservative evangelical, mostly Pentecostal, background who have grown up on a literal reading of the Bible and on premillennialist messianic expectations. Upon arriving in Jerusalem, such persons relate to the city not as the earthly, contemporary place that it is, but rather as the city where Jesus walked and suffered and sacrificed himself for the sake of humanity, or as the future messianic city where Jesus will walk the streets as the triumphant king. Those suffering from the syndrome may wander the streets in euphoria, forgetting who they really are.[55]

At the turn of the new millennium, a number of evangelical groups and individuals arrived in Jerusalem to witness the coming of the Lord at first hand. While such visits to Jerusalem have taken place for over a hundred years, the last years of the second millennium have seen the largest concentration of such messianic pilgrims in the history of the city.[56]

ESCHATOLOGY AND POLITICS

The evangelical premillennialist view of Jerusalem and its role in the events of the End Times has had a profound influence on their attitudes toward the Zionist movement, the State of Israel, and the Arab-Israeli conflict. Premillennialists responded enthusiastically to the belief that the return of the Jews to their land was a part of the events that will lead to Jesus' return. They saw in Zionism not merely a secular movement of national renewal, but a vehicle to help prepare the scene for the apocalyptic events of the End Times. Since the late nineteenth century, they have interpreted events and developments in Jerusalem in particular and the Land of Israel in general as "signs of the time," indicating that the current era was ending and the messianic age was at hand. Such occurrences as the rejuvenation of the Hebrew language, the new Jewish settlements in Palestine, and the new neighborhoods of Jerusalem all proved the validity of the evangelical premillennialist reading of the Scriptures and its predication of the unfolding of history.[57]

The Balfour Declaration and the British takeover of Jerusalem filled evangelical Christians with further joy.[58] Excited by hopes for the Second Coming, they lashed out at the British for putting restrictions on Jewish immigration and settlement, and criticized the Arabs for their hostility toward the Zionist endeavor and for their violence against the Jews.[59] Trying to block the building of a Jewish commonwealth in Palestine was viewed as equivalent to putting obstacles in the way of God's plans for the End Times. Such attempts, they asserted, were futile and the Arabs would pay dearly for their rebellious attempts.[60]

After the birth of Israel, many evangelicals observed the young Jewish state with great interest in an attempt to interpret its significance for the advancement of God's plans and purpose in the ages. Although they were not enthusiastic about the secular character of the Israeli government and society, they remained hopeful that it served a purpose relating to their messianic hopes.[61] The mass emigration of Jews to Israel in the 1950s from Asian, African, and East European countries was a cause for encouragement. This, they believed, was a significant development that had been prophesied in the Bible and a clear indication that the present era was terminating and the events of the end of this age were beginning to unfold.

The Six Day War had a profound effect on evangelical attitudes toward Jerusalem. Not since the French Revolution and the Napoleonic wars in the late eighteenth and early nineteenth centuries had there been a political-military event that provided so much fuel for the engine of prophecy as the short, dramatic war between Israel and its neighbors in June 1967, a war that led to the Jews taking over the historical sites of Jerusalem. The unexpected Israeli victory, and the territorial gains it achieved, strengthened the premillennialists' conviction that Israel was created for an important mission in history and was to play an important role in the process preceding the arrival of the Messiah.[62]

After the war, it became clear to those waiting for the Second Coming that Israel now held the territory on which to rebuild the Temple and reinstate the priestly sacrificial rituals.[63] Many premillennialists expected the imminent building of the Temple as part of the events of the end of the age. One such person who decided to give God a hand was Michael Dennis Rohan, a young Australian who had joined the Church of God and became an ardent premillennialist. After spending some time as a volunteer in an Israeli kibbutz, Rohan visited Jerusalem in July 1969 and set fire to the El-Aksa Mosque on the Temple Mount in an attempt to secure the ground necessary for building the Temple. The mosque was damaged, Arabs rioted, Rohan was arrested, put to trial, found insane, and sent to Australia to spend the rest of his life in an asylum.[64] Many premillennialists learned their lesson: openly promoting the idea that the Jews should begin building the Temple would provoke Arab hostility, embarrass the State of Israel, and hurt the image of evangelical Christianity. Although many American premillennialists were happy to discover that Jewish groups such as *Ateret Cohanim* were preparing themselves for the operation of the rebuilt Temple's ritual works and sacrifices,[65] most of them refrained from openly working for the construction of that holy site. But not all.

A few organizations and groups in the 1970s, '80s, and '90s openly advocated the building of the holy Jewish shrine. Some conservative evangelical individuals and institutions have kept close contact with the Jerusalem-based Temple Foundation, the Temple Mount Faithful, and the Temple Institute, Jewish groups that openly advocate rebuilding the Temple.[66] Chuck Smith, a noted minister and evangelist whose Calvary Chapel in Costa Mesa, California is one of the largest and most dynamic evangelical churches in America, invited Stanley Goldfoot, the founder and head of the Temple Mount Foundation, to come to California and lecture in his church. He also secured financial support for exploration of the exact site of the Temple.[67]

One noted attempt to explore the Temple Mount was that of Lambert Dolphin, a California physicist and leader of the "Science and Archeology Team." Using sophisticated geophysical technological devices and methods, Dolphin tried, in the early 1980s, to locate the Temple's exact location. The Israeli police, however, refused to allow him to use his devices in a place where they could provoke Moslem resentment.[68] Some evangelicals who hope to see the Temple rebuilt have embraced the conclusions of other explorers of the Temple site, believing that the Temple stood between the two major Moslem shrines, El-Aksa and the Dome of the Rock, and that it could, therefore, be rebuilt without destroying them, thus providing a "peaceful solution" to the problem of how to build the Temple at a site holy to the Moslems.[69] Others, such as Jan Willem van der Hoeven, disagree. Van der Hoeven, a Dutch premillennialist who went to Jerusalem in the late 1960s as the warden of the Garden Tomb, remained in the city and became active in mustering Christian support for Israel. For this premillennialist activist, Islam is an idolatrous religion and its control of the Temple Mount signifies the prevailing power of evil. Van der Hoeven yearns for the removal of Islam and its mosques from the holy site and the rebuilding of the Temple.[70]

Such outlooks have had political implications. In the 1970s and '80s, evangelicals were counted among Israel's most ardent supporters in the American public arena, where evangelical influence is the strongest.[71] Evangelicals voiced their approval of American political and economic support for Israel and became involved in such Jewish issues as the demand to facilitate Jewish immigration from Russia.[72] Dozens of pro-Israeli fundamentalist organizations have emerged in the United States. Besides mustering political support for Israel among American evangelicals, they also organize lectures, distribute materials on Israel and its historical role, and organize tours to the Holy Land.[73] The years following the Six Day War also saw an increase in the physical presence and activity of conservative evangelicals in Israel. Evangelical tours to that country increased, as did the numbers of field-study seminars and volunteers going to kibbutzim.[74]

In 1981, when, following the Israeli Knesset's Jerusalem Law, which declared the entire city of Jerusalem to belong to Israel, many states closed their consulates in Jerusalem, a group of European and American evangelicals established the International Christian Embassy. Composed of charismatic premillennialists, it has become the largest of the "Christian Zionist" organizations. In addition to offering lectures and distributing material about Israel and its role in history, the International Christian Embassy has organized groups of visitors to the Holy Land and has collected money for various Israeli enterprises such as the absorption of Russian immigrants.[75]

CONCLUSION

Conservative evangelical Christians come from a tradition that does not adhere to the idea of holy sites, yet the city of Jerusalem occupies a special place in their theology and stirs their imagination: it is the site of historical biblical scenes as well as of future occurrences with cosmic significance for all humanity in its role as the central locale of messianic events. Since the nineteenth century, evangelicals have been drawn to the city, going on visits or as missionaries, and, at times, settling in the city and building their homes there. Evangelical involvement with Jerusalem influenced the development and character of Jerusalem and left its mark on the social and cultural amalgam of the city. On the political level, the evangelical understanding of Jerusalem and its eschatological role has determined much of its thinking on issues relating to the Middle East and Israel. Its messianic outlook has helped to shape American policy toward Israel.

Messianic expectations are, in this case, more than mere hopes; they shape present realities and future developments.

NOTES

[1] On the film and its political views, see David A. Rausch, *Communities in Conflict: Evangelicals and Jews* (Philadelphia: Trinity Press International, 1991), 149-150.

[2] Robert M. Grant, *Augustus to Constantine: The Rise and Triumph of Christianity in the Roman World* (San Francisco: Harper and Row, 1990); Bart D. Ehrman, *Jesus: Apocalyptic Prophet of the New Millennium* (New York: Oxford University Press, 1999).

[3] Jaroslav Pelikan, *The Emergence of the Catholic Tradition (100-600)* (Chicago: University of Chicago Press, 1971).

[4] See George H. Williams, *The Radical Reformation* (Philadelphia: Westminster, 1970).

[5] See David S. Katz, *Philo-Semitism and the Re-Admission of the Jews to England, 1603-65* (Oxford: Oxford University Press, 1982).

[6] Clarke Garrett, *Respectable Folly: Millenarians and the French Revolution in France and England* (Baltimore: The Johns Hopkins University Press, 1975); W. H. Oliver, *Prophets and Millennialists: The Uses of Biblical Prophecy in England from the 1790s to the 1840s* (Aukland: Aukland University Press, 1978; John F. C. Harrison, *The Second Coming: Popular Millenarianism 1780-1850* (London: Rutgers University Press, 1979).

[7] Franz Kobler, *The Vision Was There* (London: Lincoln's Pager, 1956); Meir Verete, "Ra'ayon Shivat Yisrael Bamahshavah Haprotestantit Beangliyah 1790-1840," *Ziyon* 33 (1968): 145-179; Barbara W. Tuchman, *Bible and Sword* (London: Macmillan, 1983), 158-223; Mel Scult, *Millennial Expectations and Jewish Liberties* (Leiden: Brill, 1978).

[8] Tuchman, *Bible and Sword*, 175-177.

[9] On dispensationalism, see Clarence B. Bass, *Background to Dispensationalism* (Grand Rapids: Eerdmans, 1960); David MacPherson, *The Incredible Cover Up: The True Story of the Pre-Trib Rapture* (Plainfield: Omega, 1975); Ernest R. Sandeen, *The Roots of Fundamentalism: British and American Millenarianism, 1800-1930* (Grand Rapids: Baher Book House, 1978).

[10] For details of the dispensationalist eschatological hope, see, for example, Hal Lindsey's dispensationalist best-seller, *The Late Great Planet Earth* (Grand Rapids: Zondervan, 1971).

[11] See, for example, Henry Ironside, *Who Will Be Saved in the Coming Period of Judgement?* (New York: Loizeau Brothers, n.d.).

[12] Arno C. Gaebelien, *Hath God Cast Away His People?* (New York: Gospel Publishing, 1905).

[13]On the spread of dispensational millennialism, see Yaakov Ariel, *On Behalf of Israel* (New York: Carlson, 1991), 30-54.

[14]George Marsden, *Fundamentalism and American Culture* (New York: Oxford University Press, 1982).

[15]Marsden, *Fundamentalism*, Sandeen, *Roots of Fundamentalism*, and Timothy P. Weber, *Living in the Shadow of the Second Coming* (Grand Rapids: Zondervan, 1983).

[16]See, for example, A. G. Mojtabai, *Blessed Assurance* (Boston: Houghton Mifflin, 1986).

[17]William E. Blackstone, *Jerusalem* (Chicago: Fleming H. Revell, 1891).

[18]See, for example, such journals as *Our Hope: The Jewish Era, The Institute Tie,* and *The King's Business.*

[19]David Klatzker, "American Christian Travelers to the Holy Land, 1821-1939"(Ph.D. diss., Temple University, 1987), 182-195.

[20]William E. Blackstone, *Jesus is Coming* (1st ed.; Chicago: Fleming H. Revell, 1878; 2nd ed.; Chicago: Fleming H. Revell, 1886; 3rd ed.; Los Angeles: Bible House, 1908).

[21]Yaakov Ariel, "An American Initiative for a Jewish State: William Blackstone and the Petition of 1891," *Studies in Zionism* 10 (1990): 87-102.

[22]On Moody and his career, see James F. Findlay, *Dwight L. Moody: American Evangelist 1837-1899* (Chicago: University of Chicago Press, 1969).

[23]Yaakov Ariel, "An American Evangelist and the Jews: Dwight Moody and His Attitude Towards the Jewish People," *Immanuel* 22-23 (1990): 41-49.

[24]Wilbur M. Smith, *An Annotated Bibliography of D. L. Moody* (Chicago: Moody Press, 1948), 141.

[25]William R. Moody, *The Life of Dwight L. Moody* (New York: Fleming H. Ravell Company, 1900), 384-392.

[26]See, for example, the brochure, "See Israel Through Jewish Eyes, Conducted by Harold and Grace Sevener" (Chosen People Ministries, 1991).

[27]See, for example, *Baedeker's Guide to Jerusalem* (Norwhich: Jarrold and Sons, 1983), 72-3.

[28]See, for example, *Pilgrims in a New Millennium: Spiritual Reflections from the Holy Land* (Jerusalem: Interreligious Council in Israel, 1999).

[29]On Jimmy Swaggart and his comeback, see Michael J. Giuliano, *Thrice-Born: The Rhetorical Comeback of Jimmy Swaggart* (Macon: Mercer University Press, 1999).

[30]*Baedeker's Guide to Jerusalem*, 72-3.

[31]Gabriel Barkai, "The Garden Tomb in Jerusalem," in *Zev Vilnay's Jubilee Volume* (ed. E. Schiller; Jerusalem: Ariel, 1984), 195-203.

[32]For example, *Pilgrim's Map of the Holy Land* (Jerusalem, 1998).

[33]Yaakov Ariel, *Evangelizing the Chosen People: Missions to the Jews in America, 1880-2000* (Chapel Hill: University of North Carolina Press, 2000), 9-76.

[34]See Gershon Greenberg, *The Holy Land in American Religious Thought, 1620-1948* (Lanham: University Press of America, 1994), 113-140.

[35]See Pliny Fisk, *The Holy Land: An Interesting Field of Missionary Enterprise, A Sermon Preached in the Old Church Boston, Sabbath Evening, Oct. 31, 1819, Just Before the Departure of the Palestine Mission* (Boston: Samuel T. Armstrong, 1819).

[36]See Barbara W. Tuchman, *Bible and Sword: How the British Came to Palestine* (London: Macmillan, 1982), 175-207; Kelvin Crombie, *For the Love of Zion* (London: Hodder and Stoughton, 1991), 36-39. For further details, see Thomas Idinopulos, "British Millenarian Missionaries in Eretz Israel," in *"A Land Flowing With Milk and Honey": Visions of Israel from Biblical to Modern Times* (ed. L. Greenspoon and R. Simkins; Studies in Jewish Civilization 11; Omaha: Creighton University Press, 2001), 285-296.

[37]David Burnet, *The Jerusalem Mission Under the Direction of the American Christian Missionary Society* (Cincinnati: American Christian Publication Society, 1853).

[38]The International Missionary Alliance was established in 1887 "to carry the Gospel to Tibet and other parts of the world," A local American organization, the Christian Alliance, was organized to support, in prayer and finance, the missionary enterprise. The two societies were virtually one in purpose and constituency. In 1897, they were formally united as the Christian and Missionary Alliance. A. B. Simpson, who directed both organizations, was elected president and superintendent. By 1893, the Christian and Missionary Alliance was operating forty stations with 180 missionaries at work in 12 countries. On the early history of the Christian and Missionary Alliance, see P. Padington, *Twenty Five Wonderful Years, 1889-1914* (New York: Christian Alliance, 1914).

[39]*Ibid.*, 18.

[40]Paul Schmigdal, "American Holiness Churches in the Holy Land" (Ph.D. diss., Jerusalem, 1996), 63-4.

[41]Saul Colbi, *A History of the Christian Presence in the Holy Land* (Lanham: University Press of America, 1988), 143-162.

[42]On the evangelical missionary endeavor in Jerusalem in the early years of the State, see Yaakov Ariel, "Evangelists in a Strange Land: American Missionaries in Israel, 1948-1967," *Studies in Contemporary Jewry* 14 (1998): 195-213.

[43]See Louis T. Talbot and William W. Orr, *The New Nation of Israel and the Word of God* (Los Angeles: Bible Institute of Los Angeles, 1948); M. R. DeHaan, *The Jew and Palestine in Prophecy* (Grand Rapids: Zondervan, 1950); William L. Hull, *The Fall and Rise of Israel* (Grand Rapids: Zondervan, 1954); Arthur Kac, *The Rebirth of the State of Israel: Is It of God or of Man?* (Chicago: Moody, 1958); and George T. B. Davis, *God's Guiding Hand* (Philadelphia: Million Testament Campaign,1962).

[44]In *The Chosen People*, 55:2 (1949): 16-17.

[45]On Israeli policy toward Christian churches in its early years, see Colbi, *History of the Christian Presence in the Holy Land*, 163-84; Herbert Weiner, *The Wild Goats of Ein Gedi* (Garden City, New York: Doubleday, 1961), 12-15, 29-111; see also Gavriel Zeldin, "Catholics and Protestants in Jerusalem and the 'Return of Jews to Zion,' 1948-1988" (Ph.D. diss., The Hebrew University of Jerusalem, 1992).

[46] On the incident and the atmosphere under which missionaries operated, see Per Osterley, *The Church in Israel* (Lund: Gleerup, 1970).

[47]Ariel, *Evangelizing the Chosen People*, 143-64.

[48]*The Chosen People*, 61:8 (1956): 8-9.

[49]Ariel, *Evangelizing the Chosen People*, 143-64.

[50]See Gershon Nerel, "Messianic Jews and the Modern Zionist Movement," *Israel and Yeshua*, (ed. T. Elgvin; Jerusalem: Caspari Center, 1993), 75-84.

[51]See Ruth Kark and Yaakov Ariel, "Messianism, Holiness, Charisma and Community: The American Colony in Jerusalem," *Church History* 65:4 (1996).

[52]Helga Dudman and Ruth Kark, *The American Colony: Scenes from A Jerusalem Saga* (Jerusalem: Carta, 1998).

[53]On Young and his enterprise, see David A. Rausch, *Communities in Conflict: Evangelicals and Jews* (Philadelphia: Trinity, 1991), 90-93, 99-100, 114, 151.

[54]Robert Stone, *Damascus Gate* (Boston: Houghton Mifflin, 1998).

[55]See Hagit Malo, "*Meshugaim Al Hair*" ["Crazy About the City"], *Makor Rishon*, May 22, 1998, 12-13. See also Stone, *Damascus Gate*.

[56]See Boaz Gaon, "*Mehakim LaMashiach*" ["Waiting for the Messiah"], *Sofshavua*, 14-18, 78.

[57]Blackstone, *Jerusalem*.

[58]For example, George T. B. Davis, *Fulfilled Prophecies That Prove the Bible* (Philadelphia: Million Testament Campaign, 1931); and Keith L. Brooks, *The Jews and the Passion for Palestine in Light of Prophecy* (Los Angeles: Brooks, 1937).

[59]James Gray, editorial in the *Moody Bible Institute Monthly* 31 (193): 436.

[60] James Gray, "Editorial," *Moody Bible Institute Monthly* 31 (1931): 346.

[61]See Talbot and Orr, *New Nation of Israel*; DeHaan, *Jew and Palestine in Prophecy*; Hull, *Fall and Rise of Israel*; Kac, *Rebirth of the State of Israel*.

[62]See, for example, L. Nelson Bell, "Unfolding Destiny," *Christianity Today* 9 (1967): 1044-45.

[63]Raymond L. Cox, "Time for the Temple?" *Eternity* 19 (1968): 17-18; Malcolm Couch, "When Will the Jews Rebuild the Temple?" *Moody Monthly* 74 (1973): 34-35, 86.

[64]Jerusalem District Court Archive, Criminal File 69/173, 503, 1206.

[65]Gershom Gorenberg, *The End of Days* (New York: Free Press, 2000).

[66] Gorenberg, *End of Days*.

[67]See Donald E. Miller, *Reinventing American Protestantism* (Berkeley: University of California Press, 1999).

[68] Gorenberg, *End of Days,* 124-26.

[69] See Yisrayl Hawkins, *A Peaceful Solution to Building the Next Temple in Yerusalem* (Abilene: House of Yahweh, 1989).

[70]In a sermon, "Getting Tender Before the Lord," July 17, 1991.

[71]Michael Lienesch, *Redeeming America: Piety and Politics in the New Christian Right* (Chapel Hill: University of North Carolina Press, 1993).

[72] See, for example, Peter L. Williams and Peter L. Benson, *Religion on Capitol Hill: Myth and Realities* (New York: Oxford University Press, 1986); Allen D. Hertzke, *Representing God in Washington* (Knoxville: University of Tennessee Press, 1988); and Mark Silk, *Spiritual Politics* (New York: Torchstone, 1989).

[73]For example, Christians United for Israel and the American Forum for Jewish-Christian Cooperation.

[74]For example, *Pilgrim Maps of the Holy Land.*

[75]R. Scott Appleby, *Spokesman for the Despised* (Chicago: University of Chicago Press, 1997), 363-413.

Apocalyptic Schemes and Dreams: How an Ancient Jewish Vision of the Future Came to Dominate the Modern World

James D. Tabor

In just a few months we will all know. Will the arrival of the year 2000, and the ushering in of the third millennium, turn out to be "business as usual"—with all the media hype and apocalyptic hysteria gradually fading away into the all-too-familiar flow of daily life? Or will that magical number, so full of symbolic, cultural, and religious meaning, end up signaling something far more significant—something cosmic in its implications? While the question itself is silly to some, mildly important to others, to millions more there is no subject more serious, in this "year of the Lord,"1999, with the days ticking off as in some kind of countdown. A CNN poll taken January 18, 1999, asked, "Do you think there is some kind of significance to the date January 1, 2000?" Thirty-three percent answered yes, 64 percent no, with only three percent responding that they did not know.

In some ways the year 2000 and the decades following are already becoming somewhat ordinary. Most of us are carrying around credit cards in our wallets with expirations dates marked 00, 01, or 02—and they actually work. We commonly read all kinds of budgetary and financial projections taking us well into the twenty-first century. And in the United States we are gearing up for the presidential election in November 2000. Besides, as Arthur Clarke has reminded us, despite all our plans for transition and celebration, the new millennium actually does not begin with the passing of midnight this coming December 31, 1999—but one year later, as we enter 2001. Nevertheless, I doubt that anyone is going to alter plans for this coming New Year's Eve because of this technicality.

More than five years ago I had a telephone call from the chief religion editor of the Associated Press. He was chairing a meeting in New York of his fellow religion editors from all the major print media. They were considering how they would cover the upcoming millennium and what its relevance might be for religion in general and, more particularly, for any potential revival of apocalypticism. Someone at the meeting had raised the question as to whether the millennium actually began on January 1, 2000, or January 1, 2001. Since I had established something of a reputation for knowing such millennial technicalities, I was one of the experts consulted. I assured the group that although properly speaking the millennium would begin with the year 2001, they might as well forget it—the year 2000 had clearly already won the day.

One can rationally argue that our 2000 mark is purely arbitrary. After all, the Christian year 2000 will be the year 5760 on the Hebrew calendar, which marks the years from "creation" based on rabbinic tradition; and it will be the year 1420 by Muslim reckoning, measured in lunar years from the date Mohammed fled Mecca in 622 CE. The Egyptians, Babylonians, Greeks, Romans, Aztecs, and Mayans, not to mention the Chinese and Japanese, have all had their own separate ways of marking times and measuring the passing of historical eras. None of these give any significance whatever to the year 2000 on the Gregorian calendar, even though it has become our secular global standard.

Arbitrary or not, this extraordinary focus on the new millennium is not going to go away; it is only going to increase, involving as it does a complex set of converging circumstances and perceptions, often contradictory, that are drawing in the media, marketing, government, information technologies, politics, and religion. The *Wall Street Journal* published a special "Millennium Report" as a thick supplement to its January 11, 1999 issue. It surveyed various aspects of human culture and society over the past 1000 years and included an ingenious mock-up "front-page" of how the paper might have covered the news on January 1, 1000. The *New York Times* has announced a special series of six in-depth reports, spaced over the year and called the "Millennium Series," for their Sunday magazine. These issues will highlight ten centuries of human experience—"the ideas and achievements, profundities and absurdities that have defined our civilization over the past thousand years—and those that will lead us into the next thousand." The splashy two page ad announcing the series was headlined: "January 1, 2000 . . . The biggest birthday any of us will ever live through." Both papers are geared to an upbeat, optimistic, decidedly non-apocalyptic approach to the subject.

Whether newspaper, magazine, or TV, it seems that everyone is planning some kind of special ongoing coverage of the millennium. A simple search of the Internet yields over 390,000 Web sites that mention either the term

"Year 2000" or "millennium." The books are also beginning to appear. John Updike's latest novel, set in the year 2020, is appropriately titled *Toward the End of Time*.[1] In the spring of 1999, Robert Stone published *Damascus Gate*,[2] a novel set in Jerusalem that features a self-proclaimed messiah and his followers who plan to bring on the end through bombing the Muslim Dome of the Rock on the Temple Mount in Jerusalem. In his current bestseller, *A Man in Full*,[3] Tom Wolfe offers his analysis of American culture at the turn of the age, while pitching the restoration of the ancient Stoic philosophy of Epictetus ("Life in Atlanta on the cusp of the millennium, as Old South values collide with a new world" reads the *New York Times* piece). Stephen Jay Gould's *Questioning the Millennium: A Rationalist's Guide* and Damain Thompson's 's *The End of Time: Faith and Fear in the Shadow of the Millennium* were two of the most recent non-fictional analyses of the phenomenon.[4] At the 1998 Frankfurt Book Fair I counted over fifty titles, mostly in English, dealing in some way with aspects of the coming millennium—and that did not include the technical works addressing the Y2K (Year 2000) computer glitch. Neale Walsch's best-selling trilogy, *Conversations with God,* claims to be nothing less than "a message from God," that promises a "social, sexual, educational, political, economic, and theological revolution on this planet the likes of which we have never seen, and seldom imagined."[5] The "dawn of the Age of Aquarius" is no longer a pop-Sixties catchphrase. It is the serious agenda of millions, as witnessed by the phenomenal sales of James Redfield's *The Celestine Prophecy,* which heralds an "emerging planetary culture" set to make a "quantum leap" into the new millennium.[6]

All the main book chains have extensive sections devoted to what one might loosely call "New Age" spirituality, more often than not connected to the coming millennium. The sixteenth century writings of Nostradamus, who pinpointed the years from 1999-2003 as a time of great turmoil and transition, are enjoying a great revival.[7] The most cited passage is *Centuries* Quatrain X:72: "The year 1999, seven months, from the sky will come a great King of Terror, he will bring to life the great king of the Mongols. Before and after Mars [War] reigns with good success." This is apparently the only prediction by Nostradamus that specifies a precise date: July 1999. Some have seen the sighting of the new comet Lee, late last summer, as the predicted herald of the King of the Mongols; that is, the Antichrist. In Quatrain X:74 Nostradamus writes of "the age of the great millennium when the dead will come out of their graves," speaking of our own time—the year 1999 and beyond. At the same time the evangelical Christian book market is currently saturated with several dozen popular titles offering a completely opposite perspective. Most of them are oriented toward surviving an imminent apocalyptic disaster based upon interpretations of biblical prophecy, much in the tradition of Hal Lindsey's all-time bestseller *The Late Great Planet Earth* (sales of over 20 million since 1970).[8] Pope John Paul II has declared the Year 2000 a special Jubilee for celebration and reconciliation, and millions of pilgrims are expected to visit the Holy Land, perhaps including the Pope himself.[9]

The Israelis are pulling out all the stops to prepare for an overflow of visitors, but also to guard against what they perceive as "doomsday" groups that might turn to violence, or even suicide, in fulfillment of certain prophecies from the book of Revelation. They have set up a special task force, which includes an undercover team drawn from the Mossad intelligence agency, the Shin Bet security service, and Israeli police.[10] On January 8, 1999, the Israelis deported fourteen members of a Denver-based apocalyptic group called the Concerned Christians, based on reports that their leader, Monte Kim Miller (not among the deportees), had said he was destined to die in the streets of Jerusalem in the final days of December 1999.[11] And just this fall, a group of 25 Irish Catholic pilgrims were turned away at the Israeli port in Haifa for fear that they too shared some kind of apocalyptic visions of the future. The Irish government has issued a formal protest, holding that the whole episode is one of mistaken identity and overzealous paranoia on the part of the Israelis.[12] The Israelis have coordinated their efforts with the FBI and are sharing intelligence and information. FBI director Louis Freeh has officially warned that apocalyptic groups and right-wing extremists, whether domestic or international, might turn to violence to fulfill their prophecies of Armageddon as the year 2000 approaches. A document called "Project Megiddo" (taken from the term Armageddon, "Hill of Megiddo") was recently distributed to law enforcement agencies around the country, alerting them to the potential threats of such groups.[13] Whatever combination of merriment, mayhem, madness, and marketing the arrival of the millennium brings, it is surely to be *the* story of 1999.

WHY COUNT TIME BY MILLENNIA?

The world millennium is of course from the Latin *mille*, simply meaning "a thousand" (the equivalent term in Greek is *chilias*, producing the term chiliasm). What few realize is that our very concept of marking time in one thousand year segments, and its resulting significance, is rooted in the final chapters of Revelation, that mysterious final book of the Christian Bible. Indeed, we can trace the worldwide influence of this very Jewish notion to a single passage in the book: Rev 20:1-6. There the author describes a time when Satan, the Devil, is restrained and prevented from "deceiving the nations" of the world for a thousand years (he is bound with a great chain and thrown into a bottomless pit). This defeat of Satan is followed by a resurrection from the dead of those faithful to God, who "live and reign with the Messiah for one thousand years"(20:4). Following this thousand year rule Satan is briefly released for a final fling, just prior to the resurrection of all the remaining dead and the great and final judgment of both the living and the dead (20:11-15). This final thousand-year period is mentioned five times in these six verses.

This thousand-year period in the book of Revelation is not just any thousand-year period: it is the final one thousand years, followed by the resurrection of the dead and the last great judgment. And that is the point. If human history is to culminate in a final thousand-year period, does this not suggest a more general division of time into eras or periods of one thousand years? This is apparently the thinking that lies behind this text in the book of Revelation. We have no precise parallel to this final thousand-year period in apocalyptic Jewish sources prior to this time. What we do find, however, is the general notion of a specific period of bliss in which evil is conquered, death, disease, and suffering are no more, and the people of God are rewarded for their faithfulness (4 Ezra 6:25-28; 2 Baruch 73:1-7; Psalms of Solomon 17:21-32). In 4 Ezra (roughly contemporary with the book of Revelation) this "age of the Messiah" lasts four hundred years (7:26-30). 2 Enoch 33 has a seven thousand-year period, but followed by an "eighth day," of eternal rest. There is good reason to believe that the author of Revelation was tapping into a concept that had been developing for centuries among Jewish groups, and this general scheme of dividing history into millennial periods can be traced to Zoroastrian sources.[14] What the early Christians do is take up this general ancient Jewish apocalyptic notion of a messianic "age of bliss" and decisively quantify it—hence the classic Western concept of the Millennium!

Simply put, it is the notion—first found in the Psalms, but given a decidedly apocalyptic cast in the New Testament—that "a day with the LORD is a thousand years and a thousand years is a day" (Ps 90:4; 2 Pet 3:8-9). An analogy was then drawn between the six days of Creation in Gen 1:1-2:3 and the final seventh day, or Sabbath, upon which God rested from all his work. According to this view, human history would last precisely six thousand years and be followed by a final seventh "day" or millennium: that is, a final thousand years, which, like the Sabbath day, would be characterized by peace and "rest" (the word *Shabbat* in Hebrew means to stop or halt). In this case the "rest" or "Sabbath" would mean a relief from the toil and domination of Satan's evil grasp upon the planet. Millenarianism refers specifically to this idea of a "millennial reign of the Messiah," but more generally to any utopian view of a transformed New Age, or New World Order.[15]

There is an important section in the Babylonian Talmud that seems to reflect some vestige of such a scheme of history. Rabbi Kattina taught:

> Six thousand years shall the world exist, and one thousand, the seventh, it shall be desolate, as it is written, "And the Lord alone shall be exalted in that day." Just as the seventh year is one year of release in seven, so is the world: one thousand years out of seven shall be fallow (*b. Sanh.* 97a).

To which Rabbi Eliyyahu replies:

> The world is to exist six thousand years. In the first two thousand there was desolation [no Torah]; two thousand years the Torah flourished; and the next two thousand years is the Messianic era, but through our many iniquities all these years have been lost (*b. Sanh.*97a).

It is clear, from the apocalyptic nature of the Dead Sea Scrolls, the John the Baptist movement, and the Jesus movement itself, with its proclamation that "the Kingdom of God is near," that some Jewish groups in and around the first century CE were expecting a messiah to appear.[16] The Talmudic passage cited above looks back on such a hope and considers it somehow "postponed" in view of the Roman defeat of the Jews and the destruction of the Temple in 70 CE, and the disastrous Bar Kochba revolt in 135 CE.[17] Obviously these rabbis did not believe Jesus was the Messiah. Yet the very same scheme, in the hands of the Christians, becomes a powerful concept, giving biblical history a chronological "logic" that would culminate in Jesus Christ.

The earliest succinct and systematic Christian exposition of this idea is found in the *Letter of Barnabas*, which dates to the late first or early second century CE. This document was highly treasured by many Christians and included as part of the Scriptures by some.[18] The author writes:

> He speaks of the Sabbath at the beginning of the Creation, "And God made in six days the works of his hands and on the seventh day he made an end, and rested in it and sanctified it." Notice

children, what is the meaning of "He made an end in six days"? He means this: that the Lord will make an end of everything in six thousand years, for a day with him means a thousand years. . . . So then, children, in six days, that is in six thousand years, everything will be completed. "And he rested on the seventh day." This means, when his Son comes he will destroy the time of the wicked one, and will judge the godless, and will change the sun and the moon and the stars, and then he will truly rest on the seventh day (*Barn.*25: 3-5).

This notion becomes commonplace in the early church and is repeated by the earlier Church fathers.[19] Indeed, Christians came to understand this as a primary meaning of the Sabbath day. Just as God created the physical world in six days and rested on the Sabbath, so he will create a new world of spiritual perfection over a seven thousand year period. There is no doubt that the book of Revelation reflects this precise notion, even though our text mentions only the terminal thousand-year period. The author clearly assumes that his audience is familiar with the idea as a whole and can easily fill in the blanks on its own.

This idea of six thousand years of human history was most compelling within Jewish and Christian apocalyptic circles. It strongly reinforces the general notion that history unfolds according to a divine plan and an ordered sequence, orchestrated by the will of God. But there is another, far more alluring, possibility—the possibility of calculation. After all, if one could determine precisely where one lived in this unfolding sequence of millennia, the idea of the "time of the end" drawing near would take on a much more concrete meaning. And this brings us back to the year 1999.

WHY IS THIS MILLENNIUM DIFFERENT FROM ALL OTHER MILLENNIA?

The millennium we are now leaving behind (the eleventh through the twentieth centuries CE), the second millennium as dated from the birth of Jesus, is the sixth based on a literal chronology of the Hebrew Bible:[20]

Adam to Noah's Flood:	1656 years
Flood to birth of Jacob:	454 years
Abraham to Exodus:	430 years
Exodus to First Temple:	480 years
First Temple to Exile:	393 years
Exile to Second Temple:	72 years
Total:	3485 years

This takes us to the time of Haggai and Zechariah and the completion of the rebuilt Temple in Jerusalem in 516/515 BCE (the sixth year of Darius [Ezra 6:13-15]). That works out to about 2515 years ago. If we add the numbers together—2515 years taking us back to the time of Darius and another 3485 years taking us back to Adam—you guessed it: we are sitting on the cusp of the 5999th year of world history as based on a literal reading of the traditional text of the Hebrew Bible. But the modern Jewish calendar has 1999 as the year 5760 rather than 5999. How can we account for this 240 year difference, since the rabbis also began their count with Adam and Eve? The answer is that the traditional Jewish calendar, based on the ancient rabbinic text called *Seder Olam Rabbah*, is rooted in rabbinic tradition and theology, not the literal numbers taken directly from the Hebrew Bible and correlated with historical research.[21] The rabbis have 163 fewer years for the Persian period, with the result that rabbinic chronology dates the Babylonian Exile to 423 BCE.[22] This is not a possible date, as we know with certainly that the nineteenth year of Nebuchadnezzar, when he destroyed Jerusalem and burned the Temple, was 587 or 586 BCE. The rabbis also calculate Israel's time in Egypt, based on Exod 12:40, differently than I have done above, resulting in an additional difference of 77 years in the two systems. Taken together, these add up to exactly 240 years!

It is worth noting that some Kabbalistic or mystical Jewish sources find significance in this twentieth century of the Christian era, even though they accept the year of the world as 5760 based on the standard Jewish calendar. The Zohar predicts that "in the year 600 of the sixth millennia [5600 on the Jewish calendar or the year 1840] the gates of wisdom from above and below will be opened to [begin] to rectify the world to prepare it to enter into the seventh millennium" (1.117A).[23] By this analogy of a thousand years as a day, the year 1999, although 240 years from the seventh millennium by the Jewish calendar, is just "hours" before arrival of the cosmic seventh millennium or Sabbath. Just as pious Jews prepare for the Sabbath each week several hours before sundown, the events of the late twentieth century (especially the establishment of the State of Israel in 1948 and the Six Day War in 1967) can be seen by ardent Jewish fundamentalists as just such a Sabbath preparation—the "footsteps of the Messiah" as it were. By such a cosmic measure, 1999 would be equivalent to the Friday afternoon of human history, about five hours before sunset! Ironically, one mystical rabbi of the sixteenth century, Abraham Azulai (1570-1643), in contemplating such matters, actually came up with the precise year 5760 (1999 CE!) as having significance. He reasons that the measure of the world is the same as the measure of the *mikvah* [ritual bath], or 40 seah. Since a "seah" is "144 eggs" (these are Talmudic measurements of volume), then 40 multiplied by 144 equals 5,760. Thus:

> The length of days of this world shall be 5,760 years. Then shall the world be renewed. For as the mikvah purifies the unclean, at this time, the Holy One, Blessed Be He, will remove the unclean spirit from the world . . . but this is only the beginning of the redemption.[24]

Who, we might well ask, would take such numbers literally? After all, has not the myth of Adam and Eve been shown to lack all historical validity? Homo Sapiens surely existed many hundreds of thousands of years ago, so that a mere six thousand is a blink of an eye against human and planetary evolution. Well, the answer is yes and no. First, there are millions of Creationists who do take these numbers as absolutes and believe the first human beings with a human soul can be traced back to a literal Adam and Eve around 4000 BCE. But beyond that, there are others, more sophisticated, but nonetheless biblically conservative, who fully accept the evolutionary timetable of millions of years for the development of life on this planet (interpreting the "days" of Genesis 1 as ages), but nonetheless see civilization (literate humans in Egypt, Sumer, and China) as dating back to approximately 4000 BCE. Thus one can still maintain that human history has about run its course, with God having allowed us six thousand years to wander outside the Gates of Eden.

Some have found cryptic hints of this six thousand year period elsewhere in the Hebrew Bible. I mentioned above Ps 90:4, which speaks of a "day with the LORD as being a thousand years." There is also the statement in Gen 6:3, where Yahweh, grieved over the wickedness of human beings before the flood, appears to put a chronological cap on things: "My Spirit will not always strive with humans, their days shall be 120 years." What is the meaning of the 120 years? Does it refer to human life span? An ingenious apocalyptic reading has also been suggested. The reference to a year here has been understood as a "Great Year" or a jubilee year, not a calendar solar year. One hundred twenty multiplied by fifty such jubilee years equals six thousand years, the chronological *terminus ad quem* of permissible human wickedness. In other words, just as God sent the flood as a temporary check on evil, he has determined that human freedom to build its "Babylonian" society will be permitted only for a predetermined time.[25]

What is particularly fascinating about the general chronological scheme of the Hebrew Bible (our Year 2000 equals 6000 years after Adam) is that it does not have the slightest relationship to the birth of Jesus. All the numbers are taken from the Hebrew Bible, down to the return from Babylonian Exile, and then plugged into our modern historical and archaeological understanding of the Persian period (the sixth year of Darius equals 516/ 515 BCE). And yet, there is a fascinating correlation.

JESUS BORN "BEFORE CHRIST"?

My students are always puzzled when I try to explain to them that Jesus was likely born anywhere from 7 to 3 BCE; that is, several years before his "birth." This odd circumstance goes back to an error in calculation made by a sixth century CE scholar and monk, Dionysius Exiguus ("Dennis the Little").[26] In his time the years were dated from the reign of the Roman emperor Diocletian (284 CE), who had actually persecuted the Christians. Dionysius believed that the calendar should be recalculated from the birth of Jesus. He concluded that the Roman year 754 AUC (the system used for centuries that numbered years from the founding of Rome) would be 1 AD, or Anno Domini ("year of the Lord"), the first year following Jesus' birth (since there is no year zero). Gradually this system of calculating years caught on, and the Emperor Charlemagne made it almost universal by the ninth century CE. One often hears that the turn of the first millennium, that is the year 999 CE, caused widespread apocalyptic foreboding that the end of the world was near. Although we can find some isolated examples of such expectations, this new calendar, with its altered way of counting years, was just coming into vogue.[27] We should not imagine that the illiterate peasant masses were focused on the number 999, and its magical click over to 1000, on the night of December 31st that year.

The Gregorian calendar we use today, adjusted slightly in 1582 by Pope Gregory and his scholars, maintains the calculations that Dionysius had determined for the birth of Jesus. Unfortunately, Dionysius was a few years off in his calculations. Scholars are convinced that Jesus was born several years earlier than the year we designate as 1 CE, most dating his birth around 7-5 BCE, and some later in 3 or 2 BCE.[28] The calculations turn on Matthew's reference to the birth of Jesus as occurring before the death of Herod the Great.[29] There is also the matter of the "Christmas Star," which Matthew says the Magi or astrologers from the east observed, prompting them to travel to Palestine (Matt 3). Johannes Kepler, in 1630, proposed that Matthew refers to several extraordinary conjunctions of Jupiter and Saturn that took place in 7 BCE. More recently, Ernest Martin has argued that even more striking stellar events took place during the years 3 and 2 BCE, involving conjunctions of Jupiter and Venus (the "morning star") that were so spectacular they would have appeared in the sky as a single bright light, with Venus rising in the east.[30] The author of Revelation does refer to Jesus as "the bright morning star" (Rev 22:16). Martin's "Christmas Star" phenomenon has been accepted by many of the observatories in the world, including the Griffith in Los Angeles, for their annual Christmas programs.

What this means is that if we mark our millennia from the birth of Jesus, as we can now more accurately determine it, we already entered the new millennium some time between 1994 and 1998. It all depends on where we place the birth of Jesus in this range of possibilities from 7 BCE to 3 BCE. And yet, there is not the slightest chance that anyone is going to pay attention to such technicalities when the year 2000 conveys such symbolic meaning. For all practical purposes, give or take a year or two or three, the year 2000 marks the end of the second millennium since the birth of Jesus.

But from a wider perspective, we will, ironically, culminate approximately six thousand years of our great enterprising experiment we collectively call "human civilization." And it is the Hebrew Bible that most influentially chronicles this "changing of the guard" for our culture. Whether we will face an apocalyptic meltdown or just a mild "bump in the road," as we pass this milestone, is soon to be determined. At any rate, at this day, on this hour, I say to you all: "Welcome to the new era." May it herald for us a fulfillment of the central vision of the Hebrew prophets: a world of peace, prosperity, justice, and righteousness filling the earth as the waters cover the seas.

NOTES

[1]John Updike, *Toward the End of Time* (London: Penguin, 1999).

[2]Robert Stone, *Damascus Gate* (London: Picador, 1999).

[3]Tom Wolfe, *A Man Full* (London: BBC Worldwide Limited, 1998).

[4]Stephen Jay Gould, *Questioning the Millennium: A Rationalist's Guide to a Precisely Arbitrary Countdown* (New York : Harmony Books, 2000); Damain Thompson, *The End of Time: Faith and Fear in the Shadow of the Millennium* (London : Minerva, 1997).

[5]Neale Donald Walsch, *Conversations with God. The Dominica Discourse* (ReCreation Foundation, 1997), Book 2, introduction.

[6] James Redfield, *The Celestine Prophecy: A Pocket Guide to the Nine Insights* (London: Bantam, 1996).

[7] Nostradamus was born in France in 1503. His major work, *Centuries*, a collection of obscurely phrased, rhymed quatrinas written in French, was published in 1555. See John Hogue, *Nostradamus: The New Revelations* (New York: Barnes and Noble, 1995), for a sample of recent interpretation applied to the approaching new millennium. For the original French text with translation and commentary, see Erike Cheetham, *The Further Prophecies of Nostradamus* (New York: Perigee Books, 1985), 424. The following translations are my own.

[8] Hal Lindsey, *The Late Great Planet Earth* (Santa Ana: Vision House, 1974).

[9] Numerous resources, including papal statements regarding the Jubilee, may be found on the Internet on the Catholic Information Network, online: http://www.cin.org/jp2/jubilee.html.

[10] Yossi Melman, "Mossad, Shin Bet Bust Cult," *HaAretz* (January 4, 1999). Online: http://www.haaretzdaily.com.

[11] Sari Bashi, "Israel Cult Members Deported," *Associated Press* (January 8, 1999).

[12] Dana Budeiri, "Police Say Tourists Are Members of Christian Cult," *Associated Press* (October 11, 1999).

[13] Patricia Wilson, "FBI Director Freeh Warns of Millennium Violence," *Reuters* (February 5, 1999); Paul Nowell, "FBI Warns of Possibility of Violence at Millennium's Dawn," *Associated Press* (November 3, 1999). The word Armageddon occurs in Rev 16:16 as a geographical reference to the place in northern Israel where the final apocalyptic battle takes place between all the world's armies. A summary of the report is found on the FBI Web site: online: http://www.fbi.gov/pressrel/pressrel99/militias.htm.

[14] The notion of one thousand year periods can be traced to Zoroastrianism, which was very influential in the development of Jewish apocalypticism. See Norman Cohn, *Cosmos, Chaos, and the World to Come: The Ancient Roots of Apocalyptic Faith* (New Haven: Yale University Press, 1993), 77-104.

[15] On the general development of the Messianic ideas within late Second Temple Judaism, see John J. Collins, *The Apocalyptic Imagination* (2nd ed.; Grand Rapids: Eerdmans, 1998); see also the comprehensive article "Messianism," in *The Encyclopedia of Millennialism and Millennial Movements* (ed. R. Landes; New York: Routledge, 2000), 245-251.

[16] See John J. Collins, *The Scepter and the Star: The Messiahs of the Dead Sea Scrolls and Other Ancient Literature* (New York: Doubleday, 1995); and Craig A. Evans and Peter W. Flint, *Eschatology, Messianism, and the Dead Sea Scrolls* (Grand Rapids: Eerdmans, 1997).

[17] For an overview, including archaeological discoveries and a general bibliography, see Yigael Yadin, *Bar-Kokhba* (London: Weidenfeld and Nicholson, 1971).

[18]It is included in the oldest complete New Testament manuscript, Codex Sinaiticus, now housed in the British Library in London. It was placed after the 27 books that now make up the canon.

[19]See Papias, the extravagant millenarist, as quoted in Eusebius, *Church History* 3.39:11-13; Justin Martyr, *Dialogue with Trypho* 80-81; Irenaeus, *Against Heresies* 30-36; Tertullian, *Against Marcion* 3.24.

[20]Although there are a number of ambiguities in the chronological system that runs through the Masoretic Text of the Hebrew Bible, these numbers are generally quite easy to come up with from a literal reading of the text: Gen 5, 11, 25, Exod 12:40, 1 Kgs 6:1; the reigns of the kings of Judah added together; and the exile and return from 2 Kgs 25 and Ezra. Both Josephus (a Jewish historian who wrote in the first century CE) and the Septuagint (the ancient Greek translation of the scriptures) give very different numbers throughout.

[21]See Jack Finegan, *Handbook of Biblical Chronology*, (rev. ed.; Peabody: Hendrickson, 1998), 107-11.

[22]Apparently there is a theological reason the rabbis collapse their history and lose 240 years. They insist that there are only 490 years between the fall of the first and second Temples—which is plainly impossible by any outside historical evidence, but is the apparent assumption of the "70 weeks" prophecy of Dan 9:25-27. In order to make this prophecy come out correctly, stretching from the destruction of both the First and Second Temples, and even falling on the same precise day, the 9th of Ab, such an adjustment is necessary.

[23]*The Zohar* (trans. H. Sperling and M. Simon; vol.1; London: Soncino, 1984), 364.

[24]*Chesed l'Avraham* 2.59; see Pinchas Giller, *Reading the Zohar* (Oxford: Oxford University Press, 2001), 26-27.

[25] See E.W. Bullinger, *The Companion Bible* (Grand Rapids: Kregel Publications, 1990), 27; see also online: http://bibleprophecy.net/6000.htm.

[26]See the discussion by Finegan, *Handbook of Biblical Chronology*, 218-19.

[27]See James Reston, *The Last Apocalypse: Europe at the Year 1000 A.D.* (New York: Doubleday, 1998).

[28]The date of 3or 2 BCE was universally held by the early Church fathers and has recently been embraced again by Ernest Martin, W. F. Filmer, and others, who place the death of Herod in 1 BCE. Their position has now been accepted by Finegan, *Handbook*, 291-301.

[29]Finegan, *Handbook*, 291-97.

[30]See a detailed discussion of all the proposals, including Martin's, in Finegan, *Handbook*, 306-20.

"Teach Us to Number Our Days": The Elusive Epoch in Muslim, Jewish, and Christian Calendars

Seth Ward

Rabbi Elazar ben Hisma omer: qanin ufitche nidah hen hen gufe halachot; tekufot ugematriaot parperaot lachochma. Rabbi Elazar ben Hisma says: "Rules of Nests and Niddah are the essence of halacha; calculating time periods and gematrias are the desserts of wisdom." *The Ethics of the Fathers* 3:18.

In dealing with *tekufot ugematriaot*—calculations of calendrical periods and mathematical equivalents of words— we do well to remember that while the calculations are real enough, they are also arbitrary; they only have the meanings we ascribe to them. In Psalm 90:12, quoted above in the title of this chapter, the Psalmist refers to human mortality as a challenge to work to achieve "a heart of wisdom." The recent arrival of the year 2000 and its attendant celebrations provide more than adequate occasion to examine how Muslims, Jews, and Christians have "numbered their days," in the hopes that this exercise will also contribute in a small way towards obtaining a "heart of wisdom."

The minute after 11:59 p.m., Dec. 31, 1999, celebrated by millions as "the Millennium," did not celebrate an exact millennial anniversary of anything. It was an arbitrary date, determined by calendrical considerations. As purists happily pointed out, it was not the 2000th anniversary of January 1, 1 CE, the first day of our calendar. Fewer purists noted that, strictly speaking, January 1, 2001, is not either. Pope Gregory corrected the calendar only back to the fourth century, the time of the Nicaean Council, when the spring equinox was March 21. 730,487 days elapsed from the day usually considered to have been January 1, 1 CE until January 1, 2001—two more than the number of days in 2,000 Gregorian years, 730,485.[1] To make matters more confusing, the day celebrated in Rome as *Kalendae Ianuariae*, that is the beginning of January, 2,000 years before 2001 CE, was probably the day after January 1, 1 CE as given in conversion tables, due to irregularities in leap year regulation up to the year we now call 8 CE.[2]

The millennium was ubiquitous in 2000 because dating using the Gregorian calendar and the Christian era system is in nearly universal use today. This represents the ascendancy of the West, but even in Europe its acceptance is less than a century old. The Gregorian calendar was adopted in Russia only after the rise of Communism—and not without an attempt at creating a Revolutionary calendar—and in Turkey only after the fall of the Ottoman Empire.

Dating our current year as 2000 is based on the choice of Dionysius Exiguus (d. before 544 CE) to enumerate the Easter dates he calculated in terms of years "from the incarnation," rather than in the Diocletian era used by those whose tables he followed. It is further based on the choice of those after him to adopt his tables for calculating the date of Easter, including his enumeration system. Clerics would record major events of a year in the margins of the tables, making the dating of Easters convenient for marking the dating of events, but it would be many centuries before it was actually used in documents. Dionysius used his system for enumerating Easters, not years; ultimately, the reason he set the first Easter of his table as 532 after the incarnation remains elusive. The calendars of the two other monotheistic traditions, Judaism and Islam, likewise have elusive starting points, often misunderstood and misinterpreted. All three claim to date from historical events of central importance, yet none of these systems of dating manifests exact historical accuracy. Instead, the epoch reflects calendrical principles, not accurate chronology.

ISLAMIC CALENDAR
I. The Lunar Year
The Islamic calendar is a pure lunar year. There are twelve lunar months, each beginning with the visible crescent of the new moon. The average lunar rotation around the earth is a bit more than twenty-nine days, twelve hours, and forty-four minutes. For everyday purposes, a calendar is prepared with alternating months of thirty and twenty-nine days each. The twelfth month is twenty-nine days, but adds an extra day eleven times over thirty lunar years, representing the excess of the average lunar month over 29 ½ days.[3] The lunar year is thus 354 or 355 days long, ten or eleven days

shorter than the 365+ days of the solar year. In the Muslim calendar, nothing is done to keep the lunar months in sync with the sun.

Muslims rely on observation, not a prepared calendar, to determine the beginning and end of Ramadān, the month of fasting. Muslim astronomers such as al-Baṭṭānī (d. 929) were able to calculate the earliest time in which the Ramadān crescent could be sighted. This is more complicated than merely using a calculation based on the average lunar period. As the medieval Jewish philosopher Maimonides notes with respect to Jewish calculations, the actual conjunction of the moon varies significantly from the average, sometimes leading to a day or two difference as to when the moon may be sighted. But the Muslim astronomers considered this knowledge merely useful to confirm or reject actual observations as reported by witnesses.[4] Thus, unlike the Jewish system, there is no attempt to calculate the "day of the new moon" for any month.

II. Intercalation

Muslim tradition assumes that intercalation—the addition of an extra month to keep the calendar in line with the seasons—was the practice in pre-Islamic times. This practice, called *nasī'* in Arabic, may have been imposed or regulated by Quṣayy b. Kilāb (early fifth century CE), when he gained control of Mecca for the Quraysh, Muhammad's tribe. Intercalation was one of three prerogatives associated with the Pilgrimage and associated with various families. According to al-Ṭabarī's account, Quṣayy at first wrested at least one of these rights from the family which had held it, claiming he "was better entitled to it than they"—language similar to that used by Muhammad in a famous tradition about appropriating practices of Moses from the Jews.[5] But when he became master of Mecca, he confirmed all these prerogatives, including intercalation, to those who had done it before.[6] The narrative suggests that Quṣayy saw these rights as matters of religion. In any event, it does not suggest any changes in the method of intercalation under Quṣayy, but rather that he confirmed control over intercalation for the family which had held this right beforehand. Quṣayy confirmed intercalation as a traditional right of a family within the Banū Mālik b. Kināna clan, which held it until the establishment of Islam. A. Caussin de Perceval dated the introduction of intercalation to 412 CE; this was about two hundred years before the establishment of Islam.[7]

The *nasī'* was cancelled by the Qurān (9:36-37): "Allah ordained the months twelve in number when he created the heavens and the earth. Of these four are sacred, according to the true faith....The postponement of sacred months is a grossly impious practice in which the idolaters are misguided." This revelation is always assumed to have come down to Muhammad during his final pilgrimage in 632 CE, the tenth year of the Muslim era. The text of the Qurān implies that intercalation had not been abandoned prior to this time, although it says nothing about when the last intercalation was performed or the next one scheduled.[8]

III. The Epochal Event/Starting Point

The epochal event of the Muslim era is the *hijra*, the emigration of Muhammad to Medina. Hence the Muslim era is usually indicated in Western literature as AH, "Anno Hegirae." According to Islamic historiography, Muhammad left his hometown sometime well after the Pilgrimage festival in the year 622 CE. Various dates are given for his arrival in Medina, but it is most often given as Monday, the twelfth day of Rabīʿ I,[9] the third Meccan month. Other sources say it was Monday, the eighth of this month.[10] All agree that he arrived on a Monday and that the first communal prayer was four days later, on Friday. The traditional Muslim calendar assumes that no intercalation was made from the start of the year in which the *hijra* occurred; in the traditional calendar, 8 Rabīʿ Iʿ, AH 1, was a Monday, corresponding to 20 September, 622, and the twelfth was the following Friday, September 24.[11] Because the beginning of the month was determined by observation, it would be normal to have one or possibly two days' difference between the day of the week as calculated and the weekday actually given in a historical source. One presumes the weekday in the source is to be believed, adjusting the Julian or Gregorian date one or two days accordingly.[12] But a difference of four days is unlikely to be accounted for in this way.

In his notes to the translation of al-Ṭabarī 's account of the *hijra*, M. Montgomery Watt observed that three or four months were likely to have been intercalated between the *hijra* and the date intercalation was cancelled, causing "discrepancies about the days of the week on which certain events happened."[13] Although he calls attention to this problem, he gives the traditional equivalent for 12 Rabīʿ I, September 24, 622 CE, a Friday. A casual reader might think that the date needs to be adjusted by only a few days to yield a Monday, but in truth what Watt means is that the weekday is wrong because the date might be a few months off.

IV. Counting Back to the Epochal Event

'Umar (634-44) is traditionally credited with establishing the Islamic calendar.[14] He may have been preceded in this by Ya'lā b. 'Umayya, a governor of Yemen appointed by Abū Bakr (632-34).[15] Variations of the tradition say that Muhammad established the principle of enumerating years from the *hijra*.[16] 'Umar was asked how references in documents to the current month were to be distinguished from those referring to the same month in a future year. According to the accounts, he considered the Seleucid era system used by the Greeks to be too ancient and also rejected the Persian rulers' practice of instituting new dating according to their regnal years, beginning anew with each king. He determined instead to institute an era based on Muhammad's life, choosing to start not from the year of his *mab'ath* "appointment as Apostle"[17] or from his birth or death, but from the year in which the *hijra* occurred. He then had to determine the number of years since the *hijra*, suggesting that counting years from the time Muhammad arrived in Medina had not been common practice.

'Umar still had to decide what month would be the first in the year; that this debate was necessary indicates the lack of a strong prior tradition about the beginning of the calendar year. Indeed, before the fixing of the era, years were not specified—the practice about which 'Umar's officers complained. In speaking of the past, reference was made to individual events, or years were named; al-Bīrūnī has a list of the year names for Muhammad's ten years in Medina.[18] Islamic historiography uniformly dates the earliest events in Medina as occurring so many months "of the *hijra*." Presumably this was from Rabī' I; the Prophet's birth and death were also in Rabī' I. Nevertheless, the months proposed for the start of the era were Ramadān and Muḥarram.[19] Presumably Ramadān was suggested for religious reasons: it was the month of fasting and the month in which the Qurān was revealed. 'Umar, however, supported Muḥarram, noting it was one of the sacred months mentioned in the Qurān and that people return from Pilgrimage during this month. This tradition dates the establishment of the Islamic calendar to 17 or 18 AH (638 or 639 CE). 1 Muḥarram, 1 AH was determined by calculating back as if the current calendar (without intercalation) was always in force, making the starting point of the calendar equivalent to July 16, 622.[20] Yet the Seleucid and Persian eras were widespread in Arabia, and the calculation of the beginning of the Muslim epoch may have been based on determining how many years had elapsed since the year Muhammad came to Medina, in the Greek or Persian calendar, not *hijra* lunar years.

V. The Placement of the Months: The "Original" Placement and the
Placement in the Time of Muhammad

The Islamic lunar months move around the seasons; reconstructing their
"original" positions in the solar year is difficult and not necessarily relevant
to where these months fell in Muhammad's time. Attempts to determine
the original calendar have been based on such things as the Pilgrimage and
other religious observances, month names, or proposed intercalation
systems. For example, the month now called Muḥarram is often considered
to have "originally" been in the fall, making it, or the month of Pilgrimage
immediately preceding it, fall in the same season as the Hebrew month of
Tishre. Possibly this is because the *ḥajj* pilgrimage includes
circumambulations of the Kaʿba and drinking from the well of Zamzam,
reminiscent of the palm processions and water celebrations of the Sukkot
festival, called *ḥag* by rabbinic sources, and assumptions that the ʿashūrāʾ
(which occurs on the tenth day of the month) corresponded with Yom
Kippur. Yom Kippur and Sukkot are in the fall.[21] But Rajab, the seventh
month from Muḥarram, was also a holy month with its ʿumra observance
and circumambulations. Moreover, the unique rituals of the *ḥajj*—the
pilgrimage to what is today called *jabal-alraḥma,* "the mountain of Mercy,"
the sacrifice, and the other activities—do not necessarily admit a simple
seasonal parallel with a Hebrew or other festival.

There are numerous ways to reconstruct the "historic" occurrence of
Muḥarram in 622. S. D. Goitein and Arent Jan Wensinck both proposed
alignments in which this month would have fallen in the summer, based on
traditions about the ʿashūrāʾ. Goitein assumes that the famous tradition
makes Muhammad arrive in Medina on the day the Jews celebrated their
festival of ʿashūrāʾ, which he identifies as 8 Rabīʿ I =Yom Kippur, Monday,
September 20, 622. This presumes the traditional Islamic calendar starting
on July 16, 622. Wensinck, analyzing references to fasting on the ninth day
of the month of Pilgrimage, suggests that in the first year of the *hijra,* the
Pilgrimage fell in the Jewish month of Av. At the end of the first year of the
hijra, Av began July 4, 623; Tishʿa Beʾav—the Ninth of Av, a fast day—was
July 12. If this is correct, Muḥarram would have begun August 3, 623. This
implies that in the previous year it began a month later than the traditional
epoch date: August 14, 622. (Wensinck's suggestion allows for the
traditional epoch, July 16, 622, only if an intercalation had been
announced at the Pilgrimage immediately before the *hijra.*)[22]

Many scholars, including both Wensinck and Goitein outside the
contexts of the arguments just cited, assume that the actual alignment in

622 was similar to that of the traditional calendar for 632 (when intercalation was cancelled),[23] when the Pilgrimage was in March; the beginning of Muḥarram was March 29, 632. Assuming accurate solar intercalation, ten years earlier Muḥarram would have begun 18 March or 17 April—making the Pilgrimage or Muḥarram correspond in time to Easter and Passover, not Yom Kippur and Sukkot. This assumes that three or four months were intercalated between 622 and 632, as for example, in Watt's suggestion noted above.[24]

This suggests a solution to the question of the day of the week on which Muhammad arrived in Medina. Intercalating three months means that the date of the *hijra* would be eighty-eight or eighty-nine days earlier than in the traditional calendar.[25] Placing 12 Rabīʿ I eighty-eight days before the traditional date—months of twenty-nine days, thirty days, and twenty-nine days—gives June 28 622, a Monday, with Muḥarram beginning mid-April, 622. Intercalating one, two, or four intercalary months does not lead to a Monday placement of this date. Three intercalary months could have been added between 623 and 629,[26] after the *hijra* and before Muhammad's entry into Mecca in 8 AH (629/30).[27] The next intercalation would have been after the Pilgrimage in 632, but was cancelled by the Qurān. One should not make too much of this: the intercalation of seven or eight months would yield the same result (and bring the Pilgrimage closer to its supposed "original" early fall alignment). So would setting the *hijra* a year earlier—arguing, for example, that ʿUmar counted back one year too few.

All of the above assumes that the traditional material is reasonably reliable, but that is precisely the point. Even without invoking scholarship that rejects all the traditional material or the *hijra* itself, the "epoch" of the Islamic era is arbitrary. It is not clear that the year "originally" began in Muḥarram, we do not know where Muḥarram fell "originally," or where it fell in 622 CE. Possibly it occurred several months before or after the traditional date, in mid-April or March, or in September, or in February. It may have been even earlier (or later) than that and possibly 622 is not even the right year. About the only thing we can say is that the epoch of the Islamic era sets the first day of the first year of the era as equivalent to Friday, July 16, 622—based on calculating back and making the unlikely assumption that the Islamic calendar was always in force. But any attempt to determine the exact day which was actually the first of Muḥarram in Mecca—and even the solar season and perhaps even the year—remains conjectural, even according to the traditional material.

THE JEWISH CALENDAR

According to the Jewish Calendar in use today, the year 1999-2000 is 5760 "of the creation." The epochal event was the creation of the world described in Genesis, and the year is said to begin in Tishre in the fall. Unlike the Muslim calendar, the time of year assigned to the various months is reasonably stable. At least from rabbinic times, we have reports of occasional irregularities in intercalation, but the principle that the calendar should have lunar months and keep pace with the sun by adding integral lunar months from time to time never seems to have been called into question. Nevertheless, different systems have been used for the enumeration of the year and for the start of the year.

I. Eras in the Bible and Talmud

The Bible never dates from creation. Other types of dating are used: years since the Exodus, years of kings, and so forth. For rabbinic times, the Mishnah in *Gittin* 8:5 mentions various eras presumably in use or potentially in use in various Jewish communities: Persian, Greek, building of the Temple, destruction of the Temple, the Exodus. Additionally, it refers to the "era of an inappropriate monarchy." This may mean dating according to the practice of a foreign monarchy, such as using the Greek era in an area ruled by the Persians, or it may euphemistically refer to dating according to Roman emperors.[28] It would seem from these passages that there was not a single standard; different communities used different eras for dating, and a document such as a divorce order would follow local dating practice. There is no mention of the creation era. By the Middle Ages, however, at least in Europe, the creation era had become standard, thus rendering some of the strictures of the Talmud on this point no longer relevant.[29]

How did the creation era come to be established, and how did it become dominant, apparently overturning Talmudic dicta requiring local dating to be used? The creation era was preceded by interest in constructing a chronology from Adam. This was irrelevant to dating: scribes dated documents to the Seleucid era or to whatever era was in local use. Sages apparently tended to refer to the number of years since the destruction of the Temple. In developing the principles of the calculated calendar, however, a starting point at creation made great sense. The nineteen-year lunar cycles naturally started from creation. An era which allowed for easy determination of sabbatical years was useful, even if merely for convenience (sabbatical years were understood to have begun only after the Israelites settled in the land of Israel rather than as uninterrupted seven-year cycles from creation). The importance of sabbatical years, together with the practice of the eastern Mediterranean to begin years in the fall, may have contributed to the standard practice of beginning the year from Tishre. In what follows, we concentrate on issues around the determination of the epochal date of the creation era and the way the era is enumerated.

II. How Long Ago Was Creation?

Although modern scientific dating methods were not available in Roman times, people in antiquity might nevertheless have had a simple alternative to chronology for dating the creation. Abraham's Oak Tree near Hebron, known to the first century CE Jewish historian Josephus, was believed to have come from the Garden of Eden.[30] A bore through the tree could have determined the number of rings, yielding an "exact" date of the planting of Paradise. However, as noted by my colleague Don Hughes, an environmental historian who brought this passage to my attention, this technology was not available in ancient times. Moreover, Jewish and Christian calculations of the date of creation never relied on terrestrial types of data—although they would have considered celestial mechanics as appropriate sources for such deliberations. For the most part, they relied on analysis of the biblical text.

III. Figuring Back

We saw that 'Umar determined the epochal year for the new era despite the lack of a chronological tradition counting how many years had elapsed since the *hijra*. But the calculation of a chronology from creation preceded the adoption of the creation era by Jews. The version of the chronology that has become standard is found in a work known as *Seder Olam,* ascribed to R. Yose b. Halafta, of the second century CE.[31] The first century CE philosopher Philo, Josephus, the book of Jubilees, and others amply attest to Jewish interest in these issues prior to the time of Rabbi Yose. The chronology is determined by the information given in Gen 5, Gen 11, and elsewhere about the age of Adam and his descendants at the time their sons were born. From this point, the chronology resolves figures given for the age of Jacob when he went down to Egypt, the number of years spent in Egypt, and the length of time between Abraham's covenant and the Exodus. According to this chronology, Abraham was born 1948 years after Adam, and the Exodus was 2448 years after Adam. From the Exodus to the First Temple was 480 years, according to I Kgs 6:1. The First Temple stood for

410 years,[32] and there were 490 years—based on the prophecy of Dan 9:24 about "seventy weeks" of years—between the destruction of the First and Second Temples. This yields 900 years from the building of the First Temple to the destruction of the Second Temple, and 3,828 years from Adam to the destruction of the Second Temple. In other words, Adam was created in the fall of 3760 BCE, 3,828 years before Tishre 69 CE, which began the year in which the Temple was destroyed.

This places creation over seventeen centuries later than the chronology usually given by the Byzantines. Differences between the Hebrew Bible and other ancient versions, such as the Septuagint, concerning the ages of the antediluvians when they had their sons may account for a thousand years, and there are many divergent calculations of the time from the flood to Abraham, to the Exodus, and onward. Josephus has the Septuagint's 2656 years from Adam to the flood and agrees with the traditional *Seder Olam* chronography that 430 years elapsed from the time Abraham entered Canaan until the Exodus. Yet he makes the period of time from the Exodus to the Temple 592 years, not the 480 of 1 Kgs 6:2, and has both Temples last longer than the *Seder Olam*. Josephus' figures, however, do not seem to represent a consistent chronology. This may be in part due to copyists', translators', and editors' errors or "corrections," to different chronologies in different stages of Josephus' career, or to differences in Josephus' sources.[33]

As noted, the traditional Jewish chronology has only 490 years separating the destruction of the First and Second Temples rather than the historical 655. From about the time of the Greek conquest, the datings are reasonably accurate, if somewhat schematic, allowing 103 years each for the Maccabean and Herodian periods, yielding 137 BCE and 34 BCE respectively.[34] The period from the building of the Second Temple until the Greek conquest, however, is an impossibly short 34 years; in contrast, Josephus gives over two and a half centuries for this period. This allows the *Seder Olam* chronology to make the Exodus occur 1,000 years before the Seleucid era;[35] it is not clear whether this was a goal or result of this chronology. One further curiosity is that, according to the calculations used to form the Jewish calendar, the interval between Adam's birth and the destruction of the Temple is such that the first "new moon" (more accurately, the first *molad* of creation) occurred at an exact hour. The calculated time of the new moon would not occur exactly on the hour often—only once every 1,080 months, or 87 years and approximately four months (the exact number of months depending on the sequence of intercalated years).

The traditional chronology placing the destruction of the Temple 3828 years after the creation of Adam is usually taken to mean that creation occurred in September, 3760 BCE. As E. Frank noted, sometime between R. Hanina and R. Pappa, 230-375 CE, dating "after Adam" seems to have fallen into disuse.[36] Presumably this is because of the introduction of the calculated calendar, dated—on the basis of a Gaonic responsum—to 4118/357-58 CE. Even if the details used today were not all in place in the fourth century, the promulgation of a calendar required a starting point, a basis for intercalation of the months necessary to keep the lunar year in line with the seasons.[37]

Two important variations agree that creation began Sunday, 21 September 3760 BCE, but calculate the date differently. One of these sets the Rosh Hashanah of creation as Year 1—not Year 2 ("A small part of a year is not counted as a year").[38] In this system, the current year would not be numbered 5760 but 5759. A second variation enumerates the number of years elapsed since creation, reflecting the way the chronology was determined starting with the birth of Adam. As noted, September 1999 was the 5,758th anniversary of the Rosh Hashanah of creation; Adam would have been 5,758 years old.[39] Nevertheless, this system, too, is sometimes treated as an era and assigned a starting point two years after September 26, 3760. As noted below, some Jews have not adequately distinguished between "after Adam" dates and the more usual creation era. Some authors, such as Frank, have delineated two other variations as "eras."[40]

IV. When Does the Year Begin?
As mentioned above, the seasonal alignment of the months of the Jewish year seems to have been reasonably stable. The Jewish calendar, as understood today, counts years from the fall, and this has been the assumption of the calculations given above. Rosh Hashanah, or "New Year," is at the beginning of Tishre and is associated with the creation, with a liturgy full of phrases like "today the world was made" and "this day is the start of your deeds."[41]

Nevertheless, this linkage is lacking in the Torah, where this day is the beginning of the seventh month, and there is no reference to creation. Months are usually numbered from "the first month," which is in the spring,[42] and Israel is commanded to use the month of the Exodus—the spring month—as the beginning of the months (Exod 12:2). The jubilee year, which begins in the fall, starts not on the first day of the seventh month, but with the sounding of the shofar on Yom Kippur, the tenth day of the seventh month (Lev 25:9).[43] Indeed, the only biblical reference to "Rosh Hashanah" is Ezek 40:1, which refers not to the first but to the tenth of the seventh month; that is, Yom Kippur, and classical Jewish commentaries assume he is referring to the start of the jubilee year.[44] We find other terminologies, such as "the end of the year" or "the turn of the year" at the time of the harvest festival in the fall (Exod 23:16, 34:22). A similar usage, *teshuvat hashanah* or *tekufat hashanah* "the return of the year" (2 Sam 11:1, 1 Kgs 20:22, 26, parallels in Chronicles), is unclear: it is always translated by the Targum as "the end of the year" and understood by most traditional Jewish commentators as being a year later.[45]

M. D. Herr has argued that the process of moving from a year beginning in the spring to one beginning in the fall took place between the destruction of the Temple and the composition of the Mishnah,[46] but the distinction found in the Mishnah is already present in Josephus. According to Josephus, Nisan "began the year with respect to all the solemnities the [Israelites] observed to the honor of God," with the "original order of the months" used for civil activities such as buying and selling (*Antiquities* I.3.3), appropriate enough for sabbatical years. Targum to I Kgs 8:2 also considers the original order to have begun in the fall; the month Eitanim was "the month that the Ancients called first," a practice changed by divine command at the time of the Exodus.[47]

In the Mishnah, Nisan is the beginning of regnal years and Tishre is the beginning of sabbatical and jubilee years (*Rosh Hashanah* 1:1). Talmud and Midrash present materials supporting both spring and fall as the start of the year and the start of creation; other possible starting dates are briefly discussed.[48] Genesis 7:11, which describes the flood as beginning "in the second month," provided the basis in the Talmud[49]—as for Josephus[50]— for counting years from the fall, as the second month of the fall (Marcheshvan) is the beginning of the rainy season in the land of Israel. In the Talmudic passage, Rabbi Eliezer and Rabbi Joshua argued the points until it was concluded that the *tekufot* are held to be counted from Nisan, and the years from Tishre. This is why the "Blessing of the Sun" is recited in Nisan every 28 years (next scheduled for spring 2009). This passage may also suggest that the rest of the world counts years from Nisan, although others believed the rest of the world counts years from Tishre.[51] These differences were mirrored in the enumeration of years among the Byzantines and Greeks, on the one hand, and the Persians, on the other. The Byzantine civil year began in September, whereas in Babylonia the year began in the spring. This was true even in times when both the Greeks and the Persians used the Seleucid era: in the West it started 312 BCE; in Babylonia it started six months later, in the spring of 311 BCE.

If creation was in the spring, the first lunar conjunction was exactly six lunar months prior to the Tishre conjunction referred to above,[52] at about 3:35 a.m. early on the morning of Wednesday, April 2, 3760 BCE.[53] This date is sometimes given as 28 Adar, with the creation of Adam on 1 Nisan.[54] With a spring creation, and years enumerated from Tishre, it would seem hard to justify not counting the time prior to fall 3760 BCE as a year, thus the conjunction used for calculating the calendar is still in October of 3761 BCE, prior to creation.

V. 2000 CE: A Millennial Year for Jews?

Few Jews have had a Jewish reading of 2000 CE=5760 as a millennial year. There are millennial expectations, however, associated with the next year in the Jewish calendar with three zeroes at the end, 6000, which will not occur for another 240 years. These go back to rabbinic dicta in which a day is considered to be as 1,000 years, based on Ps 90:4. Six days of the week at 1,000 years each are 6,000 years,[55] or perhaps more commonly 2,000 years of *tohu* (void), 2,000 years of Torah and 2,000 years of messiah.[56] The rabbis therefore conclude that Abraham, born 1,948 years after Adam, was 52 when he began teaching Torah in Haran (a reference to Gen. 12:5), marking the end of the period of *tohu*. The end of the "two thousand years of Torah" was the writing of the Mishnah, placed 172 years after the destruction of the Temple (242 CE). This tradition is also joined to speculation about the length of the messianic era; opinions span the gamut from 40 years to 7,000 years.[57] Most Jews would probably assume that the year 6000 refers to Rosh Hashanah, 30 September, 2239,[58] but for what it's worth, the Midrash refers to years elapsed since the Rosh Hashanah of creation week, so the correct millennial equivalence is 1 Tishre, 6002, or Wednesday, September 7, 2241. Even then, Jewish tradition frowns upon and indeed forbids calculating the advent of the messianic era, proclaiming: "Blasted be the bones of one who calculates the end!"[59] Moreover, the point of many rabbinic stories is that the messiah could come at any day, even today, "if we but hearken to his voice." So while it is appropriate—and common—in some circles to express a pious wish for the speedy coming of messianic times, it would be inappropriate or even disallowed to speculate whether eschatological events might occur in one particular year or another.

CHRISTIAN CALENDAR
I. Organization of the Months
The calendar we use today, the Gregorian calendar, is based on the reform
of the calendar of Republican Rome undertaken by Julius Caesar in 46
BCE. The calendar of Republican Rome appears to have originally been
lunisolar, but by the late fifth century BCE it had ceased to have any true
relationship with the moon and "aimed at coincidence in length with the
seasons," as A. Samuel put it.[60] The average lunar cycle is about 29.53 days
long, so the months of a lunar calendar are normally nearly evenly divided
between 29 days and 30 days. At least on the eve of Julius Caesar's reform,
Republican Rome's calendar had seven months of 29 days, four months of
31 days (March, May, Quinctilis—now called July—and October), and
then as now, February had only 28, for a total of 355 days. Intercalation was
by means of an intercalary month inserted in February, beginning on what
we would call the 24th or 25th of February. The first of March was always
27 days later, adding a net of 22 or 23 days to the year, 377 or 378 days in
all. Although the presence of intercalation and the system of *nones* and *ides*
(first quarter and full moon) may reflect an ancient lunar calendar, the
Republican calendar was totally divorced from the moon as early as the fifth
century BCE.

The non-intercalated Republican year was a day longer than the
"normal" lunar year of 354 days;[61] its length and the unusual lengths of the
months no doubt reflect Roman superstitions about odd and even
numbers. Were the non-intercalated year 354 days long, intercalating
twenty-two days every other year would produce the same result as a 365-
day year, and adding alternately twenty-two and twenty-three days would
result in the Julian year of 365 ¼ days. The 355-day year required
intercalation only five times every eleven years, slightly more than half of
which were 23-day additions. If done this way, the calendar would never be
more than eleven days off the solar year. But comparison of Republican
dates with eclipse and other data indicate the calendar may have been off by
a month in 217 BCE, by four months in 190 BCE, and two months in 168
BCE. It may well have been correctly regulated in the late second and early
first centuries BCE, up to Pompey's times (66 BCE). But it had fallen three
months out of alignment by the time of Julius Caesar's reform. Not the least
of the reasons was that, as pontifex, it was his prerogative to intercalate, but
he was off fighting in Gaul. But there is also evidence of pontifical
corruption and lack of clarity about intercalation up to a few days before it

was to take place.[62]

The problems experienced in regulating the Republican calendar show how easily an advanced society could be confounded by its calendar. Julius Caesar's reform added ten days to the Republican year, bringing it to 365 days. Three months, January, Sextilis (later renamed August), and December, were extended to 31 days each, and the remaining four months gained one day each, to have 30 days. The intercalary month was cancelled, and instead a 366th day was added in February every fourth year to keep it in tune with the seasons. A onetime addition of 90 days was needed to bring the year back into alignment. Those in charge of the intercalation had misunderstood Caesar's directions at first and intercalated every three years instead of every fourth year. Augustus Caesar canceled the intercalation of February 29th for three leap year cycles to correct for this error. Other than Augustus' correction of leap year, and the renaming of July and August, the calendar functioned as designed until the reforms of Pope Gregory, and the month lengths remain unchanged from Julius Caesar until today.[63]

II. When Does the Year Begin?

There are memories of an early Roman system in which the calendar began in March, reflected in the numbered month names from Quinctilis, the fifth month counting from March. Today such names are preserved from September, the "seventh month" from March. But in the times of Julius Caesar, the Roman calendar year began in January, dated by the names of two consuls who served for one-year terms beginning the first day of January; the Julian reform kept the January start of the year. The Julian system became widespread throughout the Empire, but even when non-Roman months came to be identical to those of the Julian year or oriented so that a given day of a given month was always aligned with a particular Roman one, few adopted January 1 as the beginning of the year. Indeed, Augustus' birthday in the fall became a far more common starting point. In Christian times, there was still great variation.[64]

III. Eras

In the Republic, the Romans dated by consuls, two individuals who entered office on January 1st and stayed in office for a year. Although Romans made reference to the number of years since the founding of their city, the founding of Rome (*AUC, "anno urbis conditae"* or *"ab urbis conditae"*) was not used as a formal dating system. Thus AUC "dates" are often inconsistent and are more like dates given from the signing of the

Declaration of Independence or number of seasons a cultural organization has presented. In the period of the empire, Romans continued to date by consuls (although the system underwent some change) and by the years of the emperors. In the late third century, the era of the Emperor Diocletian (in which year 1 equals 284/5 CE) achieved a degree of stability. In early Christian circles, chronographers and computists used local eras and occasionally referred to events as being a specific number of years after creation. Other Christian datings were according to Christ's passion, or the year of grace, or years of Christ, or the year of Christ's incarnation. Alexandrian churchmen typically used four eras, all of which began in the fall: those of the World (year 1 equals 5494/3 BCE), Diocletian, Grace (year 1 equals 360/1 CE), and Incarnation (year 1 equals 8/9 CE). Other dates for the incarnation or birth of Jesus existed: Eusebius gives 5,199 after creation, in 1 BCE, and, in Alexandria, Panodorus set year 1 at 5,494 years after creation (which he considered to have occurred in 5493 BCE) = 1 AD. Others gave the twenty-eighth year of Augustus, and 1,548 years from the Exodus, dated in 1552 BCE, or 4 BCE.[65]

The Christian calendar used today is signified by the letters A.D., or *Anno Domini* ("in the year of our Lord"). Although referring to Jesus, this does not tell us precisely whether it starts with his birth or with his conception nine months earlier. (The alternate form *CE* stands for Christian Era, although it is sometimes given as Common Era.)[66] The Hebrew *lefi sefirat hanotzrim*, "According to the Christian count," means the same thing, although the Arabic *mīlādī* specifies the point of reference exactly: "pertaining to the birth [of Jesus]." In the year we now call 525, Dionysius Exiguus calculated Easter tables to continue the last set that had been adopted by the Church. He replaced the enumeration of Easters by the Diocletian era, as had been the case in the model he had before him, with enumeration "from the incarnation." The previous calendar went up to the Easter of year 247 of the Diocletian era (530-31), so Easter of 532 was the first new date calculated. Other than the replacement of the Diocletian era enumeration, his calculation of Easter dates continues exactly as that of his model, which is printed together with it in the edition of the *Patrologia Latina*.[67] In his discussion of the tables, he gives detailed guides for calculating indiction years (a fifteen-year tax cycle), lunar and nineteen-year cycles, leap years, and "concurrents" (which determine the weekday for the fourteenth day of the lunar month given in the table), and all used in previous calculations.[68] He cites the Nicaean council, and Exod 12:2 and 13 and Deut 16:1-2, verses that control the determination of the date of

Passover.[69] But nowhere does he explain how he enumerated the Easter of 248 of the Diocletian era as "532" when using the count "from the incarnation of Christ." He notes that the conception of Christ was on 25 March: according to Dionysius' tables, in AD 1, March 25 was a Friday and Easter would have been on March 27;[70] thus, the incarnation would have been on the vernal equinox and at the time of Easter—but these two did not coincide. Similarly, he suggests an argument for the nativity on Tuesday, December 20 (sic!),[71] as it occurred in 1 AD, but in the same passage he also sets the nativity on the solstice, December 25. As for the cycles, there is no reference to the starting point of the lunar or solar cycles—which do not start evenly from 1 AD; even his Easter cycle does not start from there but from the previous year, 1 BC. Dionysius referred to the "passion of our redeemer" as the cause of the repair of humanity, but does not say why he chose the incarnation rather than the passion for his Easter dates.

The dating to the incarnation pertained to Easters, not years, and Dionysius did not employ it in the cover letter which is dated to indiction and consulate.[72] 532 was the first new Easter date calculated. The product of cycles based on seven days of the week, the 4-year leap-cycle, and the 19-year cycle is 532, meaning that after 532 years the cycle of Easters repeats. Perhaps this played a role in suggesting to him to enumerate from the incarnation, but this does not seem to figure in his report.

Dionysius' calculations continued those of a system which used Diocletian and indiction years, both of which start in the fall. The authors of the *Oxford Companion to the Year* muse that Eusebius dated the nativity to 2 BCE, and the first March following the year going from autumn 2 BCE to autumn 1 BCE would be in the year 1 CE.[73] The authors of this volume do not point this out, but using Eusebius' date in this way made December 25, 1999, the 2,000th anniversary of the incarnation—providing a Christian justification for the celebrations between that date and January 1, 2000. If the incarnation is taken to have occurred in March 1 CE, the 2,000th anniversary of the nativity is just a few days before January 2002.

The Easter calculus has been much studied, but comparisons between the Easter and Jewish calculus are much less common. Like the Muslim and Jewish calendars, the Easter calculus relies on the moon, whose phases occur approximately eleven days earlier each solar year. There are some important parallels with the calculation of Passover and Rosh Hashanah—issues about the day of the week, whether Easter should be postponed if it occurs before a certain solar date or on certain lunar dates, and so forth; and a nineteen-year cycle is used in both systems to keep the lunar dates in line with the solar year. The Easter calculations never seem to worry about the exact time at which the new moon could be sighted, but instead rely on the net gain or loss in number of days over time. The Jewish system, using the *molad*, ultimately does the same: although it is very precise about the average length of the lunar month, it uses this average instead of the exact new moon or a calculated "earliest visibility" of the crescent moon. Moreover, despite the traditional insistence that the *molad* is a lunar conjunction with the sun, expressed to the nearest 1,080th part of an hour in Jerusalem time, this is rarely the case and may not even be the case on average.[74] In the system used by Dionysius, the solar year is either eleven days longer than the twelve month lunar year or nineteen days shorter than the thirteen month lunar year. To reconcile the exact average lunar month with both the nineteen year lunar cycle and the Julian leap year cycle, only one day needed to be skipped every nineteen years. This is much like numerous Talmudic texts that talk about the possible number of days between a particular holy day and its occurrence the following year or the number of added days needed to take into account the excess of the average lunar month over 29½ days.

If the relationship of a particular day of the Jewish year is compared to the *tekufat*, the computation becomes even more similar: the Easter calculus' epact is the number of days before the *tekufat* and the concurrent would be the weekday of the *tekufat*. The major difficulty is determining a method to prevent the festival from falling on the wrong weekdays while retaining the correct average month-length; perhaps this is what made using the *molad* necessary. Finally, I am struck by the parallel between *molad* Tishre and Dionysius' Easter enumeration. Dionysius began his Easter enumeration from before the first Easter and was very cognizant of the calendrical calibration with astronomical events, placing the nativity of Jesus on the winter solstice and the conception on or near both the equinox and the calculated Easter date. So, too, the calculated Jewish calendar is calibrated so that Adam's creation on Friday can fall on or near Rosh Hashanah and correspond with the *molad*.

Most important, the calculus was being developed in similar time frames. Calculating Easter became necessary as a result of the determinations of the Council of Nicaea—before the time of Hillel II. During this period, according to the usual accounts, Jews still determined Passover by actual observation and by the declaration of the patriarch. It seems unlikely that Jews would remain unaware of the benefits of a calculated Passover.

IV. The Adoption of the Dionysian Era for Use in Dating
Dionysius' Easter tables, dating of Easter from the incarnation, gained widespread use quickly. Already in Italy in the 500s there is some attestation of the use of the Dionysian system for dating events and documents. In Britain, the use of Dionysian dating is attested in the 600s (his tables were adopted at Whitby in 664), but was universally adopted for England only at the Council of Chelsea in 816.[75]

The most important influence in the adoption of the AD era was its use by the Venerable Bede. This era was known to Charlemagne, although claims of his imposition of this era for all official purposes are overstatements; he, and later the Holy Roman emperors, dated by regnal years. In Spain, the Dionysian era was rather late in application: although apparently promoted or adopted by the Council of Tarragon in 1180, non-Dionysian dating persisted in Spain and Portugal into the fifteenth century. In Russia, dating was by the Era of the World until Peter the Great, who adopted the Dionysian era in its Julian form. Dionysius' era was not used in non-Christian countries, of course, such as the Ottoman empire. In Turkey, the Gregorian calendar and the Dionysian era were adopted as part of a pattern of Westernizing reforms in the twentieth century.

Thus, enumeration of the years of the Christian era is based on Easter computations. Dionysius may have used a previously-existing chronology, much as the Jewish calendar used that of the *Seder Olam*. And it is possible that the *Seder Olam* style chronology reflects a calibration to a *molad* on Friday of creation, just as the Dionysian first Easter date would be March 27: calibrations that make more sense for calendrical principles than as chronology. Like the Jewish calculated calendar, Dionysius' Easter calculations were not designed to define an era for general use—the Jews still used the Seleucid and destruction eras and the Christians still used the Diocletian era—but to determine the date of the festival calendar. Only later did they come to serve this purpose.

CONCLUSION
In the three systems considered here, the historical basis for the starting point of the calendar is elusive. The Muslim era is based on the emigration of Muhammad from Mecca to Medina, the start of the organized Islamic polity. The calendar's starting point is 1 Muḥarram 1, Friday, 16 July, 622 CE, but Muhammad's arrival in Medina may well have occurred prior to this point. Muslim calculation of the epoch is arbitrary and religious. The

choice of Muḥarram as the first month was justified on the basis of Qurān and Pilgrimage, not age-old practice, and the calculation of the epochal year anachronistically applied the Qurānic principle that intercalation was idolatrous even before its historical revelation in the year 632. Liturgically, the actual observance of the moon, not the calculated date, determines the start of the months. Perhaps the close link between Muhammad's arrival in Medina and the establishment of Islamic prayer four days later is another link emphasizing the religious nature of the era. In a sense, the Muslim calendar embeds the value of reliance upon God. Although some Muslim sources refer to the corruption of those who regulated the intercalation, ultimately the reason it was stopped is that God created the world with twelve months in a year. So too the liturgical months begin when God wanted them to—with the moon—and human intervention to determine a calculated calendar is to be rejected.

The starting point of the Jewish calendar, as it is most commonly understood today, has been determined to be a lunar conjunction whose time and date are precisely determined—except that, according to the calendar, neither moon nor sun had been created, and this date did not exist. The "mean conjunction," immediately before the first Rosh Hashanah which actually existed, occurred at an exact hour: a good starting point, but one which came only once every 87 ¼ years. The current Jewish era, in which the year 5760 began in fall 1999, reflects a system necessary to make calculated intercalation work. According to a rabbinic compromise, years are dated as if creation occurred in the fall, whereas the blessing of the sun, for example, is formulated and recited as if creation occurred in the spring. Jewish calculations take the trouble to go back to creation, but ultimately they are followed not because they are right but because of rabbinic authority. Karaites, rejecting rabbinic authority, rely on direct observation; the rabbinic tradition is that God taught Moses to recognize the newborn crescent and sanctify the month, a prerogative passed on to the Sanhedrin. Thus it is not God who determines the calendar, as in the Qurān, but rather the community—acting on divine command to be sure— sanctifies the month and thus determines the dates of religious events. Perhaps the choice of a Tishre start to the year reflects a view about when creation really did occur. This view achieved ascendancy at least for calendrical purposes and allowed the calculation to work smoothly.

The Christian era is based on Dionysius' dating of Easters. Curiously, he provided no indication as to precisely how he came to determine that Easter in the year 248 of the Diocletian era would be numbered 532. The process of adoption of Dionysian counting was inextricably linked to the use of his system in setting Easter dates and took until the late Middle Ages, even in Christian Europe. Authority was not vested in the fiat of a pope or emperor, but rather the broad adoption of the Dionysian era was based on a slow process of councils and decisions by individual rulers. Scholars debate whether Dionysius referred to nativity or conception in dating the incarnation, but January 1 reflects neither choice. Today the practice of the Roman Republic to date from January 1st, kept on in Latin dating formulae in the Middle Ages, is well-nigh universal, but it took most of the two millennia since Caesar to achieve this.

The Jewish, Christian, and Muslim eras are often considered to date from a specific epochal event—and that is certainly how they are presented. But in each case we have found that there are arbitrary considerations which are more of a calendrical and ideological nature than simply chronological. Calculations and celestial calibrations also show there was a scientific and technological aspect. But most important, during the times these systems came to be delineated, people had come to want and need an era which was suitably universal, but suited to the central truths of their societies. The process by which they came to broad acceptance was slow, but very sure.

Today as well, time is more a question of scientific, technological, and economic concerns than history or chronology. Local time was standardized by the railroads, and the hour and year are now regulated not so much by the motion of the sun and moon as by the oscillations of cesium atoms. It is perhaps fittingly ironic that millennial anxiety about the 2000th year of our era has been essentially dwarfed by centennial angst about a a technology which could not properly handle dates after "99."

NOTES

[1]January 1, 1 CE is day 1,373,427 from October 6, 3761 BCE, the start of the Jewish creation calendar. January 1, 2000 is day 2,103,914. The number of days from creation was calculated by using a calendar program I published in *Jewish Language Review* 7 (1987): 234-60, with updates in *Jewish Linguistic Studies* 2 (1990): 23-31.

[2]A. Samuel, *Greek and Roman Chronology: Calendars and Years in Classical Antiquity* (Munich: Beck'sche Verlagsbuchhandlung, 1972), 156.

[3]This takes into account only the 44 minutes: 44 minutes times 12 lunar months times 30 years equals 15,840 minutes. 15,840 minutes divided by 60 minutes perhour, divided by 24 hours per day, equals exactly 11 days.

[4]J. Oberman, "Introduction" to S. Gandz, *The Code of Maimonides: Sanctification of the New Moon* (New Haven: Yale University Press, 1956), xlvi and l. Other astronomers mentioned by Obermann in this connection are Ibn Y nus (d. 1009) and Jābir b. Aflaḥ , a near contemporary of Maimonides. See also Neugebauer's commentary in this work, 140-41.

[5]Muhammad claimed he was "better entitled to Moses" in celebrating the ʿāshūrāʾ, or "Fast of the Tenth" than the Jews. This is cited and discussed, for example, by S. D. Goitein, in "Ramadān, the Muslim Month of Fasting," in S. D. Goitein, ed., *Studies in Islamic Institutions and History* (Leiden: Brill 1968), 95-96; al-Bīrūnī, *al-thār al-bāqiya ʿan al-qurūn al-khāliya* (Arabic ed. E. Sachau; Leipzig: Harrasowitz, 1923), 330; English trans.: *Chronology of the Ancient Nations* [trans. Sachau; London, 1879, rpt. Lahore: Hijra, 1983], 327. This hadīth is found in Bukhārī, *Saḥīḥ*, Ṣawm ch. 70 and many other places. Goitein, 97, posits that the statement that Muhammad was "better entitled to Moses" may have been the authentic core of this tradition. This tradition has been used in suggesting calendrical calibrations; we will return to it below.

[6]al-Ṭabarī, *Taʾrīkh al-rusul wal-mulūk*, (Leiden: Brill, 1879-90), 1:1096-98; English trans.: *Muhammad at Mecca* (vol. 6; trans. and commentary W. Watt and M. McDonald; Albany: SUNY Press,1984), 23-25. (al-Ṭabarī cited below in both Arabic and SUNY English translation by volume and page number).

[7]Caussin de Perceval, writing in *Journal Asiatique* 4:1 (1843), 368, see also al-Bīrūnī, Arabic, 11.

[8]Several verses of the Qurān refer to use of the sun or moon in reckoning time: 2:189, 6:96, 10:5, and 53:5. Examination of the exegetical tradition to see whether these verses were taken by Muslim or Western scholars to refer to intercalation is beyond our scope here.

[9]Ibn Hisham, *al-Sīra al-Nabawiyya* (Cairo: Muṣṭafā al-Bābī al-Ḥalabī, 1955), 492; al-Masʿūdī, *Murūj al-Dhahab* (ed. ʿAbd al-Ḥamīd; Beirut: Dār al-Fikr, 1973), 2:286; and Ibn al-Athīr, *al-Kāmil fī al-Taʾrīkh* Ibn al-Ath r, vol. 2 (ed. C. Tornberg; Leiden: Brill, 1868), 101, 107, report Monday, 12 Rabīʿ I. Ibn al-Athīr does not specifically say 12 Rabīʿ I was a Monday, but quotes (separately) the famous adage associating the Prophet's birth, death, call to prophecy, and pilgrimage with Mondays.

[10]The second and the twelfth of this month are cited as dates as well. Carra de Vaux, "Hidjra," *Encyclopedia of Islam*, 3:302.

[11]Dates have usually been calculated by Jewish and Muslim calendar programs referred to in note 1, above.

[12]As, for example, nicely stated by Bonnie Blackburn and Leofranc Holford-Stevens, *Oxford Companion to the Year* (New York: Oxford, 1999), 731. The program mentioned in the previous note (written many years before the *Oxford Companion*) allows for this adjustment.

[13]W. M. Watt, "Introduction," in al-Ṭabarī, vol. 7 (trans. Watt and McDonald; Albany: SUNY Press, 1988), xxxviii.

[14]al-Ṭabarī, 1:1251-56/ Eng. 7:155-62; al-Bīrūnī, 29-30; Ibn al-Athīr, 1:10ff., see de Vaux, "Hidjra," 3:302.

[15]al-Ṭabarī 1:1253/ English: 6:159.

[16]*Ibid.*

[17]The Mabʿath era, however, appears to have been known at least in certain circles, see, for example, E. S. Kennedy, "Two topics from an astrological manuscript" in *Astronomy and Astrology in the Medieval Islamic World* (ed. E.S. Kennedy; Ashgate: Aldershot, 1988).

[18]al-Bīrūnī, Arabic 31. Despite this tradition, however, it seems that the accounts of ʿUmar's determination of the calendar assume he determined the year, rather than used the ready-made tradition of ten named years.

[19]al-Ṭabarī 1:1251-52, Eng. 6:158.

[20]The correspondence between the Seleucid and the Persian (Yazdegerd) eras was well known to Islamic writers on the subject such as al-Bīrūnī, and al-Masʿūdī (although the latter has a mistaken date, probably a copying error). These writers, of course, reflect the traditions of a time when the era had been long-established. The Seleucid and Persian eras would have been familiar to the Arabs of ʿUmar's time, but the calendar correspondences noted by later writers do not imply that reference was made to the Seleucid or Persian calendars to *determine* the era. Sources given, for example, in F. K. Ginzel, *Handbuch der Mathematischen und Technishen Chronologie* (Leipzig: Hinrichs'sche Buchhandlung, 1906), 1:258. On the Arabian use of Seleucid era, see also Samuel, *Greek and Roman Chronology*, 245-46. On the correspondence between Jewish and Muslim calendars: often the dates are exact, as in al-Bīrūnī, and sometimes not. See, for example, Ibn al-Athīr, 1:14, "The Jews say based on all of what is confirmed for them in the Torah that 4642 (another reading is 4342) years elapsed between the creation of Adam and the *hijra*." (al-Ṭabarī 1:18, English 1:184, with references to parallels in the notes). In the system used today, this is exactly 40 years off, as year 4342 of the creation corresponds with 581/2 CE. The difference may come from incorrect information or scribal error, but more likely from adding approximate dates. It may also refer to the time of year; al-Ṭabarī and Ibn al-Athīr's Christian source noted that it was 5992 years and a month (although a variant says, "and some months"). The implication that Adam's creation and the *hijra* occurred in the same month probably assumes a Jewish fall creation, and the traditional Islamic calendar in which Rabīʿ I corresponded to Tishre of 622 CE. Yet that some Muslims believe that creation began on a Sunday and was completed with Adam's creation, on Friday, Nisan 6, presumably the Julian month of April, usually called Nisan in Arabic, not the Hebrew Nisan; al-Ṭabarī 1:117, English 1:288, al-Masʿ d 1:34. Making the *hijra* correspond with a

spring creation seems unlikely in this context but corresponds with a proposal made below.

[21] See, for example, "Introduction," in Seth Ward, ed., 'Avoda and 'Ibada, Liturgy and Ritual in Islamic and Judaic Societies (vol. 5, no. 1, Medieval Encounters: Jewish Christian and Muslim Culture in Confluence and Dialogue; Leiden: Brill, 1999), 6.

[22] See Goitein, Institutions 92-93, 95-96, 105 and Wensinck, Jews 89, 94, with notes.

[23] See Goitein, ibid. and Wensinck, Hadjdj EI and EI2.

[24] Given a Spring Muḥarram, it is curious that Goitein goes to great lengths to explain the relationship of Moses to Yom Kippur in the tradition about Muhammad finding the Jews observing 'sh r '. If the references to the 'sh r 'are removed from the tradition, it talks of the Jews observing a festival celebrating Moses' delivery of the Jews from Egypt. Passover would have fallen in Muḥarram, 632, on April 11. This reconstruction, however, would not explain how Muhammad found them celebrating this holiday when he arrived in Rabīʿ I, but then again, neither do most of the other reconstructions.

[25] This is calculated based on the average month-length of 29.53 days. It corresponds with data from rabbinic writings about the predictability of a date six months distant in a calendar based on lunar observation: Rosh Hashanah must fall on the same day of the week as the offering of the 'Omer (for rabbinic Judaism, 16 Nisan), or the following day. Tosefta 'Arakhin 1:11, Babylonian Talmud, 'Arakhin 9b. See M. D. Herr, "The Calendar," in The Jewish People in the First Century II (ed. Safrai and Stern; Assen:Van Gorcum, 1976), 834-64. Today, Rosh Hashanah always falls on the same day of the week as Nisan 17.

[26] Intercalations in 624 (=2 AH), 626 or 627 (4 or 5 AH), 629 (7 AH), and 632 (10 AH) would correspond precisely with Jewish 19-year cycle as it is traditional today, or with the intercalation scheme of Dionysius Exiguus, Liber de Paschate, Cyclus decemnovennalis Dionysii, in Migne, Patriologia Latinae (PL) 67: 495-96. The 19-year cycles of today's Jewish calendar correspond to Dionysius' luna circulus [cycle of the moon], but not to the cycle he actually used in his tables.

[27] al-Bīrūnī reports that Muhammad entered Mecca on the 19th of Ramaḍān but could not do the pilgrimage that year because of the intercalation (Arabic, 332). The Pilgrimage month is the third after Ramaḍān. Muhammad's experiences when he came to Mecca may have some bearing on the question of the cancellation of the nasīʾ. A further suggestion about this tradition is made below.

[28] See discussion Gittin 79b-80a. J. D. Eisenstein, "Chronologia," in Otsar Yisrael (New York: J. D. Eisenstein; n.d.; rpt. New York: Pardes, 1951), 291, believed that the Roman era referred to the assumption of Roman rule at the death of King Herod and associated this with the Christian era.

[29] Isaiah di Trani (d. before 1260), in Piskei Ha-Rid (called Tosafot haRid in traditional Vilna Talmud editions), Gittin 80a, and the Baʿalei ha-Tosafot (12-

13th century) to Avodah Zarah 10a, top.

[30]Josephus also believed Hebron was 2,300 years old, which would place its founding before the time of Abraham in his chronology, but of course would not make it as old as Eden. *Wars of the Jews*, 4.9.7. See also *Antiquities* 1.10.4 and 1.11.2. L. Ginzburg, *Legends of the Jews* (Philadelphia: Jewish Publication Society, 1953), vol. 1, 242 and vol. 5, 235, n. 137.

[31]See Yevamot 82b, Niddah 46b. Chaim Milikowsky, *Seder Olam: A Rabbinic Chronology* (Ann Arbor, 1981); Heinrich W. Guggenheimer, *Seder Olam: The Rabbinic view of Biblical History* (Northvale: Jason Aronson, 1998).

[32]This dating is based primarily on computing the reigns of the Davidic kings, and is probably longer than the figure given by most historians. H. Tadmor, for example, has discussed the various considerations in determining this chronology. They include various calendrical problems such as changing calendars, differing ways of denoting the era-years of individual monarchs, different starting dates for the year (Spring in Judah and Fall, at least sometimes, in the Northern Kingdom) and other issues, which readily explain how the period could be stretched out. Tadmor thinks the accession of Jeroboam—the beginning of the divided monarchy—was 95-98 years before some year from 853-841 BCE, (this yields a period between 951 and 936 BCE.). But the times of David and Solomon are so shrouded in legend that it is difficult to use Biblical dating to go back further. H. Tadmor, "The Chronology of the First Temple Period: A Presentation and Evaluation of the Sources" in *The World History of the Jewish People: The Age of the Monarchies—Political History* (Jerusalem: Masada, 1979), 44. Interestingly, 410 years before the usual Western dating of the Fall of the First Temple in 586 BCE, (not the traditional Seder Olam-based dating!), is 996 BCE., the date which was apparently—and mistakenly—used for the 3,000-year celebration of Jerusalem in 1996.

[33]Whiston, *Josephus*, "Dissertation V," Volume 4, 349-422 is about Josephus' chronology. Whiston apparently compared various editions, including Greek and Latin versions, although he also chose dates based on his own reconstructions, without a critical apparatus. I would like to extend my thanks to my colleague, Don Hughes, as well as the University of Denver Library special collections, for their assistance in allowing me to compare a 1513 Latin edition Josephus there; Don Hughes also advised me about the dates in a Greek edition.

[34]E. *Avodah Zarah* 9a. My BCE dates are based on the Temple's destruction in 70 CE.

[35]See also a discussion of this issue, *Avodah Zarah* 10a.

[36]Edgar Frank, *Talmudic and Rabbinic Chronology: The Systems of Counting Years in Jewish Literature* (NY: Feldheim, 1956), 37.

[37]In the following, I have followed the usual assumption that the basis for calculations was a *molad Tishre* before or during creation. al-Bīrūnī, however,

describes the calculation of the molad based on the beginning of the Seleucid era. Arabic, 151.

[38] *Rosh Hashana* 2b.

[39] Somewhat obviously, the result would be the same in the system in which 26 September 3760 BCE was Rosh Hashanah of the Year 1. The year which began in September, 1999, would then be 5759.

[40] Frank also delineates three Seleucid eras, beginning in 313, 312, and 311 BCE.

[41] Recited after the Shofar blasts and in the Zikhronot. See, for example, *Rosh Hashanah* 27a, Yerushalmi *Rosh Hashanah* 1:3, 57a and *Avodah Zarah* 1:2, 39c.

[42] See below for the traditional interpretation of "the second month" in the Noah story.

[43] On three calendars of ancient Israel, see S. Gandz, "Calendars of Ancient Israel," in *Homenaje à Millas Vallicrosa*, vol. 1 (Barcelona: Consejo Superior de Investigaciones Científicas, 1954-56), 623-46.

[44] See, for example, Rashi and Radak on this verse.

[45] See Rashi and Radak.

[46] Herr, "The Calendar," 834-64.

[47] See Targum Jonathan; note Rashi and Radak on the verse. "Eitanim" *the strong ones* is a poetic reference to the Patriarchs, noting traditions that some or all were born in Tishre.

[48] *Rosh Hashanah* 3a.

[49] *Rosh Hashanah* 11a-12a.

[50] *Antiquities* 3.1.1.

[51] See Radak on Gen 7:11, Radak and Rashi on I Kgs 8:2.

[52] I.e. on September 26, 3760 BCE, a Friday, at 8:00 a.m. A Midrash refers to the celestial bodies completing their cycles rapidly prior to Adam's sin (Genesis *Rabba* 10:4). Some have suggested that this is responsible for a "collapsing of time" between Adam's creation in April and his Fall in September 26. The purpose of this is to harmonize the two opinions about the season of creation. For sources, see Meir David Hertzberg, *Or ha-Hamah* 6b-7b, cited by J. David Bleich *Birkas HaChammah* (Brooklyn: Mesorah, 1980), 64.

[53] 4th day, 9 hours and 642 parts (35 1/3 minutes). On the moment of creation of the Moon, see, for example, Rashi to Rosh Hashanah 12a. "642 parts" has an interesting history; it is the difference in time between the meridians of Babylonia and of Jerusalem (about 9 degrees of longitude) and was the focus of the famous calendar controversy of Sa'adia and Ben Meir. See Arnold A. Lasker and Daniel J. Lasker, "642 Parts: More concerning the Sa'adia- Ben Meir controversy" *Tarbiz* 60 (1990-91): 119-28. R. Landau, in "Romancing the Old Moon," *Meḥqere Ḥag* 10 (October 1998): 8-19, wonders about the meaning of the strange statement in *Rosh Hashana* 20b that if the *molad* is before "*hatzot*" the crescent can surely be seen

before sunset. The lunar crescent can usually not be seen, even under excellent conditions, as soon as six hours after conjunction. He has calculated that postponing Rosh Hashanah if its *molad* fell anytime after 18 hours and 642 parts (12:35 p.m.) assures the *molad* will not fall on the second day of any month during the year. Tradition rounds this out to 12:00 noon, but the postponement, argues Landau, would not be necessary if the *molad* fell after 12:00 but before 12:35 p.m.

[54]In the current calculated calendar, in which Nisan 1 cannot fall on a Wednesday or Friday, Nisan 1 occurred on Thursday April 3. But if the following Tishre 1 was a Friday, and the month-lengths as in our current calendar, Nisan 1 would be a Wednesday. As noted above, traditions about creation preserved in Arabic sources, when they give dates, give "1 Nisan" (Probably to be understood as 1 April) as the Sunday of creation and 6 Nisan as the date of Adam's creation, with differing reports of the number of years between creation and the *hijra*.

[55]*Sanhedrin* 97a.

[56]*Avodah Zarah*, 9a.

[57]*Sanhedrin* 99a-b.

[58]See, for example, Rabbi Benjamin Bleich, "Are your ready for Y2K?" which first appeared in *Olam* (Winter 1999): 5. It was later circulated widely on the Internet (and posted at http://innernet.org.il). Bleich gives the date 2240—presumably a reference to a year beginning September 2039.

[59]*Sanhedrin* 97a. The classic study of calculating the end time is by Abba Hillel Silver, *A History of Messianic Speculation in Israel* (New York: Macmillan, 1927). See part I regarding speculation about the end and 195 for opposition to such speculation.

[60]Samuel, *Greek and Roman Chronology*, 160.

[61]As noted above with the Muslim calendar, 12 lunar months average about 354 1/3 days, in other words, 11 out of 30 years are 355 days long.

[62]Samuel, *Greek and Roman Chronology*, 157, 162-64; Agnes K. Michels, *The Calendar of the Roman Republic* (Princeton: Princeton University Press, 1967), 171-2.

[63]Nevertheless, one sometimes finds references to February having had a 30th day, or having had a 29th in Julius Caesar's time, or to Augustus adjusting lengths of months and/or distribution of 30- and 31-day months, all of which are incorrect. On 30-day February in Sweden in 1712 and in the Soviet Union in 1930 and 1931, see *Oxford Companion to the Year*, 98-99; on Augustus' reform, see Samuel, *Greek and Roman Chronology*, 156-68.

[64]*Oxford Companion to the Year*, 784-85, lists various dates used as the beginning of the year.

[65]Most of these eras are given in *Oxford Companion to the Year*, 765-66. On the 28th year of Augustus, as the source of Dionysius era, and mistakenly taken by him to be the year Octavius took the name Augustus rather than the Battle of Actium,

see John J. Bond, *Handy-book of Rules and Tables for Verifying Dates with the Christian Era* (New York: Russell and Russell, 1966), *x*, 203-4, 212.

[66] *Oxford Companion to the Year*, 782.

[67] Migne, *PL* 67, 494.

[68] *PL* 67:497-508.

[69] *PL* 67:489.

[70] This was still during the time Augustus had canceled intercalations to bring the calendar back in line, so the date that would have been recorded by Romans for that Friday would not have been "the eighth day before the Kalends of April"!

[71] This is what I take to be the meaning of 3 *feria*, thirteen days before the Kalends of January. *PL* 67:506.

[72] *PL* 67:494. But note the headings to the letters, printed 67:19, and 23, with AD dates.

[73] *Oxford Companion to the Year*, 778-79.

[74] Using tables prepared by the National Observatory in Washington, DC, I compared new moon times with *molad* Tishre, really the only important *molad* in this system; to be fair, I also compared the *molad* times for every month over a short period, attempting to find an "average new moon." I found the September new moons inconclusive at best; the year-round new moons yielded an average time which was still several hours off the *molad*, when corrected for Jerusalem or Baghdad time. Astronomers have advised me, however, that due to the complexities of the moon's motion as observed from the earth, in order to get a fair figure for comparison, one would have to calculate and compare many more years than I was prepared to do.

[75] Bond, *Handy-book of Rules*, 212-13. This would have been a "great cycle" of 532 years after the beginning of the Diocletian era.

Antichrist and His Predecessors:
The Incorporation of Jewish Traditions
of Evil into Christian End-Time Scenarios

Matthew Goff

INTRODUCTION

Christian conceptions of evil are shaped by a rich lore of legends. Christian eschatology (that is, the study of final things) holds that a period of wickedness will precede salvation and the final judgment (see, for example, Dan 7, Mark 13, Rev 20-21). It is commonly held that in the end-time Antichrist will reign on earth. His political prominence is part of an ordained end-time scenario. If a fundamentalist Christian believes that the end is near, he/she may have identified a contemporary political figure as Antichrist. Nero, Muhammad, Napoleon, and Hitler, among others, have all been identified as Antichrist.[1]

Where did Christianity get such ideas? Christianity and its precepts need to be understood in the context of the Judaism from which they evolved. The Judaism of the time of Jesus had well-developed apocalyptic concepts such as the final judgment, messianism, and the resurrection of the dead.[2] It also had conceptions of eschatological opposition to God. To understand what Christianity contributed to the Antichrist legend, we must understand what it inherited. Relevant Jewish and Christian texts suggest that Antichrist is a christological crystallization of various Jewish traditions of eschatological adversaries.[3] In this paper we examine texts that attest these Jewish traditions and speculate on how authors of early Christian literature appropriated them. The Antichrist legend throughout history will also be examined, including how it is used in our own day.

EVIL IN THE BIBLE

In the Hebrew Bible, evil, like everything else, comes from God: "I am the Lord, and there is no other. I form light and I create darkness; I produce well-being and I create evil" (Isa 45:6-7).[4] The Hebrew word for woe [ra']

91

can be translated as "evil," as in the King James Version. But the "evil" that God creates was not written with the modern understanding of evil in mind. Often in contemporary thought evil denotes a supernatural enemy that is dedicated to destruction and locked in an age-old struggle with God. The "Satan" of the Hebrew Bible does not refer to a specific individual, but is a common noun, *satan*, which means "adversary." In the story of Balaam's ass, the angel of the Lord stands in the middle of the road, blocking the way. To describe this act of obstruction, he is called a *satan*: "The angel of the Lord took his stand in the road as his adversary [*l-stn*]" (Num 22:22). The angel is opposed to Balaam and his donkey, but he is clearly not a mythological figure of evil. When the Philistines worry that David might become a military enemy, they call him a *satan*: "He [David] shall not go down with us to do battle, or else he may become an adversary [*stn*] to us in battle" (1 Sam 29:4). The term can also refer to an "adversary" in God's heavenly court. In Job 1, the *satan* is a heavenly being ("son of God," Job 1:6) who questions God in order to make him wonder if Job would continue to be upright and blameless if his life were no longer comfortable and prosperous: "You have blessed the work of his hands, and his possessions have increased in the land. But stretch out your hand now, and touch all that he has, and he will curse you to your face" (Job 1:10-11; compare Zech 3:12).[5] The *satan* ruins Job's life, but does so with God's permission (1:12). He is not the "Prince of Darkness." The Hebrew Bible has no such creature. The evil that Isaiah attributes to God refers to anything that harms God's people. That which improves their lives is also attributed to him. All facets of the human experience are attributed to God, without appeal to a mythic adversary that can be blamed for human misery and misfortune.

The God of the Hebrew Bible does, however, fight a cosmic battle. This opposition is not "evil" in the sense that it comprises a mythic enemy dedicated and organized to overthrow God's dominion. Rather it is chaos—the primal waters that existed before God's creation. The creation of the world in the first chapter of the book of Genesis is described as God's imposition of order over chaos. The account has very little of the mythic drama that colors other creation stories of the Ancient Near East. For example, in the Babylonian creation epic *Enuma Elish*, the god Marduk creates the world by slaying the primal serpent, Tiamat.[6] There is no sense of a cosmic battle between deities in Gen 1. The chaos there is not a primal force that is dedicated to the overthrow of God, but rather represents aspects of the cosmos that are not ordered by his dominion. Elsewhere in the Hebrew Bible creation is depicted with a greater sense of a mythological struggle between two foes. The primeval waters are depicted as a sea dragon, with names such as Behemoth or Leviathan (Ps 74, 89; Isa 51).[7] God's creation of the world is understood as a victory over these enemies, and in that sense it is similar to the presentation of creation in *Enuma Elish*. It is a matter of debate whether Behemoth or Leviathan should be considered "evil." I argue that they should not. They do not do the kinds of things that will be attributed to Antichrist. They do not negatively influence events in the human realm. They are beings whose defeat represents the imposition of God's mastery upon the universe. In the Hebrew Bible the presence of "evil" in this world is attributed to God, as Isaiah 45 makes clear. Nevertheless, the chaos/dragon tradition is perhaps the earliest attested tradition of mythological opposition to God. This cosmic conflict is an important precursor to the later development of an evil force that is opposed to God and dedicated to adversely affecting the human realm.

In the Hebrew Bible there are other precursors to the modern understanding of evil as denoting a supernatural enemy opposed to God. One involves the word *satan*. First and Second Chronicles are postexilic[8] retellings of events in Israelite history also found in the books of Samuel and Kings. In 2 Sam 24, God requires King David to begin a census of the nation: "Again the anger of the Lord was kindled against Israel, and he incited David against them, saying, 'Go, count the people of Israel and Judah'" (2 Sam 24:1). Censuses were often unpopular in antiquity because they were usually undertaken for taxation or military conscription. In the retelling in Chronicles, however, Satan, not God, inspires David to call for a census: "Satan stood up against Israel, and incited David to count the people of Israel. So David said to Joab and the commanders of the army, 'Go, number Israel, from Beer-sheba to Dan, and bring me a report, so that I may know their number'" (1 Chron 21:1-2).

Another antecedent to the tradition that there is an evil force opposed to God is the legend of the final tyrant of Ezekiel 38-39. These texts, written in the sixth century BCE, tell the story of God, king of Magog, a country far to the north of Israel. One day Gog will lead his country and other nations in an ultimate battle against Israel; then God will vanquish Gog and his armies. This story was incorporated into Jewish and Christian traditions about the dominion of evil in the world just before the final judgment. For example, the Dead Sea Scrolls text *Pesher on Isaiahᵃ* (4Q161)[9] interprets Isa 11:1-3 as referring to a messianic figure, the "Branch of David," who will appear at the end-time. God shall ordain the kingship of this figure over the nations. In a fragmentary portion of the text, Magog is mentioned in relation to this "Branch" ruling the nations with his sword.[10] This interpretation of Isaiah, probably written in the first century BCE, is one of the earliest examples of the incorporation of Gog and Magog into an end-time scenario. This is also the case in the New Testament book of Revelation: "When the thousand years are ended, Satan will be released from his prison and will come out to deceive the nations at the four corners of the earth, Gog and Magog, in order to gather them for battle" (Rev 20:7-8). Gog and Magog are opponents in an eschatological war that was believed to precede the judgment. The Gog and Magog tradition helped shape the belief that the end of days will feature both the powerful reign of a wicked ruler and an eschatological war.[11]

EVIL IN SECOND TEMPLE JUDAISM

In the two centuries before the Common Era, Jews increasingly began to believe that there was an evil entity, separate from God, who was responsible for the wickedness of the world. This period of Second Temple Judaism is dualistic. In dualism reality is dominated by two opposing forces, one good, one evil. Whether Judaism developed this idea independently or from foreign influence is a matter of debate. In terms of foreign influence, the most likely candidate is Persia. Persian religion was strikingly dualistic, and there was some degree of cultural correspondence between Israel and Persia.[12]

figure 1: Hans Holbein the Younger: *Daniels Vision von den vier Tieren*

The Book of Daniel, written in the second century BCE, provides important background material for the Antichrist legend.[13] In chapter 7, Daniel has a dream in which he sees four strange beasts: a lion with eagle's wings, a bear with tusks or ribs among its teeth, a leopard with four bird's wings and four heads, and a beast with iron teeth and ten horns. (See figure 1).[14] Later in the chapter an angel interprets the vision and we are told that the four beasts represent four kingdoms (Dan 7:23-24). Scholars generally take them to represent Babylonia, Media,[15] Persia, and Greece, which were successive political empires. In the vision, a "little horn" then sprouts from the fourth most powerful of the beasts, displacing three of the original ten horns. The fourth beast represents a tyrannical kingdom. The little horn represents a vicious despot who wages war against the faithful and blasphemes God:

He shall speak words against the Most High, shall wear out the holy ones of the Most High, and shall attempt to change the sacred seasons and the law; and they shall be given into his power for a time, two times, and half a time. Then the court shall sit in judgment, and his dominion shall be taken away, to be consumed and totally destroyed" (Dan 7:25-26; see also 11:36).

The cryptic expression "a time, two times, and half a time" probably refers to three and a half years (Dan 7:25).[16] Daniel 9:27 also refers to this length of time, during which "the desolating abomination" is placed in the Temple.[17] After this length of time the horn will be dethroned and judged, and the faithful will rule the entire world.

The book of Daniel is concerned with the Seleucid and Ptolemaic empires that formed as a result of the breakup of Alexander the Great's empire after his death in 323 BCE. The Seleucid Empire is understood by Daniel as the fourth beast. Daniel thus provides an account of Hellenistic history that culminates in the reign of Antiochus Epiphanes IV, who ruled the Seleucid Empire from 175 to 164 BCE. He was vilified by many in Israel because of his egregious promotion of Hellenization and disdain for Jewish tradition (see 1 Macc 1:10-15; 2 Macc 4:7-38).[18] According to 1 Maccabees, he demonstrated this in part by forcing Jews to sacrifice swine upon the altar of the Temple, by attempting to destroy all copies of the Torah (1 Macc 1:56), and by suppressing Jewish festivals. Most radically, he pillaged and desecrated the Temple (1 Macc 1:37; Dan 11:31). These events in part led to the Maccabean Revolt, the Jewish war of independence led by Judah Maccabee against Seleucid Rule.[19] The Temple was desecrated for roughly three and a half years, which may be related to the "three and a half years" of Daniel. The rededication of the Temple in 164 BCE is celebrated today as Hanukkah. Daniel, a book compiled for Jews who were suffering from persecution and whose religious traditions were under attack, is also a survey of history. It places Daniel's own day at the end of the sequence and identifies his period as the one in which evil climaxes just before God delivers his people.

This form of writing is a way of endowing the present moment with import. The apocalyptic interpretations of Antiochus Epiphanes found in Daniel were to make important contributions to the Antichrist legend. Christianity would adopt the Danielic tradition that the reign of a wicked ruler will characterize the end-time and signal the coming judgment and vindication of the righteous.

The *Book of Jubilees*, a text often dated to the second century BCE, also has an evil figure.[20] *Jubilees* is a retelling of Genesis and Exodus with embellishments in keeping with the priorities of the author's own day. For example, it portrays the patriarchs as observing the law and keeping the Sabbath—which is not explicitly the case in Genesis. Quite often it inserts an evil figure. When it narrates the story of the binding of Isaac (Gen 22), the suggestion for Abraham to kill his son does not come from an angel of God, but from "Prince Mastema" and is understood as an attempt to trick Abraham (*Jub.* 17:15-18:19). In the retelling of Exodus, Mastema aids the magicians of Egypt and kills the firstborn of Egypt (*Jub.* 48:9; 49:2). There are also apocalyptic motifs in this book. *Jubilees* 23 describes the wicked generation that will precede the final judgment. After the final judgment "there will be no Satan and no evil (one) who will destroy" (*Jub.* 23:29). "Satan" is thus parallel to an "evil" one who will no longer be around in the idealized future after the deliverance. However, in *Jubilees* the wickedness of the final generation does not culminate in a final tyrant, as in the case of Daniel. *Jubilees* shows us that in the Second Temple period there were free-floating, even competing, conceptions of eschatological adversaries. An apocalyptic scenario could accord a central role to such an adversary, as in Daniel, but depictions of the end-times did not require it.

Another important eschatological opponent mentioned in the literature of the Second Temple period is Belial.[21] This name is found already in the Hebrew Bible, often used to describe the wicked. For example, in Deut 13:13 (Heb.: 13:14) we read: "scoundrels (literally, "sons of Belial") from among you have gone out and led the inhabitants of the town astray, saying, 'Let us go and worship other gods,' whom you have not known" (see also 1 Sam 25:25; 2 Sam 16:7-8; Prov 19:28, inter alia). The term is associated with death in Ps 18 (see also 2 Sam 22), invoking associations with the myth of God's struggle against chaos, the "mighty waters." But there is no personification or anthropomorphic treatment of Belial in the Hebrew Bible. In the Second Temple period, however, Belial is often understood as the main eschatological adversary to God. He is perhaps the most important precursor to Antichrist and Satan. This is explicit, for example, in the medieval Jewish text, the *Book of Zerubbabel*, where Belial is called the father of Antichrist.[22]

Belial is mentioned quite frequently in the Dead Sea Scrolls as a figure to be feared.[23] According to the *Rule of the Community*, which explains how the group lived, these rules are to be followed "in order not to stray from following him [God] for any fear, dread, grief, or agony (that might occur) during the dominion of Belial" (1QS 1:18; see also 2:19). The *War Scroll* describes the final eschatological battle, led by angels, between the Gentiles and the Dead Sea community. Gentiles represent wickedness manifest in the world and are the "army of Belial" (1QM 1:13).[24] Belial is called the "prince of the kingdom of wickedness" (1QM 17:5-6) and the "angel of malevolence" (1QM 13:10-13). According to column 13, his rule "is in darkness and his purpose is to bring about wickedness and iniquity."[25] He also is the leader of the "angels of destruction" (see also 1QM 14:9).[26] 11Q13 (11QMelch) is another Qumran text that features Belial. This text describes the judgment and persecution of the wicked at the end of days being carried out by Melchizedek, an enigmatic agent of heavenly salvation.[27] Melchizedek will save his people from Belial's dominion (11QMelch II, 15). He will also lead a company of divine beings who will "devour Belial with fire" (11QMelch III, 7). In the Dead Sea Scrolls the Belial myth is used to explain the prevalent wickedness of the world the Qumran community opposed so vehemently. The punishment for this wickedness, which they believed was imminent, was symbolized by the prediction of Belial's downfall.[28]

Much Second Temple Jewish literature was written by Jews who believed they were living in the final days. In Daniel the end-time is characterized by the reign of a wicked king who is described in mythic language. In Qumran literature the end-time is characterized by the reign of a mythological figure of evil, the ordained divine ruler of darkness and the underworld. In these bodies of literature we see variations on the theme of eschatological opposition to God. Figures such as Belial and Mastema influence the human realm, and the presence of evil in the world is attributed to his influence. This attribution of evil to a mythological being was richly elaborated in the Second Temple period. This tradition was a seminal element in the religious milieu out of which Christianity originated.

ANTICHRIST, THE NEW TESTAMENT, AND EARLY CHRISTIAN LITERATURE

Like the Qumran community, the first Christians believed that they were living in the end-times. They continued and elaborated upon Jewish traditions discussed in the previous sections. These traditions influenced the development of the Christian Antichrist.

The word "Antichrist" occurs only five times in the New Testament. These occurrences are found in 1 and 2 John, which were probably written at the end of the first century CE. The author believed that there are many antichrists: "You were told that an antichrist was to come. Well, many antichrists have already appeared, proof to us that this is indeed the last hour" (1 John 2:18). Since 1 John 2 makes clear that its audience was expecting an 'antichrist,' it apparently did not invent the term. This letter uses 'antichrist' primarily as a term for heretics, those who deny "both the Father and the Son" (1 John 2:22; 4:3; 2 John 7). For many New Testament texts, heretics are portrayed as a feature of the end-times; false prophets and preachers will lead many astray (for example, Matt 24:5, 23; Mark 13:22; Rev 13:14).

2 Thessalonians, which is often dated to the second half of the first century CE,[29] also attributes end-time apostasy to a mythological figure of evil. It attributes this rise of waywardness to "the man of lawlessness, the son of perdition, the adversary" (2:3-4). He is also called "the wicked one." He will perform "counterfeit miracles" for those who would not accept "the love of truth" or salvation, leading them astray (2:10).

The "abomination of desolation" in Mark 13:14 is taken from the book of Daniel. Mark 13, an account of the final tribulation, is often called "the Little Apocalypse."[30] The "abomination of desolation," frequently interpreted as the Antichrist (see also Matt 24:15 and Dan 9:27, 11:31),[31] is a sign that the unparalleled distress of the end-times has begun:

> But when you see the abomination of desolation set up where it ought not to be (let the reader understand), then those in Judea must flee to the mountains; the one on the housetop must not go down or enter the house to take anything away; the one in the field must not turn back to get a coat. Woe to those who are pregnant and to those who are nursing infants in those days! (Mark 13:14-17).

This text understands signs of the end of the world as the fulfillment of the prophecy of Daniel. Though the "abomination" in Mark may originally have been a reference to the defilement and destruction of the Temple in 70 CE, Mark 13 has often been read as describing Antichrist's rise to power in Jerusalem.[32]

Jewish traditions of evil are also employed in 2 Corinthians. In 2 Cor 6:14-15 we find: "Do not be mismatched with unbelievers. For what partnership is there between righteousness and lawlessness? Or what fellowship is there between light and darkness? What agreement does Christ have with Beliar?"[33] Paul presents a Jewish eschatological adversary as the opposite of Christ. This represents the appropriation of Jewish ideas, reinterpreted christologically.

The main source for the Antichrist legend is the book of Revelation, although it does not use the word "Antichrist."[34] This book was probably written close to the end of the first century CE on the island of Patmos (Rev 1:9). It depicts the tribulations before the Day of Judgment. Rev 11 predicts that the "beast" (*therion*) that comes out of the Abyss will kill two prophets sent by God. The description of the beast, dependent upon Dan 7, portrays it with seven heads and ten horns. The people, under the beast's influence, will celebrate the death of these prophets. Rev 12 depicts a dragon that represents Satan (12:9;see also20:2). He is hurled by the archangel Michael into the Abyss. There will also be persecution of the faithful by a beast who emerges from the sea (13:1). He is generally held to be a different manifestation of the beast from that pictured in chapter 11. The dragon hands over its authority to this beast (13:2), which makes boasts and blasphemies for forty-two months, a figure equivalent to the three and half years of Daniel.[35] It also acquires power over "every race, people, language and nation" (13:7). Everyone whose name is not written in the Book of Life worships this beast.

Then another beast appears. This beast is a false prophet who will persuade Christians to worship the first beast (Rev 13:14, 16:13, 19:20, 20:10). He encourages people to construct a statue of the first beast and makes it illegal for anyone to buy or sell anything not branded with the mark of the first beast (13:17). This mark is the number 666.[36] Various solutions for the deciphering of this cryptic figure have been proposed; most likely it refers to Nero. This number in Hebrew (where each letter has a numeric value) spells out "Nero Caesar."[37] Nero is an important figure in the Antichrist legend.

Nero (b. 37 CE), emperor of the Roman Empire, was reviled by Jews and Christians alike. Mythological interpretations of his cruelty helped unify disparate traditions about eschatological adversaries. *The Ascension of Isaiah*, a Jewish text originally written in the second century BCE with sections added in subsequent centuries, identifies Nero with Beliar. It is foretold that at the ordained final period of the world, "Beliar will descend, the great angel, the king of this world ... He will descend from this firmament in the form of a man, a king of iniquity, a murderer of his mother." It continues: "This angel, Beliar, will come in the form of that king, and with him will come all the powers of this world, and they will obey him in every wish" (4:2-5;see also2:4).[38] Beliar is a "murderer of his mother," an allusion to Nero, who had his mother, Agrippina, murdered in 59 CE.[39] The tradition attested in Daniel of the wicked tyrant at the end of days and the Belial tradition of attributing evil to a mythological being are here combined into one composite picture.[40]

The *Sibylline Oracles*, which contains Jewish and Christian prophecies expressed in Graeco-Roman style, predicts that one day Nero will return to commit acts of destruction (3:63-74, 4:119-29, 4:138-9, 5:93-110, 214-27; see also 5:137-60).[41] The *Sibylline Oracles* also associates Nero with Beliar. One prediction reads:

> Then Beliar will come from the *Sebastenoi*,[42] and he will raise up
> the height of mountains, and he will raise up the sea, the great fiery
> sun and shining moon, and he will raise up the dead, and perform
> many signs for men ... But he will, indeed, also lead men astray,
> and will lead astray many faithful, chosen Hebrews, and also other
> lawless men (3:63-69).

The destruction this figure unleashes is thus understood in cosmological terms. As with the Belial of the Qumran scrolls, the presence of evil in the world is attributed to a single mythological figure. The Danielic tradition of the final tyrant is also present, in that, as in the *Ascension of Isaiah*, the mythological ruler of darkness is associated with a human king. The *Sibylline Oracles* and the *Ascension of Isaiah* rely on Second Temple Jewish traditions about Beliar and the final tyrant. Older mythologies of evil were thus used to explain Nero's well-known cruelty. Nero thus emerges as a pivotal figure in the development of the Antichrist tradition. The connection between Nero and Antichrist is explicit in Armenian, for example, where the term for Antichrist is *nerhn*, a word based on "Nero."[43]

The imagery of the beast, used in Rev 13 to refer cryptically to the Roman Emperor Nero, refers in chapter 17 to the Roman Empire. This chapter contains a vision of the Whore of Babylon riding the beast with seven heads and ten horns that was mentioned in chapter 13. She represents the Roman Empire.[44] An angel tells John that the seven heads signify seven emperors (of Rome) and the ten horns signify ten kings of nations who will be allied with Rome.

The beast is taken prisoner in the final eschatological battle between good and evil. He and the false prophet are thrown alive into the lake of burning sulfur (Rev 19:20). Then the dragon is thrown into the Abyss, after which the thousand year reign of Christ on earth begins (the origin of the term "millennialism"). The beast's rise to power signals the coming of Christ and the eventual downfall of the beast himself.

The author of Revelation viewed his own day as the end of history. In his day the most powerful force in the world was the Roman Empire. The actions of the Roman empire were attributed to Satan, the beast and the false prophet. He used Jewish traditions about a period of wickedness, dominated by an eschatological adversary, to explain the contemporary political situation. He employed traditions from Daniel about the final tyrant to interpret Nero and the Roman Empire, in order to describe a figure who is opposed to Christ.[45] The canonization of such a vivid and colorful portrayal of these traditions helps explain how the reign of an evil ruler and the dominance of a wicked empire became standard features of Christian end-time scenarios.

Other early Christian literature also includes eschatological end-time figures of evil. The *Didache*, a collection of Christian teachings from the end of the first century CE, concludes with the assertion that in the final days "the deceiver of the world" will claim to be the messiah:

> For in the last days the false prophets and corrupters will abound, and the sheep will be turned into wolves, and love will be turned into hate ... And then the deceiver of the world will appear as a son of God and "will perform signs and wonders" (Mark 13:22) and the earth will be delivered into his hands and he will commit abominations the likes of which the world has never seen before" (16:3-5).[46]

After this, according to the text's apocalyptic scenario, comes the judgment, the opening of heaven, a trumpet blast, and then the resurrection of the dead (5-6).

We see similar traditions in *The Apocalypse of Elijah*, which was probably composed in second or third century CE. It predicts that the "son of lawlessness" (a term from 2 Thessalonians) will come and perform every miracle that Christ performed, except raising the dead (3:5-13). The "son of lawlessness" will be killed by Enoch and Elijah, an action that leads directly to the beginning of the millennial reign of Christ on earth (5:30-39).[47] A similar deceiver appears in the second century CE *Apocalypse of Peter*. This text also predicts that false Christs will arise in the end-time and that there is one "deceiver who must come into the world and do signs and wonders in order to deceive" (chapter 2).[48]

This literature attests variations on the New Testament tradition that the end-time is characterized by the rise to power of an evil figure who will lead the faithful astray. These texts describe a figure who will lead the faithful astray with miracles similar to those of Jesus. They appropriate older Jewish traditions of an evil end-time figure in light of the centrality of Jesus. Unlike 1 and 2 John, the terminology these texts employ does not include "Antichrist."

In the early Church, older traditions of eschatological opposition were woven into the Christian Antichrist. The earliest systematic treatments of Antichrist were written by Irenaeus (c.130-200) and Hippolytus (c.170-236).[49] They were among the first leaders of the Christian church. Irenaeus's discussion of Antichrist is found in his five volume *Against Heresies* (ca.175-80). This is a polemical work of orthodox theology, intended to combat gnosticism (see esp. 5.30.1-4). Around 200 CE, Hippolytus wrote his *Commentary on Daniel* and *On the Antichrist*. *On the Antichrist* is the oldest known treatise on this topic. In chapter 6 Hippolytus writes:

> The Deceiver seeks to liken himself in all things to the Son of God. Christ is a lion, so Antichrist is a lion; Christ is a king, so Antichrist is also a king. The Savior was manifested as a lamb, so he too, in like manner, will appear as a lamb, though within he is a wolf.[50]

Antichrist is thus portrayed as a perverted imitation of Christ. Jewish and early Christian traditions about an evil ruler coming to power at the end of days rarely use the term Antichrist. Over time, however, Christianity came to understand these stories as describing the same personage. Irenaeus and Hippolytus examined various stories about eschatological evil and interpreted them in order to present a systematic description of a single figure—the Antichrist. This helps explain how various traditions about eschatological evil figures coalesced into the composite picture of the Antichrist.

In this period of the early Church, the second to third centuries, we see a new stage of speculation about evil at the end of days.[51] The end-time was characteristically less immediate for writers of this period than it was for authors of the New Testament. In this period Church authors often examined New Testament descriptions of eschatological opposition in order to provide exposition of Christian eschatological doctrine. Antichrist is the result of systematic reflection by the early Church.

ANTICHRIST IN HISTORY

There have been many important contributions to the Antichrist tradition throughout history.[52] For example, the Latin *Tiburtine Sibyl,* which circulated widely as early as the fourth century CE, helped popularize the belief that Antichrist will appear before Jesus' return.[53] Adso, a French monk, wrote in 950 a *vita* (life) of Antichrist, in the manner that *vitas* were written of saints.[54] In the fifteenth century *Book of Lismore,* written in Ireland, Antichrist is a monster, 600 fathoms high, with fire coming from his nose, a mouth that goes down to his chest, and wheels on his feet.[55] As an established feature of Christianity, the Antichrist legend became more elaborate over time.

While accounts of Antichrist generally agreed that he will wield power at the end of days, there were significant differences of opinion on more specific details. One tradition held that Antichrist will be a Jew, from the tribe of Dan.[56] Exegetically, this is based on Rev 7:5-8, which, when it describes the 144,000 chosen, names the tribes of Israel that will be spared from the coming destruction. Dan is not mentioned. This identification of Antichrist is also based on anti-Semitism.[57] There is also a tradition that Antichrist is a Catholic.[58] Traditionally this was an important element of Protestant polemics against Catholicism. Figure 2 is a polemical image that depicts the Pope as Antichrist. Melchior Lorch made it for Martin Luther.[59] There is also a tradition that Antichrist is a Muslim. Christian foes of Islam have often identified Muhammad as Antichrist. Some fundamentalists in recent years have believed that Saddam Hussein is Antichrist.[60]

Judaism and Islam have figures that parallel Antichrist. The Jewish figure that parallels Antichrist is Armillus.[61] The name is probably related to Romulus, the mythological founder of Rome, and perhaps the tradition of the final (Roman) emperor. Armillus will fight Israel and be slain by Messiah ben David. He will also slay Messiah ben Joseph, a tragic figure destined to be killed.[62]

Islam has many traditions about an evil being named Dajjal. He will wage war against Islam, perform miracles, and spread apostasy. According to some traditions, he is king of the Jews. Most traditions hold that Dajjal

figure 2: *Luthers Kampfbilder*

figure 3: *The Beast*

will be slain by Jesus, who is revered in Islam as an eschatological prophet. The arrival of both Armillus and Dajjal, like the Christian Antichrist, is a feature of the tribulations that characterize the end-time.[63]

ANTICHRIST NOW

Antichrist speculation shows no sign of abating. One of the basic convictions of fundamentalism and premillennialism is that we are the terminal generation, or not far from it.[64] The common conviction is that events foretold in biblical prophecy unfold in our own time. For these believers Scripture describes Antichrist's rise to world dominion. Figure 3 shows a fundamentalist depiction of Antichrist's rise to power.[65]

A fundamentalist who believes that we are living in the end of days generally accepts that current events unfold according to the "road map" to the end-times provided by the Bible. During the Cold War, for example, fundamentalists routinely wrote the Soviet Union into their views of Antichrist and the end-times. For them, the final war of Gog and Magog in Ezekiel prefigured a nuclear war between the United States and Russia.

The United Nations has been interpreted in light of the beast who will acquire power over the entire world. The European Economic Community (EEC) is similarly viewed. In his *The 1980s: Countdown to Armageddon*, Hal Lindsay interpreted Greece's induction as the tenth member of the EEC as the fulfillment of the ten horns of the fourth beast of Dan 7.[66] He asserted that Antichrist will lead the EEC and is currently a member of the EEC Parliament.[67] Pat Robertson has similar views, writing in 1981 that "[T]here is a man alive today, approximately 27 years old, who is now being groomed to be the Satanic messiah."[68] More recently, Reverend John Hagee asserted that the increase in Israeli support for the peace process prepares the way of Antichrist.[69] In a similar vein, Reverend Jerry Falwell, in January, 1999, proclaimed that Antichrist is alive today and a male Jew.[70]

As the Book of Revelation and the *Sibylline Oracles* used myths of eschatological opposition to help understand political events of their own day, so the Antichrist myth is likewise used today to interpret contemporary politics. In this way, ancient Jewish and Christian traditions of evil continue to thrive.

CONCLUSION

Naming the Antichrist is a venerable Christian practice. The Antichrist legend gives Christians a paradigm of evil that legitimates the hatred of an enemy. A Christian can thus mythologize the foe by placing him in an eschatological scenario wherein evil threatens the faithful, but is ultimately vanquished. If a Christian believes that we are living in the final days, the question is not if Antichrist will appear, but how soon.

Antichrist's precursors stem from the Jewish milieu out of which Christianity arose. Christianity adapted various Jewish traditions of a final adversary. From these Jewish traditions Christianity developed its own eschatological adversary who is Christ's opposite.

NOTES

[1] For more on the designation of these figures as Antichrist, see Bernard McGinn, *Antichrist: Two Thousand Years of the Human Fascination with Evil* (San Francisco: Harper San Francisco, 1994).

[2] John J. Collins, *The Apocalyptic Imagination* (2d ed.; Grand Rapids: Eerdmans, 1998).

[3] See Gregory C. Jenks, *The Origins and Early Development of the Antichrist Myth* (Berlin and New York: Walter de Gruyter, 1991), 363, where he views the Antichrist myth as a "christocentric adaptation of Jewish traditions." See also L. J. Lietaert Peerbolte, *The Antecedents of Antichrist: A Traditio-Historical Study of the Earliest Christian Views on Eschatological Opponents* (Leiden: Brill, 1996); Bernard McGinn, *Antichrist: Two Thousand Years of the Human Fascination with Evil* (San Francisco: Harper San Francisco, 1994); Wilhelm Bousset, *The Antichrist Legend: A Chapter in Christian and Jewish Folklore* (orig. pub. 1896; Atlanta, Ga.: Scholars Press, 1999); J. Ernst, *Die eschatologischen Gegenspieler in den Schriften des Neuen Testaments* (vol.3; Regensburg: Friedrich Pustet, 1967); William Horbury, "Antichrist among Jews and Gentiles," in *Jews in a Graeco-Roman World* (ed. Martin Goodman; Oxford: Clarendon Press, 1998), 113-33.

[4] Unless otherwise noted, all translations of biblical texts are taken from the New Revised Standard Version (NRSV).

[5] See Elaine Pagels, *The Origin of Satan* (New York: Random House, 1995), 42.

[6] For more information on this myth, see Richard Clifford, *Creation Accounts in the Ancient Near East and in the Bible* (Washington, DC: Catholic Biblical Association, 1994).

[7] See Bernard F. Batto, *Slaying the Dragon: Mythmaking in the Biblical Tradition* (Louisville: Westminster/John Knox Press, 1992); Jon D. Levenson, *Creation and the Persistence of Evil: The Jewish Drama of Divine Omnipotence* (Princeton: Princeton University Press, 1994).

[8] That is, after the exile of the Jews in Babylon, which took place in the sixth century BCE.

[9]A "pesher" is a type of commentary on biblical verses found at Qumran and elsewhere. For more information, see Maurya P. Horgan, *Pesharim: Qumran Interpretations of Biblical Books* (CBQMS 8; Washington, DC: Catholic Biblical Association, 1979).

[10]See Geza Vermes, *The Complete Dead Sea Scrolls in English* (New York: Penguin, 1997), 467. For more information on the messianic "Branch," see John J. Collins, *The Scepter and the Star: The Messiahs of the Dead Sea Scrolls and Other Ancient Literature* (Anchor Bible Reference Library; New York: Doubleday, 1995).

[11]The Gog and Magog tradition was important in speculation about the Antichrist throughout history. For example, in the Middle Ages, some in Europe held that the invading Mongols were Gog and Magog. Their excursions were seen as signaling the unfolding of end-time events. The Mongols were thus seen as the "dread predecessors of Antichrist." See Bernard McGinn, *Visions of the End: Apocalyptic Traditions in the Middle Ages* (2[d] edition; New York: Columbia University Press, 1998) 151; McGinn, *Antichrist*, 26; Bousset, *The Antichrist Legend*, 57, 195.

[12]Scholars often argue that the dualism of Second Temple Judaism is in some way related to the Persian religion of Zoroastrianism. The main reasons for this are that) Israel was a province of the Persian empire for the first portion of the Second Temple period (from the end of the exile in 538 BCE until the conquest of the region by Alexander the Great in the late fourth century BCE); this political situation was a context in which an exchange of ideas between Persia and Israel could have taken place; and 2) there are some striking similarities between Persian and Jewish apocalyptic literature. Persian apocalyptic texts, like some of their Jewish counterparts, have an eschatological savior figure, heavenly journeys, and a final cataclysm. They also often understand the world to be in the middle of a struggle between two opposing forces of good and evil. The struggle is between Ahura Mazda (good) and Ahriman (evil), who are described in terms of light/dark symbolism. See Collins, *The Apocalyptic Imagination*, 29-33.

The identification of Persian thought as a source for Jewish dualism cannot be proved because the date of the Persian texts in question cannot be accurately estimated. The basis of the opinion that they are such a source rests on the strength of the parallels and the assumption that the Persian texts preserve material that is quite old. For a maximalist account, see Norman Cohn, *Cosmos, Chaos, and the World to Come: The Ancient Roots of Apocalyptic Faith* (New Haven/London: Yale University Press, 1993). Cohn argues that the apocalyptic world view first developed in Persian religion. Scholars who do not make this claim are often willing to posit that Persian religion is a source for the dualism of the Dead Sea Scrolls. For example, the War Scroll (1QM) describes the eschatological war as between the "sons of light" and the "sons of darkness" (1:1). See Paul J. Kobelski, *Melchizedek and Melchiresaʿ* (CBQMS 10; Washington, DC: Catholic Biblical Association, 1981); John Collins, "Persian Apocalypses," *Semeia* 14 (1979): 207-17; David Winston, "The Iranian Component in the Bible, Apocrypha, and Qumran: A

Review of the Evidence," *History of Religions* 5:2 (1966): 183-216; Edwin Yamauchi, *Persia and the Bible* (Grand Rapids: Baker Book House, 1990).

[13]See John J. Collins, *Daniel* (Minneapolis: Fortress, 1993); Peerbolte, *The Antecedents of Antichrist*, 224-38.

[14]This illustration is from Henry Green, ed., *Hans Holbein's Icones Historiarum Veteris Testamenti: A Photo-Lith Reprint from the Lyons Edition of 1547* (Manchester/London: A. Brothers/Trübner, 1869). More recently it was reprinted in Hans Holbein, d.J., *Die Druckgraphik im Kupferstichkabinett Basel* (ed. Christian Müller; Basel: Verlag Swabe, 1997), 166.

[15]This is an ancient Iranian empire that ascended to power in the seventh century BCE. It joined with Babylon and overthrew the Neo-Assyrians in 612 BCE. It was incorporated into the Persian Achaemenid Empire by Cyrus II in the sixth century BCE.

[16]Collins, *Daniel*, 322.

[17]For this translation, see Collins, *Daniel*, 357. It is also often referred to as the "abomination of desolation." See McGinn, *Antichrist*, 40. See also 1 Macc 1:54. 1 Macc 1:54 and Dan 9:27 refer to a pagan altar placed inside the Temple by the Seleucid ruler Antiochus Epiphanes in 167 BCE as part of his effort to attack fundamental elements of Jewish religion. Later texts read "the desolating abomination" in the Temple as a reference to the beginning of the final cataclysm. See the section of this paper, "Antichrist, the New Testament, and Early Christian Literature."

[18]Apparently he also forced Jews to eat pork and sacrifice pigs (1 Macc 1:41-63, 2 Macc 6:6-11; see Collins, *Daniel*, 62-64). Regarding the chronological sequence the book puts forth, Collins writes that Antiochus Epiphanes "clearly represents the peak of wickedness. He is the ultimate representative of sinful human dominion, and therefore the confrontations with God takes place in his time." See his *The Apocalyptic Vision of the Book of Daniel* (Harvard Semitic Monographs 16; Missoula, Mont.: Scholars Press, 1977), 160. The excesses of his politics and personality led to his acquiring the nickname "Antiochus The Mad." See also Ida Fröhlich, *"Time and Times and Half a Time": Historical Consciousness in the Jewish Literature of the Persian and Hellenistic Eras* (Sheffield: Sheffield Academic Press, 1996), 69.

[19]The *Animal Apocalypse* can also be dated to the Maccabean Revolt (see *1 Enoch* 83-90). This work features an allegory in which figures of biblical history are represented by animals. Adam, Noah, Seth, Abraham are depicted as white bulls. The Jews are represented by sheep; God gives them seventy shepherds. It alludes to Judah Maccabee (90:9). A sword is given to the sheep. The nations bow down to the Jews, and the Jews are resurrected and transformed into white bulls. The righteous are accorded a military role. This apocalypse provided a basis for action by placing the current situation within a broader eschatological horizon. For more on the

Animal Apocalypse, see P. A. Tiller, *A Commentary on the Animal Apocalypse of 1 Enoch* (Atlanta: Scholars Press, 1993). See also J. H. Charlesworth, *Old Testament Pseudepigrapha* (2 vols.; New York: Doubleday, 1985), 1:61-71.

[20]For more information on this text, see Collins, *The Apocalyptic Imagination*, 79-84; Peerbolte, *Antecedents*, 239-45. See also J. C. VanderKam, *The Book of Jubilees* (2 vols.; Louvain: Secrétariat du CSCO, 1989); Charlesworth, *Old Testament Pseudepigrapha*, 2:35-142.

[21]S. D. Sperling, "Belial," *Dictionary of Deities and Demons in the Bible* (ed. K. van der Toorn, et al.; 2[d] ed.; Leiden/Grand Rapids: Brill/Eerdmans, 1999), 169-71. See also Theodore J. Lewis, "Belial," *ABD* 1:654-656.

[22]Bousset, *The Antichrist Legend*, 136.

[23]See Michael Mach, "Demons," *Encyclopedia of the Dead Sea Scrolls* (ed. L. Schiffman and J. VanderKam; 2 vols.; Oxford: Oxford University Press, 2000), 1:189-192.

[24]These translations can be found in Vermes, *Complete Dead Sea Scrolls*.

[25]In the *Florilegium* (sometimes called the *Midrash on the Last Days*) (4Q174), the wicked who are opposed to the "sons of light" (a term for the Dead Sea Scrolls sect) are described as being subject to Belial.

[26]For more information on the *War Scroll*, see John J. Collins, *Apocalypticism in the Dead Sea Scrolls* (London and New York: Routledge, 1997), 93-109.

[27]Melchizedek also appears in Gen 14:18-30 and Ps 110:4 as a priest. In Gen 14 he is Salem (Jerusalem) and blesses Abraham after battle. The Hebrew Bible attestations of Melchizedek present him as an important figure, but do not provide the reader with a great deal of information about him. This textual situation led Jews in the Second Temple period to speculate about him and provide elaboration, as texts such as 11QMelch demonstrate. In the New Testament, see Heb 7. For more information, see Paul J. Kobelski, *Melchizedek and Melchiresa'*.

[28]This translation is from Florentino Garcia-Martinez and Eibert J. C. Tigchelaar, *The Dead Sea Scrolls Study Edition* (2 vols.; Leiden: Brill, 1997-1998).

[29]2 Thessalonians is often dated to this period, although it itself has no historical markers. It is assigned to this date because it is generally understood to be an adaptation of 1 Thessalonians, which is widely regarded to have been the earliest extant Pauline writing and is dated to the 50s CE. For more information, see Edgar Krentz, "Thessalonians, First and Second Epistles to the," *ABD* 6:515-23.

[30]The parallel accounts of Mark 13 are found in Matt 24 and Luke 21.

[31]Peerbolte, *Antecedents*, 24-51.

[32]See McGinn, *Antichrist*, 38-41; Bousset, *The Antichrist Legend*, 22. Peerbolte, *Antecedents*, 36, reminds us that one reason for this speculation is that *esth,kota* is masculine whereas "abomination" is neuter. He suggests that the participle refers to Titus, the one who actually destroyed the Temple. He also argues that this material

in Matthew is reorganized to emphasize the theme of wakefulness.

[33]Beliar is a variant of Belial. See, for example, *Jubilees* 15:33; *Ascension of Isaiah* 4:1-7; *Sibylline Oracles* 2:167; 3:63.

[34]Peerbolte, *Antecedents*, 114-69; Collins, *The Apocalyptic Imagination*, 269-79. See also Adela Yarbro Collins, *Crisis and Catharsis: The Power of the Apocalypse* (Philadelphia: Westminster, 1984); Leonard L. Thompson, *The Book of Revelation: Apocalypse and Empire* (New York: Oxford University Press, 1990).

[35]This is a symbolic length of time taken from Dan 7:25 that represents a period of persecution.

[36]Although many believe that this is the mark that will identify the beast, in Revelation the mark is a sign of the beast that is upon all the people who are under his power.

[37]Peerbolte, *Antecedents*, 150-51. Some manuscripts have the number "616," which spells out "Caesar-God." Herman Gunkel, in an effort to demonstrate the influence of the primeval dragon/chaos myth upon the New Testament, proposed to read "666" as "primeval monster." See Bousset, *The Antichrist Legend*, 11. While Gunkel's work made important insights on such passages as Rev 12, this reading of "666" has not found support.

[38]For more information on this text, see Charlesworth, *Old Testament Pseudepigrapha*, 1:317-472; Jonathan Knight, *The Ascension of Isaih* (Sheffield: Sheffield Academic Press, 1995).

[39]See Suetonius, *Nero* 34, 39.

[40]McGinn, *Antichrist*, 45-51; Bousset, *The Antichrist Legend*, 128-30.

[41]For more information on this text, see Charlesworth, *Old Testament Pseudepigrapha*, 1:317-472; John J. Collins, *The Sibylline Oracles of Egyptian Judaism* (Missoula: Scholars Press, 1974).

[42]"*Sebastenoi*" refers to the line of Augustus, which is Nero's line. See Bousset, *The Antichrist Legend*, 96-97.

[43]McGinn, *Antichrist*, 291; Bousset, *The Antichrist Legend*, 253.

[44]Since Rome destroyed the Second Temple in 68 CE, it is often referred to symbolically as Babylon, since Babylon destroyed the first temple in 586 BCE.

[45]Peerbolte, *Antecedents*, 152. The parity is made clear, for example, when the Beast has ten diadems, 13:1, and Christ does as well, 19:12. This parity may also explain why the Beast has a monstrous wound from which he recovers (13:3).

[46]This translation is from J. B. Lightfoot and J. R. Harmer, eds., *The Apostolic Fathers* (2nd ed.; Grand Rapids: Baker Book House, 1992). For more on this text, see Kurt Niederwimmer and Harold W. Attrige, *The Didache: A Commentary* (Minneapolis: Fortress Press, 1998).

[47]For more on this text, see Charlesworth, *Old Testament Pseudepigrapha*, 1:721-53; David Frankfurter, *Elijah in Upper Egypt: The Apocalypse of Elijah and Early*

Egyptian Christianity (Minneapolis: Fortress, 1993).

[48]For the translation of this text, see William Schneemelcher, *New Testament Apocrypha* (rev. ed.; 2 vols.; Louisville: Westminster, 1991), 2:620-38. For more on this text, see Henriette W. Havelaar, et al., *The Coptic Apocalypse of Peter* (Nag-Hammadi-Codex VII, 3; Berlin: Akademie Verlag, 1999).

[49]McGinn, *Antichrist*, 58-63; Bousset, *The Antichrist Legend*, 25-28.

[50]This translation is found in McGinn, *Antichrist*, 61. It is taken from the edition of Hippolytus' *Antichrist* treatise found in G. N. Bonwetsch, *Hippolytus Werke* (Leipzig: J. C. Hinrich, 1897).

[51]Peerbolte, "Antichrist," 63.

[52]See McGinn, *Antichrist*, for a concise survey of traditions of Antichrist speculation in the history of Christianity. See also Roberto Rusconi, "Antichrist and Antichrists," in *The Encyclopedia of Apocalypticism* 2:287-325.

[53]The *Tiburtine Sibyl* is generally regarded as proof of the revival of apocalypticism in the Christian Roman empire. For more information, see McGinn, *Visions of the End*, 43-50.

[54]McGinn, *Antichrist*, 100-103.

[55]McGinn, *Antichrist*, 72-73; J. Massyngberde Ford, "The Physical Features of the Antichrist," *Journal for the Study of the Pseudepigrapha* 14 (April 1996): 23-41.

[56]Charles E. Hill, "Antichrist from the Tribe of Dan," *Journal of Theological Studies* 46 (April 1995): 99-117.

[57]The presentation of Antichrist as a Jew, given authority in part by the *vita* of Antichrist written by Adso in the tenth century CE (see above), was richly elaborated in the Middle Ages. It was routine to depict Satan as having Jewish features. For more information, see Norman Cohn, *The Pursuit of the Millennium* (rev. ed.; New York: Oxford University Press, 1970), 78-79.

[58]For more on the Protestant tradition of identifying the Antichrist as Catholic, see McGinn, *Antichrist*, 200-226; Cohn, *The Pursuit of the Millennium*, 80-84.

[59]For the frogs spewing from his mouth, see Rev 16:13. This is reprinted in McGinn, *Antichrist*, 210. It can be found in H. Grisar and F. Heege, *Luthers Kampfbilder* (vol. 4., Tafel II; Freiburg im Breisgau: Herder, 1923).

[60]For more on the designation of Saddam Hussein as the Antichrist, see Paul Boyer, *When Time Shall Be No More: Prophecy Belief in American Culture* (Cambridge: Harvard University Press, 1992), 327-30. See also Bob Ross, *Not One Stone* (West Jefferson: Armageddon Books, 1993).

[61]Joseph Dan, "Armilus: the Jewish antichrist and the origins and dating of the *Sefer Zerubbavel*," in *Toward the Millennium: Messianic Expectations from the Bible to Waco* (ed. P. Schäfer and M. Cohen; Leiden: Brill, 1998), 73-104.

[62]For examples of messianism in the Babylonian Talmud, see *Berakhot* 17a and *Sanhedrin* 98a. For more information on Jewish messianism, see Harris Lenowitz,

The Jewish Messiahs: From the Galilee to Crown Heights (New York: Oxford University Press, 1998). See also Raphael Patai, *The Messiah Texts* (Detroit: Wayne State University Press, 1979). Following is example of Armillus in rabbinic literature:

> Satan will descend and go to Rome to the stone statue and have connection with it in the manner of the sexual act, and the stone will become pregnant and give birth to Armilus. He will rule forty days. And his hand will be heavier than forty se'ah (measures). And he will issue evil decrees against Israel, and men of good deeds will cease while men of plunder will multiply If Israel is worthy, Messiah ben David will sprout up in Upper Galilee and will go up to Jerusalem, and will build the Temple and offer sacrifices (from *Midrash 'Aseret haSh'vatim*; Patai, *The Messiah Texts*, 157).

[63]There are numerous *hadith* (traditions about sayings and customs from the early period of Islam) that involve Dajjal. One of the most common features of the legend is that Jesus will descend from heaven to slay him. For more information, see McGinn, *Antichrist*, 109-13; Bousset, *The Antichrist Legend*, 116-17.

[64]Fundamentalism is the blanket term for various strands of right-wing Christianity that consider themselves to be interpreting the Bible literally. For the background of the term "fundamentalism," see Boyer, *When Time Shall Be No More*, 93. Premillennialism holds that the tribulations are at hand and that Christ will return before His millennial reign begins. See Robert C. Fuller, *Naming the Antichrist: The History of an American Obsession* (New York: Oxford University Press, 1995), 100.

[65]*The Beast* (Ontario, Calif.: Chick Publications, 1988), 9-10.

[66]Hal Lindsey, *The 1980s: Countdown to Armaggedon* (King of Prussia: Westgate, 1980).

[67]McGinn, *Antichrist*, 261.

[68]Fuller, *Naming the Antichrist*, 166.

[69]Hagee depicts an elaborate scenario, in which the increase of Israeli support for the peace process, in the wake of Yitzhak Rabin's assassination, leads to a less defensive posture on their part. In their "euphoria" the Israelis rebuild the Temple, which the Antichrist seizes. Texts such as Mark 13 and 2 Thess 2 place the center of his dominion in the Temple. This is dependent on the "abomination of desolation" tradition of Daniel. Since this rebuilding involves the destruction of the Dome of the Rock, this will unleash an eschatological war between Israel and the Arabs, who will be allied with Russia. See John Hagee, *Beginning of the End: The Assassination of Yitzhak Rabin and the Coming Antichrist* (Nashville: Thomas Nelson Publishers, 1996), 139-41. He summarizes his view of the Antichrist's plan for world domination in this way:

> The Antichrist's three-point plan for world domination consists of a one-world economic system in which no can buy nor sell without a mark

sanctioned by the Antichrist's administration; a one-world government, now being called 'The New World Order'; and a one-world religion that will eventually focus its worship on the Antichrist himself (see *Beginning of the End*, 118).

[70]See "Falwell sorry for saying the Antichrist is a Jew," *Christian Century* 116 (1999): 176-77.

The Apocalypse According to the Rabbis: Divergent Rabbinic Views on the End of Days

Richard A. Freund

INTRODUCTION

The apocalyptic view of the world or "the end of days" concept in both the Hebrew Bible and rabbinic literature can be summarized as follows: it is defined by a goal which is at once the personal salvation of an individual and the cosmic salvation of the world. This salvation is to be achieved in two contexts: a temporal context (an end period that is usually imminent and beyond the confines of history) and a spatial context in a "meta-physical realm" (different from and beyond the physical world). While different sections of the Hebrew Bible contain some elements of this view, the full-blown version of the "apocalypse" is apparently not indigenous to most of the Bible and emerges only as a result of contact with outside forces such as Greek philosophy. Platonic and Aristotelian concepts of "ideas" and "forms" as separate entities and realities are fundamental to this developing concept of the apocalypse. Although we can point to passages in Isaiah, Ezekiel, and Zechariah as representing a form of prophetic eschatology (usually on the heels of great communal suffering), it is clear that in the Hebrew Bible and the ancient Near East in general a cosmic notion of a metaphysical end of both time and space would have been rare if not difficult to comprehend during much of the classical biblical period. In short, the "end of days" in the earliest parts of the Bible meant the end of some specific suffering or overbearing tyrant. It may even have meant some period of time when a judgment of enormous personal concern would occur, but it was not as extensive as it became after the advent of the Greeks in this region.

It is the development of the post-Platonic world and contact between the Near East and the Greek world which gave rise to the true fully developed apocalyptic genre in the biblical book of Daniel, Hellenistic

Jewish writings, and eventually rabbinic literature. This genre needed first to have the dichotomy between a physical and a metaphysical realm and a concept of time and "meta"-time which developed in the Near East only after the rise of Hellenism. The Greek and the developing Jewish apocalyptic view of the world was both personal and communal in nature and can be indirectly linked with the Socratic and later Stoic concept of duty.[1] In Greek thought, perhaps as early as Plato[2] and Aristotle,[3] the view of dying for an ideal became established. By contrast, in the earliest sections of the Bible one generally finds a host of circumstances in which the patriarchs and matriarchs, as well as prophets, judges, kings, and religious leaders, saw their physical lives as more important than theoretical constructs.[4] The Greeks created moral and legal justifications for the giving up of one's life and theologically created for Judaism a metaphysical realm (heaven or spiritual redemption) to which one should aspire and in which one would reside at the end of one's physical life.[5] In short, the developing apocalyptic view of the world in the Greco-Roman period meant that an ideal realm existed and that one should be willing to live and die in pursuit of this ideal. It is a view of the world which on occasion encouraged martyrdom and even allowed for speculation and predictions about the imminent end. It is also a view which apparently inspired some Bible writers, especially the author of Daniel.

THE EFFECT OF HELLENISM: TRANSFORMING BIBLICAL VERSES AS A MEANS TO AN END

There appear to be two separate visions which Greco-Roman Jewish writers developed and which later the rabbis maintained in the period directly before and following the destruction of the Temple of Jerusalem and the exile of the Jews in 70 CE. One view holds that the destruction and exile scenario is directly associated with the "70 CE event" and was to be a precursor to the messianic "end of days"; in the other view it was not. The first view holds that the Temple needs to exist and will be restored in a short period of time, that a "messiah-like" figure will lead the exiles back to Israel (which is by now a messianic kingdom), and that this will signal the end of days. This view is maintained in some of the Jewish apocalyptic works written following the destruction, such as *2 Baruch, 4 Ezra, 3 Baruch*, and the *Apocalypse of Abraham*. G. W. E. Nicklesburg classifies these works as first century CE responses to the destruction of the Temple in 70 CE, with *2 Baruch* and *4 Ezra* especially close to the 70 CE event.[6] *2 Baruch* concentrates on the role of the Temple and Torah in this scenario. The account of Adam and Eve in Genesis 3 and the connection of this event to an ongoing "original" sin and punishment are mentioned as reasons for the ultimate apocalypse in both *2 Baruch* and *4 Ezra*. Although the messiah is never mentioned in *4 Ezra*, a servant who is messiah-like does appear in 7:11-12. He is presented as a warrior, judge, and protector; his characteristics were incorporated into the "messiah" figure proposed by the rabbis. The *Apocalypse of Abraham* has only an "elect one" who will reestablish the Temple, and then judge and execute the enemies of the righteous of Abraham's descendants. Only *3 Baruch* is silent on the question of restored Temple and sacrificial system. The others all have a restored Temple and sacrificial system, together with a "messiah-like" protector and guardian as the main figure in this drama.

The second view holds that the destruction and exile associated with the "70 CE event" are already an anticipated part of some broader, divine plan. The Temple and the sacrifices were not a necessary part of the redemption, the Temple was not necessarily to be restored in short order, and the messianic redemption is developed as a slow process of inculcating the values and teachings of the Torah. This view is found in *3 Baruch* and *Pseudo-Philo* and is shared by more pragmatic rabbinic teachers such as Rabbi Yishmael ben Elisha and other early and medieval rabbinic traditions. Scholars such as Jacob Neusner hold that the latter view was already part of the consciousness of some Jews before 70 CE:

> But long before 70 the Temple had been rejected by some Jewish groups. Its sanctity had been arrogated by others and for large numbers of ordinary Jews outside of Palestine as well as substantial numbers within, the Temple was a remote and, if holy, unimportant place.[7]

The remainder of this paper investigates two distinctive approaches to this question in the rabbinic system: apocalyptic and non-apocalyptic. Various types of rabbinic and synagogue literature will serve to illustrate these points.

One example of the effect Hellenistic apocalypticism had is found in the Aramaic translations used by rabbinic Jews. Greek translations were circulating in the same first and second century context as well, but official Aramaic translations became standard in the synagogue, perhaps to avoid theological variation. Translations were more influential than the Hebrew text itself since they were traditionally read in the synagogue in parallel to the biblical text. We have a taste of just how far the "end of days" apocalyptic vision has come in the Aramaic translations of Onqelos and

Yonatan ben Uzziel. For example, in the Hebrew Bible, Gen 49:1 reads
simply: "And Jacob called to his sons, and said, Gather yourselves together,
that I may tell you that which shall befall you in the last days."
Although Onqelos does not embellish his translation, Yonatan ben Uzziel
(Neofiti 1 manuscript) reads:

> And Jacob called his sons and said to them: Gather together and I
> will tell you the concealed secrets, the hidden ends, the giving of the
> rewards of the just and the punishment of the wicked and what the
> happiness of Eden is. The twelve tribes gathered together and
> surrounded the bed of gold on which our father Jacob was lying,
> after the end was revealed to him, that the determined end of the
> blessing and the consolation be communicated to them. When the
> end was revealed to him, the mystery was hidden from him. They
> hoped that he would relate to them the determined end of the
> redemption and the consolation. But when the mystery was
> revealed to him, it was hidden from him, and when the door was
> open to him, it was closed from him.

This esoteric view of the truth of the end extending to a hidden area of
interpretation is key to the variance in rabbinic literature. The Neofiti/Ben
Uzziel translation articulates the view that the revelation of the end was
revealed to Jacob alone, who was incapable of relating it to the sons. The
view that the end could be revealed to only a select few led the rabbis into
a new area of speculation, where only a few would be capable of
understanding the message.

The biblical text of Gen 49:9-12 reads:

> Judah is a lion's whelp; from the prey, my son, you are gone up; he
> stooped down, he couched as a lion, and as an old lion; who shall
> rouse him up: The staff shall not depart from Judah, nor the
> scepter from between his feet, until Shiloh come; and to him shall
> the obedience of the people be: Binding his foal to the vine, and his
> ass's colt to the choice vine; he washed his garments in wine, and
> his clothes in the blood of grapes: His eyes shall be red with wine,
> and his teeth white with milk

Neofiti presents an expanded and interpreted version of verse 9:

> Judah, you will your brothers praise, and according to your name
> shall all the Jews be called Jews...I compare you, Judah, my son to
> a whelp, to a lion's whelp; you saved my son Joseph from his
> murderers. From the judgment of Tamar my son, you are
> innocent; you will rest and dwell in the midst of battle like the lion

and like the lioness, and there is no nation nor kingdom that shall stand against you. Kings shall not cease from among those of the house of Judah, and neither shall scribes teaching the Law from his son's sons until the time King Messiah shall come whose is the kingship; to him shall all the kingdoms be subject. How beautiful is King Messiah who is to arise from among those of the house of Judah. He girds his loins and goes forth to battle against those that hate him; and he kills kings with rulers, and makes the mountains red from the blood of their slain and makes the valleys white from the fat of their warriors. His garments are rolled in blood; he is like a presser of grapes.

These additions or interpretations are not only remarkable, but also extremely illustrative of how pervasive the apocalyptic view of the world was among Jews in the post-70 CE era. They suggest an entire hierarchy of apocalyptic symbols that were somehow sanctioned by their inclusion in this official translation. In Neofiti and Onqelos we discover the basis for later rabbinic disputes over the messiah.

Targum Onqelos translates Gen 49:9-11:

From the house of Judah dominion shall come forth in the beginning and a king shall be raised in the end; because you, my son, withdrew from the sentence of death. He shall rest and dwell with strength like a lion and like a lioness, and there is no kingdom that could move him. The ruler shall never depart from the House of Judah, nor the scribe from his children's children for evermore—until the Messiah comes, whose is the kingdom, and him shall the nations obey. He shall lead Israel round about His city, the people shall build His Temple. The righteous shall be round about him and they that carry out the Law shall be engaged in study with him. Let his raiment be of fine purple and his garment all woolen, crimson, and multicolored.

In these two translations are contained many of the elements of later rabbinic views. A human ruler of the house of Judah (or better, from Judah) would lead the people into the divine kingdom awaiting them. Until the messiah comes, Onqelos states, the righteous will be engaged in the study of the Law. This pacifistic, almost "quietist" view contrasts with Neofiti, which associates violent battles and proactive behavior with its messiah figure. These two interpretations or visions continue in (and perhaps are a reflection of) the writings of two major first and second century CE rabbinic figures, Rabbis Akiva and Yishmael, as they waged a debate over the "job description" of the messiah.

THE SECOND TEMPLE APOCALYPSE

As noted above, an apocalyptic view of the world existed in Judaism before the destruction of the Temple and was manifested both communally and personally, but it was not the prevalent view of history before the end of the Second Temple. Most Jewish writers gradually adapted it by the end of the Second Temple period. In some ways, a highly personalized apocalyptic view is apparent in Jewish writers who advocated giving one's life when faced with the violation of fundamental Jewish ideals, a particularly Stoic view (as mentioned above). In the *Testament of Moses,*[8] *I Maccabees,*[9] *II Maccabees,*[10] *IV Maccabees,*[11] Josephus Flavius,[12] the New Testament,[13] the writings of Qumran,[14] and others, one finds examples of how Jewish writers attempted to deal with developing issues of the apocalypse on a personal level. It seems that some type of apocalypse was expected in this period and one's personal conduct in anticipation of end-time reckoning was what motivated this attention to ideals. The question was how and when. Gnosticism[15] and the dualistic formulations present in this pan-oriental movement affected Jews at a theoretical level, but at a practical level the influence seems to have been strategic and psychological. Unfortunately, it is difficult to construct a fully developed rabbinic view because often our information on many rabbis is so spotty. Only a few rabbinic figures have provided enough information to provide a full understanding of their system. One notable exception is Rabbi Akiva. The apocalyptic personality is what seems to have driven Rabbi Akiva, and he is also the first rabbi to fully articulate a personal and communal apocalyptic view. He may only be one spokesperson for a much larger movement, but the extensive number of his of views canonized in various collections demonstrates his overarching influence. Almost all rabbis and Jewish writers from the Roman period through the modern period have reacted to him—positively or negatively.

Rabbi Akiva lived most of his early adult life during the time of the Temple's existence, and his death is associated with the failure of the Bar Kokhba movement in 135 CE. According to his own telling, he was a person who came to religious leadership late in life, although his influence from the beginning of the second century onward was enormous. He was the teacher of the major rabbinic figures who organized the Mishnah, the Tosefta, and many of the Midrashic collections, and his traditions figure prominently in the arguments of Babylonian and Palestinian Talmudim. Rabbi Akiva was a clear supporter of Bar Kokhba; another prominent leader of this period, Rabbi Yishmael, was not. They had a number of methodological and ideological differences between them. Both Rabbi Akiva and Rabbi Yishmael seem to have produced midrashim on most of the major legal works.

The major difference between the methods of Yishmael and Akiva is that Akiva applied analogies—*gezerah shavah* (an important type of verbal analogy), inclusion and exclusion, linguistic peculiarities, duplication of expressions, particles, letters, and even early forms of *gematriot* (substitutions of letter and number values for recalculation of different words)—as divine evidence or support for creating new ordinances, interpretations, and meanings. These forms of reasoning were not necessarily irrational or mystical, but did imply a totally different method for rabbis to achieve an understanding of the divine will, which often bordered on personal revelation over logic. Rabbi Yishmael, on the other hand, used a series of logical principles of deduction, together with some basic preconceptions about the Torah's meaning ("the Torah speaks the language of [regular] human beings"), to justify an extremely conservative approach to new ordinances and interpretations.

To Rabbi Yishmael's teacher and patron, Rabbi Joshua ben Hananiah, is attributed the most famous anti-Temple statement:

> Once Rabbi Yohanan Ben Zakkai went out from Jerusalem and Rabbi Joshua went after him and saw the ruined Temple. Rabbi Joshua said: Oh, it is awful for us because of the destruction (of the Temple), the place which would repent for the sins of Israel. Rabbi Yohanan said: My son, don't feel so bad, we have another repentance which is like it, and what is that (asked Rabbi Joshua), it is loving kindness, as it is said: Because of this kindness which I desire and not sacrifice (Isaiah) (*Avot DeRabbi Natan, Nusah A'* 84, *Halachah* 5).

Rabbi Akiva's view of the Temple and its reconstruction is quite different. He held that the Temple should be reconstructed and that certain people possessed the ability to divine the path to redemption.

Rabbi Akiva is perhaps best known for his encounter with the divine in the Babylonian Talmud (BT) Tractate *Hagigah* 14b:

> Our rabbis taught: Four men entered the 'Garden,' namely, Ben 'Azzai and Ben Zoma, *Aher*, and R. Akiba. R. Akiba said to them: When ye arrive at the stones of pure marble, say not, water, water! For it is said: He that speaketh falsehood shall not be established before mine eyes. Ben 'Azzai cast a look and died. Of him Scripture

says: Precious in the sight of the Lord is the death of His saints. Ben Zoma looked and became demented. Of him Scripture says: Have you found honey? Eat so much as is sufficient for thee, lest thou be filled therewith, and vomit it. *Aher* mutilated the shoots. R. Akiba departed unhurt.

The commentary on BT *Hagigah* 15b states:

R. Akiba went up unhurt and went down unhurt; and of him Scripture says: Draw me, we will run after thee. And R. Akiba too the ministering angels sought to thrust away; [but] the Holy One, blessed be He, said to them: Let this elder be, for he is worthy to avail himself of My glory.

This rabbinic section implies that the other rabbis did not possess the personal characteristics to absorb the divine message. In a sense, it assigns to Rabbi Akiva (and apparently those who followed his teachings) a special power or insight in matters regarding apocalyptic knowledge. It is a form of justification which held that the messianic/apocalyptic scheme was a real and present possibility which was not to be achieved through slow and progressive non-violent means, but by a military leader who would initiate the end. Rabbi Akiva was a well-known supporter of Bar Kokhba, and his view of Bar Kokhba as the messiah is unsurpassed in the rest of rabbinic literature.[16]

The question is, why was Rabbi Akiva a supporter of Bar Kokhba when most rabbis were not? Was his apocalyptic vision the result of his own personal view of the world or was the apocalyptic vision the dominant view of the rabbis of this period? During the period of the first revolt against Rome, Rabban Shimon Ben Gamliel and John of Gischala, the messianic leader of the first revolt, enjoyed a relationship of mutual respect, according to Josephus.[17] This implies that during the first revolt at least one main rabbinic figure, Rabban Shimon ben Gamliel, was in favor of the pro-activist approach. Rabban Shimon Ben Gamliel exercised influence upon Anan ben Anan and Joshua ben Gamla, the former high priests, and John played a leading in Galilee before he escaped to Jerusalem in 69 CE. John brought with him many Jews from Galilee for the defense of Jerusalem.[18] The near messianic power attributed to him by the Zealots and the traditional leadership of Anan ben Anan allowed him to desecrate the inner precincts of the Temple and, according to Josephus, to bring the final destruction of the Temple.[19] His religious conviction held that ultimately God would aid his efforts, and so his apocalyptic zeal was apparently respected by some of the rabbinic leadership.[20]

Rabbi Akiva was living during the second revolt some sixty years later. The apocalyptic zeal had abated somewhat in the aftermath of 70 CE, but Rabbi Akiva saw those events primarily as a failure in the area of messianic leadership. Unlike some of his colleagues, Rabbi Akiva held that divine miracles were profound and prevalent, comprising a major part of God's work on earth. Rabbi Yishmael held that miracles were rare and not intrinsic to the divine mission. Rabbi Akiva was known for having a "martyrdom" wish. His final torture and death are captured in a number of versions,[21] which reveal that he relished this opportunity to sanctify the name of God. He held that this was somehow a part of the extreme measure of expectation set by the apocalypse. He was apparently executed at the end of the Bar Kokhba Rebellion:

> And when Rabbi Akiva was executed in Caesarea, the news reached Rabbi Yehudah ben Beva and Rabbi Haninah ben Teradion....Rabbi Akiva was executed only as an omen....In a short time from now, no place will be found in the Land of Israel where bodies of slain will not have been cast....Not long thereafter, it is said, war came and put the entire world into chaos.[22]

His apocalyptic interpretation of Lev 18:5, "You shall love the Lord your God with all your heart, with all your soul and with all your might,"[23] was meant to suggest that total commitment to the divine entailed the possibility of giving of one's life for divine principles. In a period when other rabbis were trying to limit self-sacrifice and martyrdom to very specific cases, he was apparently expanding the definition. To him, the commitment was one which stretched to public and private moments and even to circumstances which might otherwise be ignored.

The vast majority of rabbis interpreted Lev 18.5 to mean that if a Jew was given the choice of survival or observing the law, physical survival took precedence over observance: "You shall therefore keep My statutes, and My ordinances, which, if a man do, he shall live by them." "He shall live by them" and not "die by them" is the interpretation of Rabbi Yishmael. Most rabbis interpreted this to mean that no one should be obligated to give his life in order to observe the laws of God. This rather open-ended view did have three caveats: if one were being forced to commit idolatry, incest, or murder, one was obligated to give one's life rather than commit these heinous crimes against humanity.[24]

What makes Rabbi Akiva so compelling as an apocalyptic figure is that he could not or would not wait for the end of days to be initiated by the divine. Following in the line of other biblical and post-biblical writers, he held that the end of days would be ushered in by human beings and was in need of human institutions. Only later would there be a final divine intervention. Rabbi Akiva also held that this was not necessarily a group action, but could be accomplished by individuals. The *Mechilta de Rabbi Yishmael* delineates the differences between him and Rabbi Akiva.[25] The stark contrasts between the views of Rabbi Akiva and Rabbi Yishmael become clear. It is Rabbi Akiva who interpreted Num 24:17, "A star (*Kokhav*) shall come out of Jacob," as: "A *Kozba* shall come out of Jacob."[26] It is Rabbi Yishmael who taught that revelations of this sort were "among the seven things that are kept from human beings until they are the day of his death...and the kingdom of David, when it will return and the Kingdom when it will be pulled up."[27]

Rabbi Yishmael's thinking against apocalyptic speculation and its messengers is found in *Shir HaShirim Rabbah* 32.7, where he states: "Four oaths were given by the Divine...one was that they should not rebel against the kingdoms and not to work out the end of days." (See also *Shemot Rabbah* 20.) In *Derech Eretz Rabbah* 11, the tone of Rabbi Yishmael's opposition to any speculation about apocalypse is clear:

> He who works out the end does not have a part in the world to
> come. An example is Benai Ephraim who worked out the end while
> in captivity in Egypt and went forward in war because of that and
> fell in great numbers.

Apart from Rabbi Akiva and Rabbi Elazar of Modiin, no other sages explicitly mention Bar Kokhba.[28] Rabbi Akiva's hailing of Bar Kokhba as the messiah was attacked by Rabbi Yohanan Ben Torta, who said: "Akiva! Grass will grow in your cheeks and the son of David will still not have come."[29] It was, however, this same Ben Torta who held that the Temple would be rebuilt in his own lifetime.[30] The movement of the Sanhedrin to Bethar in the days of Rabbi Akiva signaled the important influence (BT *Sanhedrin* 17b) of Rabbi Akiva, but it is nearly impossible to say if Rabbi Akiva commanded a large following of sages in the issue of Bar Kokhba's messiahship, since most of the materials about Bar Kokhba were edited after the failure of the rebellion and its disastrous results. Many other sages, however, were arrested at the time of the rebellion for defying decrees[31] associated with the Bar Kokhba rebellion. The overall reaction of the rabbis to the Bar Kokhba rebellion is measured but clearly felt. A whole series of enactments by late second century rabbis seems to confirm an attempt to cap apocalyptic speculation. The late second century sage Rabbi Yosi ben Yehudah, for example, ruled that one may not make a replica of the

Menorah out of any metal or even wood.[32] Another sage of the same period, Abba Shaul, ruled that the use of the Tetragrammaton should be limited in the provinces and synagogue service from his time onward.[33] Only the priests in the future holy Temple would be allowed to use the divine name again. This was intended to insure the curtailing of religious passions for the reinstatement of the Temple, sacrifice, and biblically-ordained leadership, which were rampant during the Bar Kokhba Rebellion.

THE MYSTICAL TRADITION OF THE RABBIS AND THE APOCALYPSE

It is not a coincidence that a major trend in Jewish mysticism which began at the end of the second century CE also involved Rabbi Akiva and Rabbi Yishmael. In *Maaseh Merkavah*, an ancient anthology of mystical hymns and prayers, a young Yishmael is introduced to the semi-divine, Yuphiel, and he is enlighted to revelations of the secrets and depths of the Torah which others could not attain. In *Heichalot Zutartei* [The Lesser Book of Palaces], attributed to Rabbi Akiva and dating from the end of the same period, it is Rabbi Akiva who receives the divine call, not Rabbi Yishmael. Here Rabbi Akiva ascends to the seven palaces of heaven. Ultimately, after overcoming the many hardships placed before him, Rabbi Akiva reaches the final palace, beholds the king in his beauty, and is then overcome by the many sacred names and manifestations of the deity. Rabbi Akiva is apparently well known as a figure capable of achieving such knowledge.[34]

Another ancient mystical text, *Heichalot Rabbati,* includes Rabbi Nehuniah ben HaKanah and the central hero, Rabbi Yishmael, the main adversary of Rabbi Akiva in most of the rest of early rabbinic literature. Rabbi Yishmael here is given the improbable title of "high priest,"as if the Temple were still in existence and priests were still called to do sacrificial service. He is the regular "worker" of the old system, and Rabbi Akiva is the revolutionary figure who storms heaven. The book is ahistorical (as is most mystical literature of this genre) and combines many traditions and figures from different historical periods into one account. *Heichalot Rabbati* deals indirectly with the Bar Kokhba revolt by presenting the tale of an emperor of Rome, who decides to execute ten rabbis as punishment for a biblical crime committed thousands of years before. In this account Rabbi Yishmael is chosen by his teacher, Rabbi Nehuniah, to ascend to heaven to verify if the decree of the emperor is somehow a part of the divine plan or is simply the initiative of the emperor himself. A hybrid version is found in *Shiur Qomah*. In this book, Rabbi Yishmael and Rabbi Akiva present two interlocking parts of a description of the divine in measurements and in numbers which are intended to overwhelm the reader. Finally, *Sefer Heichalot* (known alternatively by the name 3rd Enoch[35]) presents Rabbi Yishmael as the interlocutor with the mysterious Metatron. In the *Alfabeta de'Rabbi Akiva* it is Rabbi Akiva who now has the seventy names of God and Metatron which he can use for mystical or magical deeds.

In the last part (chapters 27-30 in the Jellinek edition) of the printed versions of the *Heichalot Rabbati*, another seemingly independent Rabbi Akiva/Rabbi Yishmael work is appended, the *Sar Torah*. In it Rabbi Yishmael presents the view that the full Torah has not been given up until his own time and awaits "the last Temple." Rabbi Akiva and Rabbi Eliezer, together with Rabbi Yishmael, discuss the divine's command to build the Temple and study Torah. They claim that both cannot be done simultaneously. The divine demands both study and building. More importantly, in this synthetic work of the mystical "Rabbis Yishmael and Akiva," it is Akiva who is called Moses, while it is Yishmael who is apparently Aaron. It is Moses who speaks to God, and Aaron who has to translate the words of Moses to the people. It is the person who receives the revelation versus the one who ritually carries out the day-to-day cult. There is no final conclusion in this work, no final apotheosis which reveals the end time. Just an esoteric non-linear system of history, which appears to indicate that a regular flux of divine energy in the world can be accessed with proper magical or mystical formulae. It is the beginning of a tradition which continues far beyond the period of the early rabbis. It is another way for apocalyptic and non-apocalyptic views of the rabbis to be expressed. There are apparently two forms of mystical power which they propose. One is an active, Akivan, encounter, while the other is the passive, Yishmael, system of normative—but still mystical— study. Although the messianic movement of the historical Rabbi Akiva is not necessarily apparent, the two figures, Akiva and Yishmael, are presenting an ongoing debate as to the way that the end of days will be initiated among the mystics.

MEDIEVAL TO MODERN EXAMPLES OF THE APOCALYPSE AND NON-APOCALYPSE OF THE RABBIS

Among medieval rabbis, Rabbi Yishmael's view seems to have predominated. Rashi, the Alfasi, and most of the medieval codifiers followed his view. Such a "non-apocalyptic" stance was not necessarily anti-apocalyptic, but often bordered on it. Some rabbinic traditions moved back and forth between the two stances in a very unsystematic way, as if to indicate that the two—the passivity or quietism of Rabbi Yishmael and the radical apocalyptic activitism of Rabbi Akiva— are part of a greater whole. In this category can be noted Saadiah Gaon (tenth century),[36] Joseph Qaro (sixteenth century),[37] and, in recent times, Rabbi Abraham Isaac Kook (twentieth century).[38]

The key figure for creating a synthesis between Rabbi Akiva's apocalypticism and Rabbi Yishmael's quietism is Maimonides. In the Thirteen Principles of his *Mishnah Commentary to Sanhedrin* 10, Maimonides accepts the necessity of a messiah figure and also the idea that one cannot be proactive about his arrival:

> The twelfth principle concerns the Days of the Messiah. It consists of believing and recognizing as true that he will come and not thinking that he will delay. 'Though he tarry, wait for him.' And one must not determine a time for him nor speculate on biblical verses in order to bring about his coming. And the sages said: 'May the spirit of those who calculate the End be extinguished.' One should rather believe in him...magnify and love him, and pray for him, in accordance with the words of all the prophets from Moses to Malachi. And whoever is in doubt concerning him or belittles his glory, he has denied the Torah which explicitly promises his coming.

This was the youthful Maimonides writing. Some years later, when faced with the real challenge of a messianic figure, he hedged somewhat and turned into a supporter of Rabbi Akiva's activism in his *Epistle to Yemen* (1172):[39]

> But his unique characteristic is that when he appears God will cause all the kings of the earth to tremble and be afraid at the report of him. Their kingdoms will fall; they will be unable to stand up against him, neither by the sword nor by revolt....All the words of Scripture testify to his success and to our success with him.

In all of this, Maimonides steadfastly maintained that the messiah's coming will be unexpected, miraculous, and not the result of public agitation in his favor.

The last Jewish millennium was initiated in 1240, the year 5000 in the traditional Jewish calendar. Before and directly following this period, messianic speculation was rampant. In Prague and France, Jews were expelled for such speculations.[40]

David Gans, reporting in the sixteenth century chronicle *Zemach David*, recalls:

> Rabbi Lemlein announced the advent of the messiah in the year
> 1500, and his words were credited throughout the dispersion of
> Israel....My grandfather, Seligman Gans, may his memory be for a
> blessing, smashed the special oven in which he baked Matzot,
> being firmly convinced that in the next year, he would bake Matzot
> in the Holy Land.[41]

David Reubeni appeared in 1522, claiming to represent the ten lost tribes. He, together with the Marrano Diego Pires (who took the name Shelomo Molkho), failed to reach the Holy Land, but their activism and their ability to raise small armies of followers show the difference between the earlier Ashkenazi and the Sephardic views of the messiah. While Ashkenazic apocalyptic accounts included theoretic planning and liturgical issues, no real recruitment of followers took place. Reubeni and Molkho, both Sephardim, prepared shields, holy names, flags, and the like, and even requested permission to draft Jews into the battle against the Turks. According to a widely-attested medieval doctrine, in the correct cycle of time one can understand the "correct" meaning of earlier revelations. What this meant in practice was that the standard ritual, social, legal, and ethical interpretations of Judaism's major revelatory works, especially the Bible, could be transformed by symbolic reworkings under the guise of mystical interpretation. The most radical examples of this can be found in the ministries of Shabbatei Tzvi and Jacob Frank.

Drawing upon diverse antinomian tendencies, Shabbatei Tzvi and Jacob Frank radically transformed many of the standard interpretations of biblical and rabbinic practices. In the case of the seventeenth century figure Shabbatei Tzvi, for example, totally new laws as well as new commandments, rituals, and legal standards became prevalent in Asia Minor, certain areas of Europe, and the Middle East. Among the ritual and legal changes practiced or advocated by Tzvi was the celebration in one week of all the three pilgrimage festivals which were usually celebrated throughout the year. In addition, he eliminated fasts, ate forbidden foods, denigrated the rabbis and rabbinic practices, pronounced the Tetragrammaton in unusual settings, performed new rituals such as a symbolic marriage between himself and the Torah, dressed up a large fish as a baby and placed it in a cradle, and declared antinomian meanings for ancient blessings.[42] The mystical rationale for such actions was already in existence when Tzvi and his prophet, Nathan of Gaza, began their movement in the early 1660s. Three ideas— a coming messianic kingdom unlike the material world, the need to see beyond the literal words of revelation to their spiritual meanings,[43] this world and its laws as a means to a greater end rather than an end in themselves—were all generally accepted parts of medieval, Zoharic, and Lurianic mysticism. When Tzvi combined them into actual ritual and social practices, however, this form of antinomianism came to represent the extreme of mystical speculation. Tzvi and his movement were officially excommunicated by many Jewish communities even before his conversion to Islam, but the social and religious changes in the earlier part of his career seem to have made it impossible to accomodate this group even within Jewish mysticism.

The effects of the antinomianism of Sabbateism continued to be felt into the eighteenth and nineteenth centuries. Rabbinic apocalypticism was minimized almost to the point of extinction: in the Reform movements of the nineteenth and twentieth centuries apocalypticism was formally eliminated, while even in the Orthodox versions such ideas are downplayed.[44] The only exception was in Religious Zionism, where messianic apocalyptic thought still presented itself in the writings of Rabbi Abraham Isaac Kook in the 1930s:

> Jewish original creativity, whether in the realm of ideas or in the arena of daily life and action, is impossible except in Eretz Israel....While the life and thought of Israel is finding universal outlets and is being scattered abroad in all the world, the pristine well of the Jewish spirit stops running, the polluted streams emanating from the source are drying up, and the well is cleansing itself, until its original purity returns. When that process is completed, the exile will become a disgust to us and will be discarded. Universal Light, in all its power, will again radiate from the unique source of our being; the splendor of the Messiah who is to gather in the exiles will begin to be manifest....The time is ripe. Everlasting light, the true light of God, the Light of the God of Israel revealed by his wondrous people must rise to the level of consciousness....Our nation is called to drink not from alien wells but from its own deeps. Let it fill its vessels with will from the depth of its prayers, with life from the well of its Torah, with courage from the roots of its faith, with order from the integrity of its reason, and with heroism from the might of its spirit, for all that arises under the canopy of its skies derives form the spirit of God that is hovering over the universe, from the beginning unto the end of time. All the civilizations of the world will be renewed by the renascence of our spirit. All quarrels will be resolved, and our

revival will cause all life to become luminous with the joy of fresh birth. All religions will don new and precious raiment, casting off whatever is soiled, abominable, and unclean; they will unite in imbibing of the dew of the Holy Lights, that were made ready for all mankind at the beginning of time in the well of Israel.[45]

CONCLUSION

In summary, it is difficult to know if these two separate apocalyptic and non-apocalyptic rabbinic positions represent a straight line which emerges in the Hellenistic and Roman periods and continues unbroken until the modern period or whether it is just a series of different movements within rabbinic tradition which only seem similar. Certainly, the classical rabbinic tradition as articulated by the seminal figures of Rabbi Akiva and Rabbi Yishmael had an enormous influence upon the formulation of some of the classical texts. These texts in turn were used as the basis for ongoing speculation in rabbinic tradition, which in some periods emphasized or minimized one or the other trend. In the end, the existence of both traditions tended to offset and balance one another. The apocalyptic trends did not usually get out of hand because they represented only a part of the rabbinic tradition. The dynamism provided by the apocalyptic tradition did, however, encourage speculation and raise significant hope for many Jews in times of serious despair. The violent nature of apocalypticism was oftentimes moderated in mystical and rational speculation, but more often than not, the passion and activism of the apocalyptic tradition contributed to the development of a more dynamic Jewish community with an eye to its own autonomy.

NOTES

[1]J. M. Rist, *Stoic Philosophy* (Cambridge: Cambridge University Press, 1977), 252. An example of the public manifestation of principle is found concerning the Stoic Epictetus. If Epictetus was forced to shave off his beard, meaningless for most people but compromising his status as a philosopher, he should prefer death to shaving off his beard!

[2]Two passages discuss suicide and draw distinctions: *Phaedo* 61B-62D, *Laws* 873 CD.

[3]See, for example, *Nichomachean Ethics* 1116a and 1138a.

[4]See Richard A. Freund, *Understanding Jewish Ethics* (vol. 1; New York: Mellen, 1990), 81-127.

[5]See, for example, Cicero, *Tusculans* 1.71-75, 118; Plutarch, *Cato* 67-68; Seneca, *Moral Epistles* 71.8-16.

[6]G. W. E. Nicklesburg, "Apocalyptic Responses to the Fall of Jerusalem," in *Jewish Literature Between the Bible and the Mishnah* (ed. G. Nicklesburg; Philadelphia: Fortress, 1987), 280-309.

[7]Jacob Neusner, "Judaism in a Time of Crisis: Four Responses to the Destruction of the Second Temple," *Judaism* 21 (1972): 314.

[8]9.4-7.

[9]1.44-52, 2.33-37, 6.44.

[10]6.1-7, 10-12, 18-20, 7.2, 12.39-45, 14.42-46.

[11]5.29-32, 12.19, 14.42-46,17.21-22, 18.3-4.

[12]See the martyrdom accounts of Jotapata, Gamla, and Masada in *Jewish Wars* 3.3-83, 141-339, and 7.320-406.

[13]There are numerous examples, including the martyrdom of John the Baptist, Stephen, and others in Acts and Paul's writings. So, for example, Phil 1:19-26 and, even later, Rev 1:5, 3:13, 5:9-11, 11:32-40, 16:6, 17:6.

[14]*The Community Rule* and the *War Scroll* have references to communal and personal salvation in an end time.

[15]H. Jonas, *The Gnostic Religion* (Boston: Beacon Press, 1958), 226-36.

[16]*Tana DeBei Eliyahu* 28, 154, Friedman edition.

[17]*Life* 192.

[18]*Life* 354.

[19]*War* 5, 36, 100.

[20]*War* 6, 98-99.

[21] *p. Ber.* 14b, PT *Sotah* 20c, *b. Ber.* 61b.

[22] *Sem.* 8.9, ed. Higger, 154-55.

[23] *b. Ber.* 61b. He said to them: "All my days I have been troubled by this verse, 'with all thy soul,' [which I interpret,] 'even if He takes thy soul.'" I said: "When shall I have the opportunity of fulfilling this? Now that I have the opportunity shall I not fulfil it? He prolonged the word *ehad* [one]." Other Akiva martyrdom quotes include: BT *Eruvin* 21b: Our rabbis taught: R. Akiba was once confined in a prison-house and R. Joshua the grits-maker was attending on him. Every day, a certain quantity of water was brought in to him. On one occasion he was met by the prison keeper who said to him, "Your water to-day is rather much; do you perhaps require it for undermining the prison?" He poured out a half of it and handed to him the other half. When he came to R. Akiba, the latter said to him, "Joshua, do you not know that I am an old man and my life depends on yours?" When the latter told him all that had happened [R. Akiba] said to him, "Give me some water to wash my hands." "It will not suffice for drinking," the other complained, "will it suffice for washing your hands?" "What can I do," the former replied, "when for [neglecting]

the words of the rabbis one deserves death? It is better that I myself should die than that I should transgress against the opinion of my colleagues." It was related that he tasted nothing until the other had brought him water wherewith to wash his hands. When the Sages heard of this incident they remarked: "If he was so [scrupulous] in his old age how much more must he have been so in his youth; and if he so [behaved] in a prison-house how much more [must he have behaved in such a manner] when not in a prison-house."

[24] *b. Sanh.* 74a.

[25] *Shirah* 3 (Horowitz, 127).

[26] *p. Ta'an.* 68d.

[27] *Mech. R. Yis.* Beshalah, chapter 5.

[28] In Tosefta *Eruvin* 2 (3), 6, for example, a statement by Rabbi Judah ben Tema may be interpreted to mean that Rabbi Judah was having indirect contact with the rebels.

[29] *p. Ta'an.* 68d.

[30] Tosefta *Menahot* 8.23.

[31] *b. Ta'an.* 18a lists Rabbi Judah Ben Shammua and his colleagues in opposition to the decrees of Hadrian.

[32] *b. Menah.* 28b, *b. Rosh Hash.* 24a.

[33] Mishnah *Sotah* 7:6, *b Qidd.* 71a.

[34] E. E. Urbach, "The Tannaitic Traditions of Esoteric Lore," (Hebrew) in *Studies in Kabbalah and the History of Religions Presented to G. Scholem* (Jerusalem: Magnes, 1968), 1-28. Rabbi Akiva is also the hero of several other non-normative rabbinic works, including *Havdalah D'Rabbi Akiva.* See G. Scholem, *Tarbiz Jubilee Volume* (1980-81): 243-81.

[35] P. S. Alexander, *The Old Testament Pseudepigrapha* (vol. 1; ed. J. Charlesworth; Garden City: Doubleday, 1983), 223-315.

[36] Saadiah Gaon's mystical-moral ideas can be found in *Doctrines and Beliefs (Emunot VeDeyot),* Chapter IV, "*Shaar HaPerishut*" ["Chapter on Asceticism"]. He also wrote a commentary on *Sefer Yetzirah.*

[37] Joseph Qaro's diary is published in *Magid Mesharim* ["Teller of Upright Words"].

[38] *Orot HaQodesh.*

[39] David Hollub, ed., *Iggeret Teman* (Vienna: Domb, 1875), 48.

[40] David Berger, "Three Typological Themes in Early Jewish Messianism: Messiah Son of Joseph, Rabbinic Calculations, and the Figure of Armilus," *AJS Review* 10:2 (1985): 160.

[41] M. Breuer, ed. (Jerusalem: Mass, 1983), 137, #1530.

[42] All of the examples can be found in G. Scholem, *Sabbatai Sevi* (trans. R. J. Zwi Werblowsky; Bollingen Series 93; Princeton: Princeton University Press, 1973), 140-1, 159-67, 221, 250, 319-24, 413-14. The prayer which he changed is part of

the Amidah, said three times per day. It is usually translated: "...who releases the captives." Shabbatei Tzvi's 1658 pronouncement and reinterpretation of the Hebrew was: "...who permits the forbidden," which was intended to provide divine sanction for his antinomianism.

[43]G. Scholem, *Kabbalah* (New York: Meridian, 1978), 119, 137, 142, 329.

[44]From the Orthodox side, see Samson Raphael Hirsch's Siddur. See also S. C. Reif, *Judaism and Hebrew Prayer* (Cambridge: Cambridge University Press, 1993), 251-55, 271, 275, 281.

[45]A. Hertzberg, *The Zionist Idea* (New York: Atheneum, 1969), 420-23.

The New-World Pilgrimage of the Church: Millennial Hopes and Disappointments in the Franciscan Mission to New Spain

David E. Timmer

THE DEBATE OVER FRANCISCAN MILLENNIALISM

In 1541, the Franciscan missionary friar Toribio de Benavente—also known by his self-chosen Indian name Motolinía, "the poor one"— sent a treatise on the indigenous peoples of Mexico, the *History of the Indians of New Spain*, to his relative, the Duke of Benavente. A passage in Book III of the *History* describes the range of mountains which encircles the city of Mexico, calling it "a country very suitable for hermits and contemplatives." He predicts that like Egypt, which in the early history of the church was transformed from idolatry and sin into the center of monastic holiness, Mexico "will flower and will be filled with hermits and contemplative penitents" drawn from the ranks of the new Indian Christians. Motolinía continues:

> And we may see how the faith and Christianity have come from Asia, which is in the east, to arrive at the utmost limit of Europe, which is our Spain, and from there it comes striding briskly to this land, which is at the farthest point of the west. Can it be that the ocean obstructs it? Certainly not, for the ocean creates no division or separation to the will and desire of him who created it. Shall not the desire and grace of God reach as far as the ships? Yes, and much further, for in all the wide circle of the earth shall the name of God be praised and glorified and exalted; and as at the beginning the church flourished in the east, which is the beginning of the world, just so now, at the end of the age, it must flourish in the west, which is the end of the world.[1]

Having said this, Motolinía notes that he digressed and returns to his geographical description.

Like many digressions this one may open up the mind of its author to us more deeply than his routinely relevant remarks. Some modern interpreters of Motolinía and his missionary colleagues would argue that this passage reveals an underlying current of eschatological expectation which is fundamental to their enterprise of evangelization and which must be recognized in order to account for much that is otherwise puzzling about that enterprise. John Leddy Phelan described this expectation memorably in the title of his study of Motolinía's protégé, Gerónimo Mendieta, as *The Millennial Kingdom of the Franciscans in the New World*.[2] As such scholars as Phelan, Marcel Bataillon, and José A. Maravall understand it,[3] the eschatological views of the Franciscan missionaries were shaped by late medieval currents of millennialism mediated by the Spiritual Franciscans, a faction of the order that that insisted on uncompromising adherence to the ideals of St. Francis. These currents in turn found their source in the thought of Joachim of Fiore (d. 1202), the Calabrian abbot and exegete who claimed to read in contemporary events the onset of the final chapter in human history.[4] Two crucial features of Joachim's vision of the end could be adduced to explain Motolinía's digression: first, the expectation of apocalyptic conversion, a massive influx of unbelievers into the church before the final crisis of history; and second, the emergence of the contemplative life as the dominant motif of the renovated church of the end-times.

More recently, Georges Baudot[5] has employed this millennial hypothesis to account for several features of the Franciscan missionary enterprise which might otherwise appear to be paradoxical. First, the Franciscans supported the Spanish conquest and the imposition of Spanish rule and tribute on the Indians—unlike their Dominican contemporary Bartolomé de las Casas.[6] Yet they also insisted on missionary control over the religious lives of the natives, opposing their "Hispanization" and resisting the creation of a parish system dominated by the ordinary diocesan clergy and funded by the imposition of the tithe on the Indians. Within the millennial framework, this policy was coherent, according to Baudot. The Spanish conquest was providentially willed by God to set the stage for the apocalyptic conversion of these new peoples; nevertheless, the millennialists were convinced, God did not will that the Indian Christians should simply replicate the corrupted religion of the Spaniards, but rather that they should become the renovated, contemplative church which would herald the end of history.[7]

Second, the Franciscans labored mightily to uproot the native religion, which they considered to be a satanic invention compounding idolatry with human sacrifice. At the same time, however, they devoted themselves to a massive project of what we would term "ethnography"—studying and recording the cultural heritage of the Indians, including their religion, sometimes even writing their accounts in Nahuatl, the language of the Aztecs. Again, Baudot claims, the millennial hypothesis accounts for the seeming paradox. An intimate knowledge of Indian culture and religion was vital for two reasons: to help in the extirpation of idolatry by enabling missionaries to identify pagan ideas and practices, and also to engender a truly Indian Christianity, an *iglesia indiana*, which was not simply imposed from the outside, and hence not alien in language and sensibility to a people whose culture and character prepared them in a unique way for the Christian faith.[8]

The millennial hypothesis has enjoyed wide acceptance, especially among North American and French scholars, but that acceptance is no longer universal. While never without its critics, especially within the Spanish milieu, more recently it has been subjected to a concerted counterattack. According to the revisionists, the evidence for a millenarian program within the Franciscan mission is weak, with too much dependent on speculation and inference. Further, they contend, no clear links can be established connecting the Franciscan missionaries of Mexico to Joachim of Fiore and his late medieval followers, especially as these were manifested in the Spiritual Franciscans, stigmatized as heretical and schismatic by the Church. Finally, on this view the apparent instances of millennialism in the missionaries' writings can be explained satisfactorily in terms of orthodox Franciscan spirituality or ideas of divine providence common within the milieu of sixteenth century Spain.[9]

The dispute is one which does not seem to hinge on specific pieces of documentary evidence. Both sides read the same texts and often cite the same passages, but each side interprets the evidence within its own distinct framework of assumptions. Supporters of the millennial hypothesis read eschatological intent into the often ambiguous texts, arguing that the submerged presence of a millennial goal, even if unacknowledged by the missionaries themselves, makes better sense out of the data than any alternative. In addition, they welcome evidence which indicates that the Franciscan missionaries were more than mere agents of European conquest, that they had their own indigenist and even revolutionary purposes. In contrast, critics recoil from the notion of a heterodox or schismatic subtext to the revered Mexican mission and spin every ambiguity in the direction of theological orthodoxy and ecclesiastical loyalty.

There is, however, one important common feature of the opposing positions. Each view assumes that "millennialism" can be defined in advance, as a known quantity whose presence or absence needs simply to be verified. Given the convoluted history of millennial ideas in late medieval Europe, this assumption is too simplistic.[10] Millennial ideas were not passed along in neat bundles like credal formulations; rather, they evolved unpredictably and combined eclectically in both the popular and theological imaginations. Millennialism should be seen as a part of a repertoire of eschatological ideas and images, some of which may more aptly be termed apocalyptic or messianic, which could be deployed in varied combinations and patterns to make sense out of the particulars of one's experiences.[11]

The controlling image of Motolinía's encomium to the mountain ranges of Mexico, the idea of the steady westward movement of the church to the end of history, can be seen as one such element in the eschatological repertoire available to the Franciscan missionaries. As we will see, similar images were used by Motolinía's fellow missionaries, Bernardino de Sahagún and Diego de Landa, and the motif is implicit in other key aspects of the literature they created. An analysis of its evolution, its use, and its relationship to other eschatological motifs may help to clarify the existence and nature of Franciscan millennialism. But its interpretation requires patient excavation of a tangled clump of medieval roots, as well as an understanding of how medieval concepts of space and time were challenged by the Columbian encounter and its aftermath. The linkage of the spatial and temporal orders implicit in the motif—what has been dubbed the "geoeschatology" of the Age of Discovery[12]—can lead past the controversy over Franciscan millennialism to a deeper appreciation of the Franciscan missionary worldview.

MEDIEVAL WORLD MAPS AND THE "TRANSFER OF EMPIRE"
Space and time were not discrete categories of perception in the worldview of the late Middle Ages. The temporal movement of human history was correlated with a movement across space; hence the charting of space included, implicitly or explicitly, a mapping of time as well.[13] The most famous of the medieval *mappaemundi*, or world maps, the one produced for Hereford Cathedral in the early fourteenth century, actually refers to itself as an *estorie*,[14] and is thickly overlaid with commentary regarding the

unfolding of human history "from Paradise in the east, through the parade of empires, to the newest cities in the west."[15] This and similar maps were elaborations of a simplified and schematic *mappamundi* sometimes referred to as a T-O map, which envisioned the world as a disc of land surrounded by ocean (forming the O); the land-mass is separated into the three known continents, Asia, Africa, and Europe, by bodies of water, the Don, the Mediterranean, and the Nile, which come together to form a T. More detailed versions of this schema note the location of Paradise at the eastern extreme (or top) of the map and place Jerusalem, site of the crucifixion and resurrection of Jesus, at the center.[16]

Mappaemundi could exist in both visual and verbal forms. Perhaps the most influential verbal *mappamundi* in the Latin west is found in Book 19 of the *Etymologies* of the seventh-century Spanish bishop and encyclopedist, Isidore of Seville.[17] Isidore's descriptive order follows the east-west orientation; elsewhere, he commented on the east-west movement of history, citing a passage from Augustine's *The City of God* which notes the westward movement of empire, with Rome beginning its rise in the west as Assyria falters in the east.[18] As a supporter of the Visigothic kings of Toledo, who had replaced the Romans in Spain, Isidore was committed to advancing their claims over against the eastern Byzantine emperors, who were attempting to establish their authority over the western Mediterranean in the wake of the barbarian invasions. His insistence on the westward flow of history, therefore, had a political subtext: it legitimized the Spanish Visigoths as successors to the western Roman Empire which they had helped to topple.

Another verbal *mappamundi*, from the early twelfth century, is found in a recently discovered treatise attributed to Hugh of St. Victor, titled *Description of the World Map*.[19] The description begins, in medieval fashion, with the site of the terrestrial paradise in the east and moves to the limits of the west. In his allegorical treatise on Noah's ark, *De arca Noe morali* (ca. 1129), Hugh commented on the east-west movement that controls the narration of both space and time, and he added an eschatological reflection:

> The order of place and the order of time seem to agree almost completely in the course of events. Thus it appears to be established by divine providence that what was done at the beginning of the ages, at the outset of the world, took place in the East, and finally, as time runs along to its end, the completion of events should penetrate even as far as the West. Hence we may acknowledge that the end of the age [*finem saeculi*] approaches because the sequence

of events has reached the end of the world [*finem mundi*].[20]

Of course, by the geographical "end of the world," Hugh had in mind the Atlantic seaboard of Europe, regarded in the Middle Ages as the westward limit of human habitability and hence of historical development. But Hugh's conviction of the approaching temporal end, while obviously eschatological, and incipiently apocalyptic, leads to no specific expectations which could be described as millenarian.

Like Isidore, Hugh appealed to the "transfer of empire" [*translatio imperii*], the idea that the locus of imperial sovereignty over nations and peoples has moved over history, from Assyria through Babylon, Persia, and Greece to Rome.[21] On the basis of Nebuchadnezzar's vision of the statue in Dan 2:31-45, the fourth kingdom, the Roman Empire (symbolized by the statue's legs of iron),[22] was expected to exist in some form until the end of history. In twelfth-century Western Europe, of course, Rome was identified with the Holy Roman Empire of Charlemagne and his Frankish and German successors. Hence, the idea of *translatio* could potentially function as a powerful legitimation of the western Empire and a symbol of the foreordained unification of political power in western hands.

A generation after Hugh, the German bishop and chronicler Otto of Freising returned to this idea in his chronicle of universal history, *The Two Cities* (1146).[23] As the half-brother of the German emperor Conrad III and the uncle of his successor Frederick Barbarossa, Otto might have been expected to use the notion of *translatio* to exalt these emperors of the Hohenstaufen dynasty as the inheritors of divinely-ordained empire. Interestingly, however, Otto adopted a pessimistic and mournful tone when discussing Roman power and its vicissitudes. He noted that in the process of repeated transfers (from Rome to Byzantium to the Franks to the Lombards to the Germans) the Roman Empire had become only a decrepit shadow of its former self.[24] He was similarly dismissive about another aspect of east-west transfer which he discussed, that of knowledge or wisdom:

> And so it is to be observed that all human power or learning had its
> origin in the East, but is coming to an end in the west, that thereby
> the transitoriness and decay of all things human may be
> displayed.[25]

With respect to a third type of *translatio*, however, Otto showed greater optimism. In addition to the westward movement of power and learning, he argued, there is a *translatio religionis*, a transfer of the religious or monastic life, from its origin in the deserts of Egypt to "the regions of Gaul and Germany." In his enthusiastic description of western monasticism,

Otto gave no hint of declension in comparison to its eastern forerunners.[26]

Like Hugh of St. Victor, Otto drew an eschatological inference from the notion of *translatio*, but not a millennial one: the world was fast approaching its end, drawing its last breath; power and learning increasingly manifested decrepitude; only those who already lived beyond the limits of ordinary human life and society, namely the monastics, continued to thrive as the end approached. Their prayers, Otto suggested, might prepare his readers to understand "what consummation awaits the City of God, what destruction the reprobate City of Earth."[27] For Otto, as for St. Augustine whose classic formulation he followed here, that consummation clearly would involve no earthly millennium, but rather would proceed directly to the final judgment and eternal life.

Alongside the Augustinian non-millennial interpretation of *translatio* which finds expression in Hugh and Otto, another more millennially-charged interpretation was also emerging, one which crystallized in the Byzantine Empire and was transmitted to the west via pseudonymous prophecies attributed to the third-century bishop and martyr Methodius or to the Sibyls, ancient prophetesses of pagan Rome. This view held that Christendom would be rescued from its tribulations by the arrival of a final world emperor who would "destroy or convert all the heathen and inaugurate an age of peace and plenty," an age which would be interrupted only by the onslaught of Antichrist and the second advent of Christ.[28] In the late thirteenth century, Alexander von Roes couched his expectation of a last world emperor in terms of the advent of a "second Charlemagne," uniting Christendom under "one sheepfold and one shepherd."[29] Competing French and German versions of the prophecy developed, often with a monarch of the other nation serving as a persecutor defeated by the last emperor.[30] By the end of the fifteenth century, such hopes had also migrated to the Spanish kingdoms of Aragon and Castille, where they would exert a powerful influence in the court of the Catholic Monarchs, Ferdinand of Aragon and Isabella of Castille, and of their successor, Charles I, who bore Charlemagne's name as well as his imperial crown.[31]

APOCALYPTIC CRUSADE AND CONVERSION

The late medieval development of the apocalyptic motif of the last world emperor was inextricably tied to the ideal of the Crusade. The movement to roll back the gains of militant Islam and re-establish Christian control over the birthplace of the Christian religion had succeeded only briefly during the first half of the twelfth century; by the end of that century, the catastrophic failures of the Third and Fourth Crusades had severely curtailed the enterprise in the "real" world of arms and diplomacy.[32] But the idea of the Crusade was to have a long half-life in the religious and political imagination of late medieval Europe. As a series of Muslim powers challenged European Christendom in the Mediterranean and on its eastern frontiers, many Christians anticipated that the last world emperor would be a crusader who would vanquish the Turks and the Mongols, recapture Jerusalem, and reunite the eastern and western churches.[33]

This notion of a final crusade was but one element in a larger program of church renewal [renovatio ecclesiae] which the last emperor would bring about, often in conjunction with a holy or "angelic" pope. Another key element was the conversion of the infidel nations to Christianity. Crusade and conversion, indeed, were often seen not as conflicting but as complementary modes for the expansion of Christendom.[34] In the Old Testament, images of universal conversion were freely combined with those of political sovereignty (see Ps 2:7-11; Isa 60:10-14), and such images were increasingly used by medieval Christians to legitimize Christian aggression.[35] Similar political implications were read into Christ's "Great Commission" to his disciples:

> All authority in heaven and on earth has been given to me. Go therefore and make disciples of all nations, baptizing them in the name of the Father and of the Son and of the Holy Spirit, teaching them to observe all that I have commanded you; and lo, I am with you always, to the close of the age (Matt 28:18-20).[36]

In Rom 11:25, Paul made universal conversion a key to the consummation of history. When the "full number" of the Gentiles has come into the church, the subsequent conversion of the Jews would signal the end of history. A mid-fourteenth century Catolonian prophet influenced by the Joachite tradition spoke of a reverse transmigration of Christianity to the end-times, "from the Roman Empire and Christendom to the gentes, that is, to the Holy Land and the other infidel nations."[37] This image suggests the necessity of a return eastward to Jerusalem in order to bring the history of humankind to its end; as the gospel had been preached from Jerusalem to the farthest reaches of the west, so now it must return to the east to complete the plenitudo gentium. But it remains ambiguous on one significant point: was the return to be a triumphant one in which a purified western church achieves the ideal of "one sheepfold and one shepherd," or did it represent a new eastern flowering of the church as the west sank into apostasy and corruption?

Such an evangelistic commitment was particularly strong within the Franciscan Order, encouraged by the missionary activities of Francis himself who traveled into Muslim lands in an effort to spread the gospel.[38] Those members of the order who strove to maintain the ideals of their founder in an uncompromised form in the two centuries after Francis's death, the so-called Spiritual Franciscans, found additional inspiration for their missionary zeal in the writings of Joachim of Fiore, who a generation before Francis had predicted the emergence of two new orders of "spiritual men" which would lead the church into the millennial age.[39] Understanding the new mendicant orders, and especially the Franciscans, as the fulfillment of this prophecy, Spirituals such as Peter John Olivi (d. 1298) gave a powerful millennial charge to the missionary enterprise.[40] Olivi's Spanish Joachite contemporary, Arnold of Villanova (d. 1311),[41] linked such hopes for missionary success both to the Franciscan order and to the kingdom of Aragon. At the same time, the Mallorcan Ramon Lull (1232-1316), theorist of missions and crusade who was influenced by both Franciscan and Dominican ideals, was developing his program of study, evangelization, and crusade under Aragonese auspices.[42]

A mid-fourteenth century Catalonian prophet influenced by the Joachite tradition spoke of a reverse transmigration of Christianity in the end-times, "from the Roman Empire and Christendom to the *gentes*, that is, to the Holy Land and the other infidel nations."[43] This image suggests the necessity of a return eastward to Jerusalem in order to bring the history of humankind to its end. But it remains ambiguous on one significant point: was the return to be a triumphant one in which a purified western church achieves the ideal of "one sheepfold and one shepherd," or did it represent a new eastern flowering of the church as the west sank into apostasy and corruption? The context suggests the latter; and indeed, precedent for such pessimism about the west can be found in Joachim himself, who foresaw the apocalyptic conversion of the Jews as a correlate of western Christian degeneracy.[44] Thus, the idea of Christianity's movement from east to west and its reversion to the east at the end of history contained within itself both an optimistic strain, which foresaw the triumph of western crusade and evangelism, and a pessimistic strain, which saw the light of faith moving away from the west.

The optimistic strain was represented at the turn of the sixteenth century by no less a figure than Christopher Columbus, the Genoese mariner who was so deeply influenced by the Observant Franciscans of Spain, orthodox heirs of the ideals of the Spiritual Franciscans.[45] In 1501, before his fourth voyage, Columbus compiled his *Book of Prophecies* [*Libro de las profecías*], a collection of biblical, patristic, and medieval prophecies designed to show that the conversion of remote peoples and the successful prosecution of a crusade to Jerusalem were imminent. Indeed, Columbus believed that the two projects, apocalyptic conversion and final crusade, were inextricably linked in his own enterprise of exploration. By sailing west, Columbus believed he had arrived in the East, that is, Asia, which now lay open to Spanish missionaries and merchants. The wealth and manpower produced by this Spanish penetration of Asia would in turn enable Spain to finance and prosecute the crusade which would bring Christianity full circle, from Jerusalem back to Jerusalem again. The Spanish monarchs who sponsored his voyages, Columbus believed, were to play a key role in this eschatological scenario—one resembling that of the last world emperor.[46]

Columbus was not alone in attributing a significant eschatological role to Spain. At least eleven prophecies dated from 1473 to 1515 refer to King Ferdinand of Spain as conqueror of Jerusalem or as universal monarch.[47] In 1509, amid the fervor which accompanied Spanish victories against the Moors in North Africa, a French Hispanophile, Charles de Bovelles, in a congratulatory letter to the warrior-archbishop Cisneros, noted that the movement of God from east to west was now ready to reverse, so that with the armies of Spain the "sun of justice" would move to the east, back toward Jerusalem: "Who can prevent the purification of the Holy Places, and their transformation into the fortress of every pure spirit, the dwelling place of the saints, and according to the word of Jeremiah the joy of all the world?"[48]

Writing at the same time, the Spanish humanist Antonio de Nebrija showed greater awareness of the impact of the Columbian encounter. Nebrija appealed to the *translatio* theme to underline his claim that the reality of world empire (if not the title itself) now resided with the Spanish monarchs, who had both begun to recover the Roman domains in Africa and also "to send their fleets westward with the movement of the heavens, touching the islands near the Indies." Obviously sharing Columbus's own view that the newly discovered islands were a beachhead to Cipangu (Japan) and the rest of Asia, he believed that "little remains in order that the extreme west of Spain and Africa may be united with the eastern point of the terrestrial ball."[49]

Another thinker who attempted to adapt the traditional east-west theme to the new discoveries was the Milanese Dominican Isidore of Isolanis. In a treatise significantly entitled *On the Empire of the Church*

Militant (1516), Isidore argued that the next step in the east-west movement of the church from Asia was to be its return to those "remotest isles which are said to lie toward the east." Although his meaning is obscure, he seems to have in mind the Indies, those islands at which Spain has arrived by sailing westward.[50] Significantly, despite the triumphalist title of his treatise, Isidore described the church as having been "displaced" toward the west throughout its history, implying that its odyssey involved loss as well as gain. As with the transfer of empire, with each step in the westward journey the previous step was effaced. Described in this fashion, the "empire" of the church militant begins to look more like a pilgrimage.

THE EAST-WEST MOTIF IN THE FRANCISCAN MISSION

By 1517, Spanish explorers had become aware that beyond the Caribbean archipelago a mainland lay which they called *las Indias*, and two years later Hernan Cortés was dispatched from Cuba on what was to become his momentous enterprise of exploration and conquest.[51] Later Franciscan chroniclers were to make much of the fact that the conquest of Mexico began at the same time as Martin Luther's schism erupted in the heart of the Holy Roman Empire, suggesting that God providentially opened up New Spain to compensate Christendom for the losses it was about to experience in Europe. At the time, of course, news of Cortés's enterprise simply expanded the range of potential evangelization far beyond the primitive and vanishing tribes of the Caribbean islands, to include the complex civilizations of the Maya and the Aztecs.

One of the earliest responses to this expansion may be recorded in Motolinía's biography of Fray Martín de Valencia, the Franciscan mystic who would eventually lead the first missionaries to New Spain in 1524. Some years earlier, while meditating on the conversion of the heathen prophesied in the psalms he was reciting at matins, Fray Martín had had a vision of the fulfillment of those prophecies:

> This servant of God said to himself, "Oh, when shall this be? When shall this prophecy be fulfilled? Would I not be worthy to see this conversion, since we are now living in the evening and end of our days and in the last age of the world?"[52]

Believing that the end times were near, Fray Martín clearly expected them to be accompanied by dramatic conversions to the Christian faith. Beyond this, we can say little about the exact nature of his expectation, in particular whether he expected these conversions to produce a millennial kingdom. According to Motolinía, Fray Martín believed he had witnessed the fulfillment of the vision during the first year of the Franciscan mission in Mexico.[53]

The more puzzling, then, that after having invested such intense expectation in the Mexican mission, Fray Martín seemed ready after a few years to abandon it. In 1532, apparently frustrated both with the progress of the Mexican mission and the policies of the Spanish authorities, Valencia set out westward on a somewhat quixotic venture to find new peoples to convert. Motolinía, who may well have accompanied him, describes the adventure in his *History* in terms which suggest that they intended to explore the Pacific coast of the continent to find people "handsomer and cleverer than these in New Spain," who could be preached to "without any previous military conquest."[54] Other accounts state that the intention was to sail across the Pacific to China— an improbable enterprise, but one which would equally confirm the "westering" orientation of the Franciscan mission. The incident is shrouded in ambiguity, but it suggests that the aged Fray Martín, who would not long outlive the adventure, maintained an apocalyptic anticipation which could not be reconciled with the mundane realities of the mission which he himself had founded in Mexico.

His disciple Motolinía appears to have kept the faith through a career which extended for another four decades after Valencia's death. We have already encountered his evocation of the east-west pilgrimage of Christianity to predict an eschatological flowering of the monastic life among the Indians of New Spain— a vision which strongly resonates with the Joachite tradition of apocalyptic conversion and the renovation of the church. Motolinía also expressed his hope for a final crusade to Jerusalem, and its connection with the enterprise of New Spain, in a pageant entitled "The Conquest of Jerusalem," which he wrote in 1539 for performance by native Christians. Designed to celebrate the Truce of Nice concluded on June 17, 1538, between the Holy Roman Emperor Charles V and King Francis I of France, the pageant was motivated by the hope that peace between these European monarchs would lead to cooperation in the conquest of Jerusalem. Significantly, in imagining this future crusade, the pageant gave a decisive role to "the armies of New Spain," who are described as Nahuas from Tlaxcalla, the native allies of Cortés in the conquest of Mexico. Ultimately, the Muslim "Sultan of Babylon" is depicted as surrendering Jerusalem to the Christian forces, and he and his armies submit to baptism.[55]

What the Indians who performed and watched the pageant made of it, we can only guess. But its significance within the context of Spanish apocalypticism should be clear. The Spanish conquest of Mexico, extending Church and Empire to this western extremity of the world, was seen as fraught with significance for Europe in its ongoing struggle with the eastern forces of Islam. Thrown into the balance of this long struggle, the armies of New Spain would bring victory to the Holy Roman Emperor, Don Carlos of Spain, and the dramatic conversions expected in the end-times would begin. These expectations are clearly apocalyptic; yet on the other hand, they are not explicitly millennial in their view of the armies of New Spain. The Nahuas were expected to play a pivotal role in this scenario, both as soldiers and as believers, but not a fundamentally different role than that played by the other armies of Christendom.

Some sixteen years after the performance of the pageant, Motolinía found himself writing urgently to the Emperor in the belief that the entire missionary effort in New Spain hung in the balance.[56] The decade from 1545 to 1555 had proved a traumatic one for Motolinía and others who shared his vision, with threats arising on two fronts. The effort by the Crown to impose the church tithe on the Indian converts, along with the replacement of the mendicant missionaries by parish priests, was viewed by the friars as the first stage in the secularization of the mission. As such, they bitterly opposed it, arguing that only the friars were adequate to the task of nurturing the Indian church. At the same time, the Dominican Bartolomé de las Casas was pursuing his radical critique of the Spanish Conquest, lobbying the crown for new laws which would weaken Spanish control over New Spain. In this case, Motolinía and his allies argued passionately for the legitimacy of Spanish control and for strengthening the power of the Viceroy as the Spanish monarch's representative in New Spain. In each case, the fundamental issue for the friars was the effectiveness of the mission.

In his letter to the Emperor, Motolinía addressed the second threat, arguing that the Spanish conquest of the Aztecs was a legitimate extension of the principle of the transfer of empire. He traced the westward course of empire from Assyria to Babylon to Greece to Rome, using as his model the vision of the statue in Dan 2, with its descending order of metals from gold to iron. Charles was held to represent, not the iron mixed with clay which formed the feet of the statue, but rather the "stone not cut with hands," which destroyed the statue and then became "a great mountain which filled the whole earth"—namely, the kingdom of Jesus Christ which had begun already "during the lordship of the Roman emperors." This successor to the four world empires would be, in its full realization, the eschatological kingdom. Motolinía made no attempt to disguise his fervent expectation:

> What I ask of Your Majesty is the fifth kingdom of Jesus Christ,
> signified by the stone from the mountain cut without hands, which
> must expand and occupy all the earth, of which kingdom Your
> Majesty is leader and captain; Your Majesty should order that all
> possible diligence be used so that this kingdom might grow and
> extend and so that it might be preached to these unbelievers.[57]

Motolinía shared the apocalyptic hopes for world dominion which so many
had invested in the Spanish monarchy, but his was not a political hope.
Rather, it was the hope for the universal extension of the reign of Christ
through the conversion of these new peoples at the western extremity of the
world.

Even as Motolinía's millennial hope reached this high tide of
expression, the signs of the tide's turning were becoming unmistakable. The
steady pressure to secularize the missions was accompanied by an attack on
the methods which the friars used in evangelization, in particular their right
to use physical punishment to discipline their Indian converts. At the same
time, some observers were beginning to have doubts about the effectiveness
of the mass conversions which had greeted the first thrust of the mission and
of the religious instruction which had ensued in the Indian church.[58] By the
end of the 1550s, Franciscan missionaries like Motolinía felt themselves
beleaguered by hostile forces in the church, the royal Council of the Indies,
and rival orders.

The first major upheaval was to occur in Yucatan, a distant outpost
where missionary work had begun only in the 1540s. In 1562, the
Franciscan provincial of Yucatan, Diego de Landa, uncovered evidence of
massive apostasy among the new Mayan converts, including— he
claimed—a reversion to the practice of human sacrifice. Landa instituted
inquisitorial procedures to discover the extent of the apostasy and to punish
the offenders. Called to account by his bishop (ironically a fellow
Franciscan), Landa defended the severity of his methods by insisting that
the apostasies were serious and extensive, that only extreme measures could
root them out, and that failure to extirpate them would result in the collapse
of Christianity among the Maya.[59]

In Landa's view, the danger was not merely to his beloved Yucatan; it
was one which involved the entire church. In a letter defending his
assumption of inquisitorial power, Landa mentioned that in 1559 prelates
in the Indies had received a royal communiqué urging them to "take great
care for matters of the faith and Christianity, because in Spain there was

great perdition."[60] Undoubtedly a response to the crisis over "Lutheran" heresy in Spain, the letter urged vigilance against Protestant infiltration of the Indies.[61] But Landa applied the warning to the new Mayan Christians and their very different apostasy. His warrant for this transferal was revealed a few years later in his book, *Account of the Affairs of Yucatan*, when he noted:

> [It] is not unreasonable to feel fear when we consider the perdition which has existed for so many years throughout the whole of the great and most Christian Asia, and in the good, Catholic and venerable Africa, and the miseries and calamities that are happening even today in our own Europe, among our own people and in our own towns.[62]

Perdition, the fall into apostasy of a once-Christian people, had overtaken the church from its origins in Asia, moved westward across Africa, and was even then afflicting Europe and Spain itself. Landa feared that, without resolute action on the part of the missionaries and the Spanish authorities, this westward march of apostasy could reach across the ocean to the new Indian church.

This pessimistic interpretation of the "westering" motif, with its emphasis on the fragility and transience of Christendom, seems far removed from Motolinía's fervent triumphalism. Yet arguably it stems from the same root of Spanish apocalypticism. The triumphs of Spain during its Golden Age were continually haunted by the possibility that they might lead, not to the millennium, but rather to a new destruction or perdition like that of the Visigothic kingdom of Spain, which had been swept away by the Moorish invasion of the eighth century.[63] That mournful heart of the national mythos could not be healed even by the brightest glories of the *Reconquista*[64] nor by the new military and spiritual conquests of the New World. Unconverted Moors, Jewish *conversos*,[65] and Protestant heretics haunted the dreams of Spaniards at home; missionaries in the New World, for their part, feared the unraveling of their careful labor of evangelization. Landa himself was determined to stand his ground against the advance of perdition, although he could not help but see Yucatan reflected in the prophecies concerning Jerusalem, "that its enemies would encircle it and encompass it and press so hard upon it that they would tumble it to the ground."[66]

While Landa pondered the future of Christianity among the Yucatan Maya, Fray Bernardino de Sahagún was similarly preoccupied among the Nahua of New Spain. Like Landa, Sahagún was the foremost expert on the native cultures within his mission-field and was at work on a massive project of ethnographic description. Although his *General History of the Affairs of New Spain*[67] would ultimately dwarf Landa's *Account of the Affairs of Yucatan*, both in its scope and in its depth of understanding, Sahagún was likewise driven by his research to the conclusion that the Indian church was in peril. But his understanding of the causes and the consequences of that peril were quite different, as was his vision of the church's future in the New World. Sahagún's conviction about the crisis of Indian Christianity seems to have emerged gradually in the 1560s, as he began the task of organizing the vast body of materials which he and his native collaborators had produced since the beginning of their research in 1547. In 1564, Sahagún still regarded the conversion of Mexico as the greatest act of God since the primitive church. The New World, he claimed, had been kept hidden by the secret judgments of God until the present time; nonetheless, its peoples and their conversion had been foreseen by some, including the fourteenth-century prophetess, Saint Birgitta of Sweden.[68] Sahagún referred vaguely to her *Revelations*, widely read in Franciscan circles; he can only have had in mind Birgitta's vision of the time when there will be "one flock and one shepherd" and when a people which does not know God will glorify him, outshining those who presently confess the Christian faith.[69] God revealed their existence and enabled their evangelization, Sahagún stated, by putting it into the hearts of the Spanish people to launch out westward on the ocean sea.[70]

Five years later, as Sahagún penned the prologue to the Spanish version of his *Historia general*, originally written in Nahuatl, he ventured a theory as to the precise nature of the mysterious providence which had opened up this New World to the Gospel. The seemingly miraculous growth of the church in Mexico shows "that in these times, and in these lands with this people, our Lord God has desired to restore to the church that which the demon has stolen in England, Germany and France, in Asia and Palestine."[71] Retracing the long pilgrimage of the church from its origins in Palestine, Sahagún—like Landa—reckoned large portions of Europe lost to the faith. The church of New Spain constituted restitution for that loss. But it is not clear whether Sahagún meant to imply more than a mere numerical equivalence, in which Indian saints would replace European heretics. The voices of Columbus, Birgitta, and the Joachite tradition, with their hopes for apocalyptic conversion leading to a universal Christendom, are muted here, but not entirely silenced.

Sahagún returned once more to the image of the church's wandering in a passage of the *Historia general* dateable to 1576. It is one of the passages usually labeled as "interpolations," since it is not a translation of the corresponding chapter in the original Nahuatl version. That original chapter described the road system of Mexico before the conquest, and perhaps Sahagún knew that the security-conscious Council of the Indies would allow no such description to be published in Europe. So he replaced the text with a reflection on "the roads along which the church has come in order to arrive at this ultimate dwelling where it now sojourns." Here he describes in detail what he terms *la peregrinación de la Iglesia*, the pilgrimage of the Church:

> The Church militant began in Palestine, and from there made its way through various parts of the world. . .The Church left Palestine, and now the infidels live, reign, and hold dominion over Palestine. From there it went to Asia, in which there are now nothing but Turks and Moors. It went to Africa, where now there are no Christians. It went to Germany where, now, there are none but heretics. It went to Europe, where, in the greater part thereof, the Church is not obeyed. Where it now has its most tranquil seat is Italy and Spain, whence, crossing the Ocean, it has arrived in these regions of the West Indies, where there was a diversity of people and languages, of which many have already been destroyed, while the rest are on their way to destruction.[72]

Up until the end of this passage, Sahagún seems intent on making the same point he had made in his prologue; namely, that the church of New Spain was providentially intended as compensation for the losses of European Christendom, and perhaps as the faith's eschatological stronghold. The last two clauses reveal a significant darkening of his vision. The intervening years had brought with them a series of realizations and reverses which had combined to alter his perspective in a fundamental way. The precipitating event was the outbreak of a disastrous epidemic among the Indians in August 1576, which had carried off vast numbers of the natives and reduced the friars to a state of exhaustion in caring for the sick and in hearing the confessions of the dying. Those very confessions had confirmed for Sahagún a suspicion which his own investigations had aroused, that the "Christianity" of the Indian church was a facade, beneath which indigenous beliefs and practices had continued unabated throughout the past fifty years of the Franciscan mission. Further, in many cases the first generation of missionaries, including the revered Motolinía himself, had through naivete or carelessness become accomplices in the charade.[73]

From this point to the end of his life in 1590, Sahagún was engaged in a revisionist project, attempting to convince his fellow missionaries of the fatal weaknesses of their alleged "spiritual conquest" of Mexico and of the need for drastic reforms in their conceptions and their methods. He warned that the soil of New Spain was "sterile and very difficult to cultivate, [a place] where the Catholic Faith has very weak roots," and he speculated that it survived only by virtue of Spanish political and military power. What then became of the providential purpose of the Indian church? Sahagún returned to that issue at the end of the chapter on "Roads," noting the recent news from the Spice Islands, where Spaniards had settled and begun to preach the Gospel, and from China, where missionaries had already attempted to establish a beach-head. It would be in China, he believed, that the faith would experience enduring growth; the West Indies, New Spain and Peru would prove to be only temporary way-stations on the Church's long journey westward to the East.[74]

In Sahagún's late reflections on the New World pilgrimage of the church, the eschatological motifs which had filled Motolinía with such fervent millennial optimism and motivated Landa to his resolute and ruthless inquisition gained a quality of humility and resignation. As so often in the history of hope, apocalyptic ideas carry within themselves the seeds of their own disappointment. Yet those seeds can often mature, in unexpected ways, to bear our hopes in more modest and enduring forms.

NOTES

[1] Toribio Motolinía, *Memoriales e Historia de los Indios de la Nueva España* (Biblioteca de Autores Españoles 240; Madrid, 1970), 303 [author's translation]. See also Elizabeth Andros Foster, ed. and trans., *Motolinía's History of the Indians of New Spain* (Berkeley: The Cortés Society, 1950), 221-22.

[2] John Leddy Phelan, *The Millennial Kingdom of the Franciscans in the New World* (2nd ed.; Berkely: University of California Press, 1971).

[3] Marcel Bataillon, *Erasmo y España: estudios sobre la historia espitual del siglo xvi* (2nd ed.; Mexico City: Fondo de Cultura Economica, 1966). José A. Maravall, "La utopia político-religiosa de los Franciscanos en nueva España," *Estudios Americanos* 1 (1949): 197-227.

[4] See Marjorie Reeves, *The Influence of Prophecy in the Later Middle Ages: A Study in Joachimism* (Oxford: Oxford University Press, 1969); Bernard McGinn, *The Calabrian Abbot: Joachim of Fiore in the History of Western Thought* (New York: Macmillan, 1985) and *Visions of the End; Apocalyptic Traditions in the Middle Ages* (New York: Columbia University Press, 1979).

[5]George Baudot, *Utopia and History in Mexico: The First Chroniclers of Mexican Civilization (1520-1569)* (Boulder: University Press of Colorado, 1995); see also his *La pugna franciscana por México* (México City: Alianza Editorial Mexicana & Consejo Nacional para Cultura y los Artes, 1990).

[6]See Lewis Hanke, *The Spanish Struggle for Justice in the Conquest of America* (Boston: Little, Brown, 1949); Juan Friede and Benjamin Keen, eds., *Bartolomé de las Casas in History: Toward an Understanding of the Man and His Work* (De Kalb: Northern Illinois University Press, 1971).

[7]See, for example, Baudot, *Utopia and History*, 308-19, on Motolinía's polemics against Bartolomé de las Casas.

[8]*Ibid.*, 86-91.

[9]See Pedro Borges, *Métodos misionales en la cristianización de América, Siglo XVI* (Madrid, 1960): 34-35; Elsa Cecelia Frost, "A New Millenarian: G. Baudot," *The Americas* 26 (1980): 515-26. See also the sources cited in J. I. Saranyana and A. De Zaballa, *Joaquin de Fiore y América* (2nd ed.; Pamplona: Ediciones Eunate, 1995), 153 and notes 26-28. Also Marco Cipolloni, *Tra memoria apostolica e racconto profetico: Il compromesso etnografico francescano e le Cosas della Nuova Spagna (524-1621)* (Rome: Bulzoni Editore, 1994), 388ff.

[10]See the works of Reeves and McGinn in note 4 above.

[11]The following definitions may be helpful: *apocalypticism* is a conviction that the culmination of history is imminent and that it will be preceded by dramatic events which those now living may experience. These events may be both positive (miraculous conversions, renovation of the church, reunification of a divided Christendom) and negative (persecution of true believers, apostasy, external or internal attack on Christendom). *Messianism* is the belief that the imminent culmination of history will include the advent of an individual or group (for example, a Last World Emperor, an Angelic Pope, a final prophet, or an evangelical order) as a divine instrument (messiah) for the accomplishment of the positive events of the apocalypse. A particular apocalyptic scenario may include more than one figure with messianic functions. *Millennialism* is the belief that the imminent culmination of history will include, as one component, a period of time during which the true church will flourish and the forces of evil will be (at least temporarily) vanquished. This "millennium" may or may not last for a literal thousand years; at its end, a reappearance of and final struggle with evil may be expected. Also *millenarianism*.

[12]Delno C. West and August Kling, trans. and eds., *The Libro de las profecías of Christopher Columbus* (Gainesville: University of Florida Press, 1991), 68.

[13]See Evelyn Edson, *Mapping Space and Time: How Medieval Mapmakers Viewed Their World* (London: The British Library, 1997).

[14]A variation of *estoire* or *istorie*, medieval forms of the French *histoire*.

[15]Edson, *Mapping Space and Time*, 140.

[16]In addition to Edson, *ibid.*, see Jerry Brotton, *Trading Territories: Mapping the Early Modern World* (Ithaca: Cornell University Press, 1998), 28-29.

[17]Isidore of Seville, *Etymologiae* (ed. W. Lindsay; Oxford: Clarendon, 1911), bk. 19. See the discussion of Isidore in Edson, *Mapping Space and Time*, 46ff.

[18]Isidore of Seville, *Etymologiae*, bk. 9.3. See Augustine, *De civitate Dei* 18,2, 18,22; and Orosius, *Historiae adversus paganos*, 2,1.

[19]Patrick Gautier Dalché, *La "Descriptio Mappe Mundi"de Hugues de Saint-Victor; Texte inédit avec introduction et commentaire* (Paris: Études augustiniennes, 1988). The text of the *Descriptio* is on 133-60.

[20]*De arca Noe morali* 4, 9 (PL 176.677f.); the translation follows Bernard McGinn, *Visions of the End: Apocalyptic Traditions in the Middle Ages* (NY: Columbia University Press, 1979), 111. See also *De vanitate mundi*, Bk. 2 (PL 176.720).

[21]The classic treatment is Werner Goez, *Translatio Imperii: Ein Beitrag zur Geschchte des Geschichts-denkens und der politischen Theorien im Mittelalter und in der Frühen Neuzeit* (Tübingen: Mohr, 1958).

[22]Modern interpreters, of course, identify Daniel's fourth kingdom with the Greek empire of Alexander the Great and his successors.

[23]Otto of Freising, *Chronica sive Historia de duabus civitatibus* (Monumenta Germania Historica [MGH]; Scriptores, vol. 45 [hereafter *Chronica*]; English trans. C. C. Mierow, *The Two Cities* (New York: Columbia University Press, 1928).

[24]*Chronica*, 7. See Hans-Werner Goetz, *Das Geschichtsbild Ottos von Freising; Ein Beitrag zur historischen Vorstellungswelt und zur Geschichte des 12. Jahrhunderts* (Cologne: Böhlau Verlag, 1984), 158-61.

[25]*Chronica*, 8. Elsewhere he uses the *translatio sapientiae* to underscore that the world is "already failing and, so to speak, drawing the last breath of extremest old age," 227; Mierow, *Two Cities*, 323.

[26]*Chronica*, 372; Mierow, *Two Cities*, 448.

[27]*Chronica*, 373; Mierow, *Two Cities*, 449.

[28]Marjorie Reeves, *Joachim of Fiore and the Prophetic Future* (New York: Harper Torchbooks, 1976), 59.

[29]See Alexander von Roes, *De translatione imperii* (1281), in Herbert Grundmann, *Alexander von Roes, De Translatione Imperii und Jordanus von Osnabrück, De Prerogativa Romani Imperii* (Leipzig: Teubner, 1930), 30-31.

[30]Reeves, *Joachim of Fiore*, 60-72.

[31]Alain Milhou, *Colón y su mentalidad mesianica en el ambiente franciscanista español* (Cuadernos columbinos 11; Valladolid: Casa-Museo de Colón, 1983), 349-401.

[32]See Jonathan Riley-Smith, *The Crusades: A Short History* (New Haven: Yale University Press, 1987).

[33]Milhou, *Colón*, 289.

[34]See Benjamin Z. Kedar, *Crusade and Mission: European Approaches to the Muslim* (Princeton: Princeton University Press, 1984). On the Franciscans, see 136-58.

Also see Elizabeth Siberry, *Criticism of Crusading, 1095-1274* (Oxford: Clarendon Press, 1985), 16-20; Norman Housley, *The Later Crusades, 1274-1580: From Lyons to Alcazar* (Oxford: Oxford University Press, 1992), 309, 381.

[35]Pope Innocent IV (d. 1254), also a prominent canon lawyer, laid down the legal principle that the universal sovereignty of the Pope justified warfare against infidels in order to pave the way for Christian missionizing; see Kedar, *Crusade and Mission*, 159-161.

[36]Here and elsewhere the Bible translation used is the New Revised Standard Version (NRSV).

[37]*Breviloquium de concordia Novi et Veteris Testamenti* (ca. 1350) in Harold Lee, et al., *Western Mediterranean Prophecy: The School of Joachim of Fiore and the Fourteenth-Century Breviloquium* (Toronto: Pontifical Institute of Medieval Studies, 1989), 269, lines 129-33.

[38]See E. Randolph Daniel, *The Franciscan Concept of Mission in the High Middle Ages* (Lexington: University of Kentucky Press, 1975), 37-54.

[39]Reeves, *Joachim of Fiore*, 29.

[40]David Burr, *Olivi's Peaceable Kingdom: A Reading of the Apocalypse Commentary* (Philadelphia: University of Pennsylvania Press, 1993), 120-21, 190.

[41]See Reeves, *Joachim of Fiore*, 63-64; Milhou, *Colón y su mentalidad mesiánica*, 372ff.

[42]See J. N. Hillgarth, *Ramon Lull and Lullism in Fourteenth-Century France* (Oxford: Clarendon, 1971).

[43]*Breviloquium de concordia Novi et Veteris Testamenti* (ca. 1350), in Harold Lee, Marjorie Reeves and Giulio Silano, *Western Mediterranean Prophecy: The School of Joachim of Fiore and the Fourteenth-Century Breviloquium* (Toronto: Pontifical Institute of Medieval Studies, 1989), 269, lines 129-33.

[44]Joachim of Fiore, *De prophetia ignota*, edited by Bernard McGinn in "Joachim and the Sibyl," *Cîteaux* 34 (1973): 97-138; see especially pp. 133-35.

[45]See Baudot, *Utopia and History*, 80ff.

[46]West and Kling, *Libro de las profecías of Christopher Columbus*, 68.

[47]Milhou, *Colón* 391-94.

[48]Quoted in Bataillon, *Erasmo y España*, 66 (author's translation).

[49]Quoted in Juan Gil, *Mitos y utopías del Descubrimiento*, 1. *Colón y su tiempo* (Madrid, 1989) 238 [author's translation].

[50]Gil, 239; see also Pedro Borges, "El sentido transcendente del descubrimiento y conversión de Indias," *Missionalia Hispanica* 13 (1956): 152, for a different interpretation.

[51]See Hugh Thomas, *Conquest: Montezuma, Cortés, and the Fall of Old Mexico* (New York: Simon and Schuster, 1993).

[52]Foster, *Motolinía's History*, 177.

[53]*Ibid.*, 178.

[54]*Ibid.*, 270.

[55]*Ibid.*, 109. See Delno C. West, "Medieval Ideas of Apocalyptic Mission and the Early Franciscans in Mexico," *The Americas* 62 (1988-89): 293.

[56]Toribio de Benavente Motolinía, "Carta al emperador" (Tlaxcala, 2 de enero de 1555), in Isacio Perez Fernandez, ed., *Fray Toribio Motolinía, O.F.M., frente a Fray Bartolomé de las Casas, O.P.* (Salamanca: Editorial San Esteban, 1989), 111-35.

[57]*Ibid.*, 121.

[58]See, for example, the critique of the Archbishop of Mexico, Alonso de Montfár, writing to the royal Council of the Indies in Seville in 1556, excerpted and translated in Charles S. Braden, *Religious Aspects of the Conquest of Mexico* (Durham: Duke University Press, 1930), 247-49.

[59]See Inga Clendinnen, *Ambivalent Conquests; Maya and Spaniard in Yucatan, 1517-1570* (Cambridge: Cambridge University Press, 1987); and David E. Timmer, "Providence and Perdition: Fray Diego de Landa Justifies His Inquisition against the Yucatecan Maya," *Church History* 66/3 (September 1997): 477-88.

[60]France V. Scholes and Eleanor B. Adams, eds., *Don Diego Quijada, Alcalde Mayor de Yucatán, 1561-1565* (vol. 2; Mexico City: Editorial Porrua, 1938), 410.

[61]Between 1557 and 1559, groups of Protestants including persons of rank were exposed in Seville and Valladolid, stimulating widespread anxiety. See Henry Kamen, *The Spanish Inquisition: A Historical Revision* (New Haven: Yale University Press, 1998), 91-98.

[62]Diego de Landa, *Relación de las cosas de Yucatán* (ed. M. Rivera; Cronicas de América 7; Madrid: Historia 16, 1985), 113-14; translation (with some revisions) follows A. R. Pagden, *The Maya: Diego de Landa's Account of the Affairs of Yucatán* (Chicago: O'Hara, 1975), 108.

[63]Milhou, *Colón* 356; see also Milhou, "El concepto de 'destrucción' en el evangelismo milenario franciscano," in *Archivo Ibero-Americano* 48 (1988): 297-315.

[64]The Spanish reconquest of the Iberian peninsula from the Moors, culminating in the taking of Granada in 1492.

[65]Jewish converts to Christianity or their descendants, often suspected of continuing to practice Judaism secretly.

[66]Landa, *Relación,* 114; Pagden, *The Maya,* 108.

[67]Bernardino de Sahagún, *Historia general de las cosas de Nueva España* (4 vols.; ed. J. Ramírez Cabañas (Mexico City: Pedro Robredo, 1938); see A. Anderson and C. Dibble, eds., *General History of the Things of New Spain: The Florentine Codex* (13 vols.; Santa Fe: School of American Research, 1950-1982).

[68]Birgitta (1303-1373), also known as Bridget, received revelations denouncing corruption and urging reform in the church, particularly the return of the papacy from Avignon to Rome. See Bridget Morris, *St. Birgitta of Sweden* (Rochester: Boydell Press, 1999).

[69]See Birger Bergh, ed., *Sancta Birgitta,, Revelaciones, Book VI* (Stockholm: Almquist and Wiksell International, 1991), 239, 244.

[70]Bernardino de Sahagún, *Coloquios y doctrinas cristiana*, (ed. M. Léon-Portilla; Mexico City: UNAM, 1986), 72.

[71]Bernardino de Sahagún, *Historia general de las cosas de Nueva España*, (ed. J. Ramírez Cabañas; vol. 1; Mexico City: Pedro Robredo, 1938), 11. Translation follows Charles E. Dibble, "Sahagún's Prologues and Interpolations," in *The Florentine Codex: General History of the Things of New Spain* (ed. A. Anderson and C. Dibble; vol. 1; Santa Fe: School of American Research, 1982), 50.

[72]*Historia general* 3:302; translation follows Dibble in *Florentine Codex* 1:93.

[73]*Historia general* 3:298, 308.

[74]*Historia general* 3:304.

THE PEOPLE MOURNING OVER THE RUINS OF JERUSALEM
How doth the city sit solitary, that was full of people! how is she become as a
widow! she that was great among the nations ... (Lamentations 1: 1)

figure 1: "The People Mourning Over the City of Jerusalem"

Mourning the End of Time:
Apocalypses As Texts of Cultural Loss

Dereck Daschke

In 1913, a year prior to the First World War, Sigmund Freud stood in the Italian Alps with some friends who were deeply affected by a sense of the impermanence of things. They complained that the coming winter lessened the joy they could find in the beauty of the countryside, its worth diminished by its ephemeral nature. Two years later, Freud reflected on the devastation brought on by the war—not just the physical and personal toll of cities destroyed and lives lost, but also the sense of desolation inflicted upon his beloved European culture, its ideals, its history, its future. In the essay in which he relates these sentiments, "On Transience," Freud states that the war:

> shattered our pride in the achievements of our civilization . . . . It made our country small again and made the rest of the world far remote. It robbed us of very much that we had loved, and showed us how ephemeral were many things we had regarded as changeless.[1]

Unlike his friends, Freud understood that loss points not only to an ending, but towards a new beginning as well. He saw that what lay ahead, a Europe built out of the ruins of the old one, could be even greater than this homeland in its lowly state. He expected his own civilization to overcome its loss, to recover and prosper as future generations came to terms with its past. He concludes:

> When once the mourning is over, it will be found that our high opinion of the riches of civilization has lost nothing from our discovery of their fragility. We shall build up again all that war has destroyed, and perhaps on firmer ground and more lastingly than before.[2]

Sadly, Freud had no way of knowing that this very sentiment would underlie the millenarian plans of the Third Reich, which would inflict

159

unimaginable loss and devastation on both of his cultural heritages—
European and Jewish.

Nearly two and a half millennia before Freud wrote these words, after
the Babylonian Conquest of Jerusalem and the destruction of its Temple in
587 BCE, a national poem of mourning was written. Known to us as the
book of Lamentations (figure 1), it bewailed the ruin brought about by war
on the very places and ideals within which the people had lived and
understood themselves. It begins:

> How lonely sits the city that once was full of people! How like a
> widow she has become, she that was great among the nations! She
> that was a princess among the provinces has become a vassal" (Lam
> 1:1).[3]

But it concludes with a somewhat less sanguine hope than the secular Jew
Freud expressed so many centuries later: "Restore us to yourself, O Lord,
that we may be restored; renew our days as of old—unless you have utterly
rejected us, and are angry with us beyond measure" (5:21-22).[4]

These two instances, though separated by centuries and ingrained in
very different contexts, produced remarkably similar understandings of
what it means to experience loss on such a terrible scale and to have done so
collectively—although the tenors of their conclusions reflect more and less
optimistic views of the future. One reason for this distinction, illustrated by
Freud's departure from his friends' feelings about loss, is that cultural
symbols have so many layers of meaning that one may not fully
comprehend exactly how deeply a traumatic loss cuts. Often it is to the very
core of a society's—and a member of that society's—identity and existence.
Freud, well aware of both the devastation's extent and the healing
possibilities of history, was not troubled by the vulnerability of beauty or
civilization to the inevitable procession of time. Those who are sensitive in
this way, he indicates, are mournful of some things of which they are not
aware. He calls the loss, with an unknown and therefore unconscious
component, "melancholia."

What does melancholia, or any type of mourning for that matter, have
to do with millennial or apocalyptic expectations? A close examination of
texts, such as the canonical book of Ezekiel and the non-canonical 4 Ezra
and 2 and 3 Baruch, dealing with the fall of the Temple at the hands of the
Babylonians or later, in 70 CE, of the Romans reveals many of the
components of the mourning process: an individual recovering the lost
Temple or City in dream, visionary, or fantasy sequences; its vilification or,
alternatively, glorification; extreme shifts in the mood of the visionary from

rage to paralytic passivity, from self-annihilation to euphoria.[5] These seers invariably require an interpretation by an authoritative figure to comprehend their situation, for once these symbols are revealed to them, their meaning is almost simultaneously concealed or obscured again. On the whole, such texts show a progression from grief to consolation. They are often replete with overt signs of mourning, such as prayerful lament, fasting, or bodily alteration.[6]

On a larger scale, the millennial impulse reveals a good deal of anxiety about loss or endings. Apocalypse, it must be recognized, is about the end of the world. There can be no greater loss. Even the idyllic New Age that is to follow marks the End of the current one, the one in which the seers or prophets actually live. Most scenarios envision this transformation as brought about by the violent destruction of much of the earth's population, sinners and righteous alike. They ask potential followers to empathize with the remnant, in that they may expect to be among them. The picture is meant to be a comfort, but in what way can Armageddon be comforting?[7]

Beyond theological reasons concerning God's justice and the salvation of the righteous, I think the structure and themes of visions of the End—which, almost without fail, bear a strong resemblance to one another—point to another answer. Their creation initially reflects a personal, individual standpoint. Their preservation and use by a community reflects their resonance with the issues of a social collective. In other words, to invoke Clifford Geertz, millennial scenarios represent both models of and models for mourning. In this sense, the word "recovery" has a double meaning: the process by which a new worldview's elements are reconstituted from an old one (a model of mourning), and the therapeutic view that with completion of the traumatic period, one should be able to negotiate satisfactorily a current and future situation (a model for mourning).[8] And in this respect, they can be viewed as texts of healing for both individual and communal traumas.

In a related manner, millennial visions are intensely concerned with time—specifically the community's past, present, and future. These three aspects of history directly inform one's sense of identity, and a disturbance in any one threatens the others. Apocalyptic and millennial visions show the process of dismantling and remaking a people's reality by recasting its history. It is for this reason that these visions typically look to a "Golden Age from the Past" to supplant a "Corrupt Present" in a "Perfect Future." The quality of loss is often betrayed in even the most forward-looking millennial programs, including that of American fundamentalist Christianity, for example, by the constant imagining that the community's or nation's greatness and moral ascendancy existed once long ago, and that they are destined for it again in the near future.[9] Not incidentally, longing for a lost time is more often than not joined by a longing for a lost place, as the examples from Freud and Lamentations illustrate. As my analyses later in this paper shows, in apocalypses this sentiment is doubly true. If apocalypses are in some way involved in healing, the illness they treat is homesickness as much as heartsickness.

APOCALYPTIC RECOVERY: THE GENERAL PATTERN
Psychoanalytically speaking, in mourning the world is empty.[10] Absence causes desire to go unsatisfied; an individual faced with loss attempts to test the reality of a world radically altered by it.[11] Inevitably, the believer will search for answers to the questions posed by the new situation in the collective memory of the culture's traditions. If tradition can offer none or if the tradition suppresses, misperceives, or fails to recognize the reality of the loss so that it remains unchallenged, a melancholic response will be evoked in the mourner. This can cause disintegrating and disorienting aftershocks for generations.[12]

The members of a culture (or at least a subgroup of it) may then seek a rapprochement of the old order and the new, restructuring the present with some of the symbols preserved yet altered from the old system, with the creation of a new symbolic order resulting.[13] For apocalyptic seers, the empty world again becomes full of precisely what they desire most, the presence of God in a divinely determined universe. The new order is left unchallenged by its displacement spatially into the heavens and temporally to the Endtime; nothing on earth, including the painful events of history, can falsify it—at least until its predictions for the Endtime pass unfulfilled.

In sum, the apocalyptic response to symbolic loss reads as follows: rupture in culture leads to a)
mourning for lost cultural symbols and idealization of the distant past; b) recovery of history and tradition and the reconstruction of worldview (with new elements) to envisage dual realities, divine and earthly, and dual, mutually exclusive moralities, righteous and wicked; and c) indication that the righteous shall vanquish the wicked and divine reality shall subsume the earthly at the Endtime, thereby wholly sealing the initial rupture.

We now explore how the theme of the end of human, or at least Jewish, history plays out in two texts concerned with the destruction of the Temple in Jerusalem, the books of Ezekiel and 4 Ezra.

EZEKIEL: DESOLATE AMONG THEM

The book of Ezekiel is part of the prophetic corpus of the Hebrew Bible and not generally regarded as an apocalypse per se. We justify its inclusion here on the basis of its form, content, and worldview. While its overall concerns are of the prophetic, here-and-now, judgment type, Ezekiel delivers them in a style and with a specific cosmic orientation that remain entirely consistent with apocalypticism (figure 2).[14]

As a member of the priestly lineage, Ezekiel drew his identity from the symbols of God, city, and people that coalesced in the edifice of the Temple and the rituals practiced therein. After his deportation to Babylon, Ezekiel sees a vision (Ezek 1-3) in which God is recovered, establishing the unmistakable presence of the divine on earth again and initiating the direct experience of another reality. Ezekiel's melancholia may first be glimpsed in the verses bracketing this call vision. He begins his book in exile on the river Chebar, and no mention is made of his state of mind. After this extraordinary vision, he is there again, only this time his emotional state is identified clearly:

> A wind lifted me and took me, and I went, bitter, my spirit raging, overpowered by the hand of God. I came to the exiles at Tel Abib, who were living by the Chebar canal and . . . there I sat seven days, desolate among them (3:14-15).[15]

This emotional description clearly indicates his desperate isolation even among his fellow exiles, as may the note on the length of time that he sat: seven days, or one *shiva* period.

This is the sequence of events: Ezekiel resides in exile, and no emotion is reported in either of two verses that situate him there. Suddenly, he has a visionary experience of the Divine Presence, which results in a call to prophesy. He is forced to ingest a scroll of "lamentation and mourning and woe" that almost completely subsumes his personality (2:10-3:3; cf. Jer 1:9; 15:16; Rev 10:8-11).[16] Because the content of the scroll is negative and mournful, this act of God's giving such a scroll to the prophet can be read as a projection, externalization, and introjection of Ezekiel's painful feelings.[17] This psychological process allows the prophet to defend against the overwhelming nature of the feelings as "not his," while still expressing and acting on them. This defense effectively suppresses Ezekiel's personality, cementing his identification with God. At the same time it displaces, through the prophet himself, his negative emotions onto the House of Israel.[18] Then the spirit of the Lord takes Ezekiel up "bitter" and "raging," returning him to where he started—but this time he is "desolate."

EZEKIEL PROPHESYING
Now it came to pass in the thirtieth year, in the fourth month, in the fifth day of
the month, as I was among the captives by the river of Chebar, that the heavens were
opened, and I saw visions of God . . . (Ezekiel 1: 1)

figure 2: Ezekiel Prophesying

The conspicuous introduction of strong emotion at the end of the vision, in contradistinction to the lack of it at its inception, indicates a catharsis of emotion through the emergence of the vision and the beginning of the mourning process.[19]

In the Temple Vision (Ezek 8-10), other elements are recaptured (the Temple, the city, the Jews as a people), but the vision distorts their representation to Ezekiel. Here the emphasis on revelation and concealment is acute. For example, the prophet must actually dig through a wall to see the goings-on in the Temple, and these activities are done intentionally in secret from God (Ezek 8). Ultimately in Ezekiel's fantasy, God's angels destroy the Temple and the idolaters in the city, a destructive response to the memory of a lost love typical of melancholia. Observing the wickedness of the inhabitants of Jerusalem as they defile the Temple with foreign cult worship provides both the theological and psychological justification to the prophet for their subsequent decimation.

The collective and personal foci of this text come together in the prophecy announcing the death of Ezekiel's wife and the imminent fall of the actual Temple in Ezek 24:15-27. God refers to both events identically, as "the delight of your eyes." God prohibits both Ezekiel and the exiles from mourning their losses; in fact, Ezekiel's actions are explicitly a sign for the people. Socially, the purpose of Ezekiel's prophetic ministry is to prepare his fellow exiles to give up their attachment to their former Temple and the security it represented. Thus, when the fall of the sanctuary becomes an impending reality, though it is still horribly shocking – as though a husband has lost "the delight of his eyes"—the followers of Ezekiel stand ready to accept a new vision of the future, for they have already been given a new vision of the past.

Eventually, the anger and resentment dissipate in the cathartic fantasies of Israel's humiliation and ruin, and the need to envision a restoration arises.[20] When the vision of the Heavenly City in Ezek 40-48 is compared to the destruction of its predecessor in Ezek 8-10, the differences are striking. There is very little ambiguous or secretive about the restored city. The long descriptive passages of its measurements, chambers, and archways stand as the very opposite of the depictions of the Temple in Ezek 8. The cultic practices are clearly described and are of obvious Israelite origin (Ezek 44). This vision is not a product of anxiety erupting in symbolic forms into consciousness, as in the early part of the book, but a carefully created picture of new hopes and expectations based on a restructured understanding of reality. It is no accident that the details of its construction are so concrete.

The end of the exile once again establishes the reality of the presence of God within his land and people. Thus, the book of Ezekiel fittingly closes with the name of the Restored Jerusalem: *Adonai Š mm h*, "The Lord Is There."

4 EZRA: "BECAUSE OF MY GRIEF I HAVE SPOKEN"

The book known as 4 Ezra also purports an exilic setting (3:1), but it is a fiction. 4 Ezra was written following the fall of the Second Temple to the Romans in 70 CE. It is pseudepigraphic, the putative narrative of a reforming scribe and priest of the early Second Temple period; unlike Ezekiel, it is not part of the Hebrew canon. It is a book from the Apocrypha, a Greek term for "secret" or "hidden."[21]

The fall of the Second Temple forced the collective memory back to 587 BCE in search of answers and to ask in the face of this insufferable loss, "Who are we now?" In Palestine near the end of the first century CE, the survival of the Jewish people was by no means self-evident. The question of why God would allow such an event to befall Jerusalem—again!—and what it meant for the chosen people must have imposed itself on anyone with a vested interest in the earthly preservation of the people of God—hence the proliferation of apocalyptic literature such as 4 Ezra and the Baruch Apocalypses that reevaluate the relationship between the people and their God. One of the fascinating aspects of 4 Ezra is that these questions are played out against a traditional Yahwistic stance, which placed the Temple at the institutional and symbolic center of the nation, representing the continuity of God's protection, presence, and the nation's prosperity since the beginnings of the monarchy more than a millennium earlier. The dialectic between the biblical figure Ezra and a divine counterpart, usually the angel Uriel, significantly end in virtual standstill.

4 Ezra begins with a scene of Ezra in bed, still greatly disturbed by the "desolation of Zion" some thirty years earlier (cf. Dan 2:29; 7:1, 15).[22] The first half of the book (figure 3) thereafter is structured by episodes of ritual mourning (usually seven days long) followed by laments, then questions and dialogue with the interpreting angel (4 Ezra 5:20f; 6:35f; 9:27-37). By tracing Ezra's emotional responses as a participant in the dialogues, it becomes apparent that much is going on in this text beneath the surface.

Ezra's plaints unmistakably establish him as the voice of experience, as one who has lived through something that demands explanation. Of the key issues he raises, one is national and one is personal, but they are both related: he laments the suffering of the Jewish people in light of the prosperity of her enemies, but also his failure to understand this situation. Both involve a

EZRA IN PRAYER

And at the evening sacrifice, I arose up from my heaviness; and having rent my
garment and my mantle, I fell upon my knees, and spread out my hands unto the Lord
my God . . . (Ezra 9: 5)

figure 3: Ezra in Prayer

question of basic fairness in the structure of the world, for God's order should be consistent and sensible. Ezra seeks merely to understand his own reality, not the heavenly reality that Uriel's loaded questions, starkly reminiscent of God's to Job, concern.[23] One of the defining characteristics of a melancholic response to loss is its disjunctive sensibility: there exists a disparity in the mind between the way reality is and the way it should be. Ezra's skepticism in his dialogues certainly reflects this disparity. The wide gap between the author's experience and his traditional expectations emerges in the oft-noted irony that Ezra is more reasonable, more oriented toward reality, than his divine interlocutor.[24] Ezra's plaintive dialogues with the angel Uriel unmistakably establish the visionary as the voice of experience, as one who has lived through something which demands explanation. Of the key issues he raises consistently, one is national and one is personal, but they are both related: Ezra laments the suffering of the Jewish people in light of the prosperity of her enemies, but also his failure to understand this situation. He definitely implicates God for neglecting to act to protect his people:

> Are the deeds of those who inhabit Babylon any better? Is that why she has gained dominion over Zion?...And my heart failed me, for I have seen how you endure those who sin, and have spared those who act wickedly, and have destroyed your people, and have preserved your enemies.

Ezra continues with the accusation: "[And you] have not shown to anyone how your way may be comprehended" (4 Ezra 3:28-31). Similar complaints also appear at 4 Ezra 4:2-3, 12, and 22-25. Although the angel's answers remain totally insufficient, Ezra is compelled to look to him for understanding. The need to return again and again to a failed expectation in hopes of mastering the reality of a loss is also characteristic of the melancholic.

Unlike Ezekiel, who avoided placing blame on any dangerous targets—for example, Babylon and God—4 Ezra asserts their culpability from the start. Overcoming the melancholic paralysis here has as much to do with a movement away from anger, and even hatred, toward God, back to love and trust in his ways. The dialogues are the mechanism for this movement. In fact, between the first and second visions, after Ezra has fasted and mourned, he laments that the "thoughts of his heart were very grievous" to him again. Yet suddenly his "soul recovered the spirit of understanding," and he begins his questioning of God once more (4 Ezra 5:20-22).

Ezra's frustration with the dialogues derives from his inability to connect with his interlocutor on a cognitive level; he is unable to sway the divine representative at all, no matter how solid, logical, and self-evident his arguments are. Yet the issues raised, defended, and avoided stir his emotional life in unexpected ways. The rage of the past thirty years becomes focused, sometimes shockingly, first on Ezra himself, then on God and his representative, expressed initially in wishes for punishment, even self-annihilation. Ezra declares: "It would be better for us not to be here than to come here and live in ungodliness, and to suffer and not understand why" (4:12). Then he makes the shocking assertion that the deity now *hates* his people; worse yet, God remains indifferent enough not to punish them himself (5:30-35).[25] One who has lost love, if at the deepest level unable to give it up, will prefer to be an object of hate, derision, and punishment rather than of indifference and total abandonment.[26]

Uriel, while not responding to Ezra's specific pleas, does strike right at the heart of the matter, asking if the seer does—i.e., could possibly—love Israel more, and be more distressed by what has transpired, than the Creator. The seer's immediate response to Uriel is no, but he adds, tellingly, that it is "because of my grief I have spoken; for every hour I suffer agonies of the heart, while I strive to understand the way of the Most High and to search out part of his judgment" (5:34). Here, Ezra essentially admits that he is lashing out in anger and frustration because of his grief. When he accuses his God of hating his people, but backs away from the sentiment quickly, he reveals more about his unconscious feelings than he realizes. Like Ezekiel, the true object of Ezra's rage is the original object of his love: his God. In the course of his disappointment, love has turned to hate, but via a psychological defense he prevents the realization of that hate by displacing it on to the object itself.

Ezra cannot say he hates God, but it is psychically acceptable, momentarily, to believe that God hates his people, the seer himself included. When the angel rebuffs him again, telling him that he cannot question God's ways or judgment, Ezra asks, "Why did not my mother's womb become my grave?" (5:35a). This almost suicidal impulse consumes his entire existence at points, where he seems to echo the sentiments of many depressed persons: "I wish I'd never been born!"[27]

THE VISION OF THE WEEPING WOMAN
Undoubtedly, the revelation of what is sometimes called the Vision of the Weeping Woman is the key to the psychology of 4 Ezra, and, not

surprisingly, it focuses on loss. After the dialogues, Ezra sees a woman who was "mourning and weeping with a loud voice, and was deeply grieved at heart" (9:38). Her only son had collapsed and died on his wedding day, and now she intends to "mourn and fast" until she herself dies (10:4). Ezra chastises her, saying:

> You most foolish of women, do you not see our mourning, and what has happened to us? For Zion, the mother of us all, is in deep grief and great humiliation. It is most appropriate to mourn now, because we are all mourning, and to be sorrowful, because we are all sorrowing; you are sorrowing for one son, but we, the whole world, for our mother. . . . Now, therefore, keep your sorrow to yourself, and bear bravely the troubles that have come upon you. For if you acknowledge the decree of God to be just, you will receive your son back in due time (4 Ezra 10:6-8, 15).

He continues with a litany of indignities the Temple and city have suffered, when suddenly the woman is transformed into a huge city (10:27). He cries out for interpretation, and Uriel tells him:

> The woman whom you saw, whom you now behold as an established city, is Zion. . . . And as for her saying to you, "When my son entered his wedding chamber he died," and that misfortune had overtaken her, that was the destruction which befell Jerusalem. And behold, you saw her likeness, how she mourned for her son, and you began to console her for what had happened. For now the Most High, seeing that you are sincerely grieved and profoundly distressed for her, has shown you the brightness of her glory, and the loveliness of her beauty (10:44a, 48-50).

When he arrives at an understanding of events, it is not through persuasive dialectic with the angel or his own gradual, conscious coming to terms with his past. The final resolution happens all at once in a vision that catches him off guard and transforms his position, as it itself is transformed from despairing mother to glorious city. In a symbolic loss approach to apocalypticism, there can be no better illustration of cultural recovery of symbol, created in fantasy and structured in narrative, to link past ideals, present desolation, and future restoration of the "True Israel" than this apocalyptic vision "encountered" by Ezra, the revered priest and scribe who helped establish the religious faith of Second Temple society.

    The answer to Ezra's prayer comes not in the now-expected form of dialogue with the angel, but with the appearance of the woman, who is not immediately thought of as anything other than what she claims. Just as in the dialogues there was an apparent disconnection between Ezra's questions and the angel's answers that propelled the visionary's psyche toward resolution and consolation, a disparity exists also in this break in form and message. The seer forgets his prayer and starts interrogating the woman. Ezra now acts in the angel's role, trying to convey the authority of traditional responses to a grieving and desperate individual.

With the woman, he confronts himself as he previously was. It is a general truth that we are unable to tolerate faults in others that we possess ourselves, especially those faults we feel we have overcome.[28] Hence the recent convert and the recovered addict are harsher than anyone else with associates who share their former problems. Like Ezra, they also come to believe that only those who have undergone the same process of transformation can understand the experience and see the world as it truly is. Ezra here is the recent convert, but a convert at a cognitive, philosophical level. He has not yet learned to accept his past, to embrace it, and to integrate it into his new worldview—that is, to mourn it and thereby finally mourn the lost Temple. His whole being has not been transformed. That changes with the metamorphosis of the woman into the image of the Heavenly City.

This image represents the solid and certain future for Ezra and his people, one which is beautiful and compelling but not yet permanently manifest. It is, unlike any work done by humans, ideal and perfect. The angel directs Ezra to explore this vision, an action to which readers are not privy, again revealing and concealing psychically weighty knowledge in the same symbol. The following chapters of 4 Ezra concern visions that structure the knowledge of the events of the future. Its audience knows that its protagonist has moved once and for all from his emotional investment in the structure of the past. Therefore, he can finally receive that knowledge not as one working through the psychological impact of a loss, but as a renewed individual working towards his, and his people's, complete recovery in a changed world.

CONCLUSION

Despite its bona fide promise, the second Temple period never offered a return to the glory of the monarchy, ensuring that the Exile would linger as a living presence long after its end. The injustices committed against the sanctity of the Temple would simmer for some, the appearance of a return to devoted Temple practice notwithstanding, with the impact of those injustices waiting to reemerge when the larger cultural context would give them new life. Under the enormous Hellenistic empire, the context in which apocalypticism properly arose, the disparity in many cultures between the past and present was pronounced. As John J. Collins notes, "The Hellenistic age was marked by widespread nostalgia for the past and alienation from the present. In a broad sense this 'Hellenistic mood' may be considered a matrix for the apocalyptic literature."[29]

The texts examined in this paper as well as apocalypses from the same period do not represent documents of complete and perfect mourning. Their fixation on an other-worldly solution to the disappointments of this world, their focus on the primacy of events of the past and the idealized nature of their visions of the future broadly suggest the melancholy at the root of their apocalyptic world view. They quite convincingly preserve the lost object—the Temple, the city, God's role in history—in a fantasy creation. Yet it is this very fantasy that can commemorate not just the physical (and therefore conscious) losses, but also the deep, core, existential losses, the loss of the continuity of the people's story, the loss of identity and expectation. For this reason these texts are concerned with the future and express it in terms of transformative ideals which draw both individuals and cultures out of the problematic past and into the real future.

The traumatic events in these apocalypses shattered certain sensitive individuals' construction of their culture's sacred reality and made its symbols vulnerable to doubt and even annihilation. These texts did what they could in their time and place, for their creators and for contemporary and future readers, to heal these wounds and to bind the ideals of "the true Israel" and "Yahweh" more firmly than before. Both during the Exile and after their dispersal by the Romans, Jews outside the land of their ancestors, having lost both their Temple and their city, continued to maintain and reflect their religious identity without those physical structures. As the work of mourning borne by apocalyptic literature eventually came to an end, ceding to the rabbis their role in structuring the Jewish world view anew, a different kind of Judaism began for those who finally came to terms with the memories of the lost Temples and the tantalizing promise of seeing Zion on earth before them once again.

ACKNOWLEDGMENT: Portions of this paper have appeared in modified form as "Desolate Among Them: Loss, Fantasy, and Recovery in the Book of Ezekiel," *American Imago* 56:2 (1999): 105-32.

NOTES

[1]Sigmund Freud, "On Transience," *The Standard Edition of the Complete Psychological Works of Sigmund Freud*, vol. 14 (London: Hogarth, 1957), 307.

[2] *Ibid.*, 307.

[3]Unless otherwise noted, all translations of the biblical text in this article come from the New Revised Standard Version.

[4]The book of Lamentations represents on the first reconsiderations of the Holy City and the religion of the Judeans in light of the Babylonian conquest. The text expresses the full extent of loss and sorrow felt by pious Yahwists left in the ruins of Judea, "so complete and honest and eloquent an expression of grief that even centuries after the events which inspired it, it is still able to provide those in mute despair with words to speak," Delbert Hillers, *Lamentations* (AB 7A; Garden City: Doubleday, 1972), xvi; see also 20-21, 44-45. In the course of the poem, the city mourns, the highways mourn, the elders mourn, the author mourns, all as if for a person (Lam 1:1, 2:10). Lamentations, furthermore, is read on the ninth of Av, the holy day memorializing the fall of Jerusalem and the exile. Thus both as national literature and as an annual festival, grief and mourning for the Temple became incorporated into the culture and collective experience of Jews long after its destruction. In fact, Ig Gous, "Psychological Survival Strategies in Lamentations 3 in the Light of Neuro-Linguistic Programming," in *Old Testament Science and Reality* (ed. W. Wessels and E. Scheffler; Pretoria: Vera Vitae, 1992), 317-41, argues that the very structure of Lamentations—a rigid acrostic construction with verses beginning with each letter for the Hebrew alphabet—may both reflect the experience of loss and draw an audience through the process of grief and consolation via neuro-linguistic strategies.

[5]The template for the psychoanalytic understanding of mourning and its vicissitudes, Freud's "Mourning and Melancholia," *The Standard Edition of the Complete Psychological Works of Sigmund Freud* (hereafter *SE*) (vol. 14; London: Hogarth, 1957), is also the keystone for interpreting the apocalyptic visions dealing with the fall of the Temple, as will be discussed below. In many ways, the issues of serious loss and mourning suggested in the apocalyptic texts can be seen more specifically under the rubric of trauma. Clinically speaking, healing from a traumatic event is associated with repetition, trust, and the concept of psychological mastery of one's environment. Psychic re-experiencing of the trauma is, in fact, indicative of the clinical condition labeled Post-Traumatic Stress Disorder, Chronic or Delayed, or PTSD, in the *Diagnostic and Statistical Manual of Mental Disorders, Fourth Edition* (*DSMV-IV*) (Washington, DC: American Psychiatric Association, 1994), 424-25. For a clinical consideration of the range of issues involved in post-traumatic healing, see Richard Tedeschi, et al., eds., *Posttraumatic Growth: Positive Changes in the Aftermath of Crisis* (Mahwah: Lawrence Erlbaum,

1998).

[6]See especially the sign acts of Ezek 3:22-6:14, the repetition of fasting and prayer in 4 Ezra, and, in another apocalypse set during the Babylonian exile, Daniel's prayer in Dan 9.

[7]For a rich source book, with commentary, of modern apocalyptic movements ranging from Earth First! to Nazism, see Ted Daniels, *The Doomsday Reader: Prophets, Predictors, and Hucksters of Salvation* (New York: New York University Press, 1999). That loss plays a substantial role in the choices of many to start or join a group undergirded by some kind of end time ideology is clear in several prominent cases. William Miller became disillusioned during his participation in the War of 1812 and spent two years in intense Bible study, through which he developed his apocalyptic beliefs and method of interpretation. See Ruth A. Doan, *The Miller Heresy, Millennialism, and Popular Culture* (Philadelphia: Temple University Press, 1987), 17-18. In Leon Festinger, *When Prophecy Fails* (Minneapolis: University of Minnesota Press, 1956), 33, the leader of the UFO cult who was the subject of the book experienced the onset of her prophetic episodes in the figure of her late father. Charles Strozier's book, *Apocalypse: On the Psychology of Fundamentalism in America* (Boston: Beacon Press, 1994), contains the autobiographical accounts of members of contemporary New York city millenarian churches, who depict various losses—financial, geographical, marital, familial—as instrumental in their decisions to align themselves with an apocalyptic set of beliefs.

[8]Clifford Geertz, *The Interpretation of Cultures* (New York: Basic Books, 1973), 93-95.

[9]Stephen O'Leary, *Arguing the Apocalypse: A Theory of Millennial Rhetoric* (New York: Oxford University Press, 1994), 134-93, examines the interrelated rhetoric of the American apocalypticism of two major figures of the 1970s and 1980s: Hal Lindsey and Ronald Reagan. Both men's world views included a conviction that the Soviet Union and the United States were locked in a struggle for the moral leadership of the world—a tension which looked to them inescapably like Armageddon, the ultimate battle between good and evil as played out in the Gog and Magog chapters of Ezekiel 38 and 39 and in the books of Daniel and Revelation. To both Lindsey and Reagan, the Soviet empire epitomized everything that had weakened the social fabric of the United States since the 1960s: godlessness, liberal elitism, the reliance on government and not faith to solve problems. If the Soviets could be defeated in the political—or more likely, military—theater, then not only would their pernicious ideas be discredited forever, but the immediate threat to the American, and Christian, way of life would be eradicated.

[10]Freud, "Mourning and Melancholia," 246.

[11]Freud, "Mourning and Melancholia," 244: "Reality-testing has shown that the loved object no longer exists, and it proceeds to demand that all libido shall be

withdrawn from its attachments to that object. This demand arouses understandable opposition—it is a matter of general observation that people never willingly abandon a libidinal position, not even, indeed, when a substitute is already beckoning to them. This opposition can be so intense that a turning away from reality . . . and a clinging to the object through the medium of a hallucinatory wishful psychosis [takes place]."

[12]The study of collective memory examines the relationship of a culture at a given time (its present) to its past—and ultimately, then, to its expectations for the future. Change brings about both the sense and the force of the past, but continuity ensures its presence; hence, texts dealing with great historical changes, as these apocalypses do, often exhibit a palpable tension between the dynamics of history and the continuity and stability of tradition, which they mediate through the grounding in narrative of a few important symbols. On the "use of the past" and the relationships among tradition, history, and memory, see Iwona Irwin-Zarecka, *Frames of Remembrance: The Dynamics of Collective Memory* (New Brunswick: Transaction Publishers, 1994) and Yael Zerubavel, *Recovered Roots: Collective Memory and the Making of Israeli National Tradition* (Chicago: University of Chicago Press, 1995).

[13]This transitional space is essentially the place in which originality and tradition can be combined anew. See D.W. Winnicott, *Playing and Reality* (New York: Routledge, 1971), 99. See also Peter Homans, *The Ability to Mourn: Disillusionment and the Social Origins of Psychoanalysis* (Chicago: The University of Chicago, 1989), 333: "Individuation [the separation of an individual or a group of individuals from a larger, once-binding group structure] has two components, return and release. In the first, there is the loss of symbols or meaningful structures, the response to which is mourning; in the second, a movement forward into consequent structure building and the creation of meaning, of new structures of appreciation, the response to loss opens up the transitional space, which is both social and historical, and in the space persons construct a bridge of symbols between inner and social worlds through fantasy activity and its implicitly narrative character."

[14]That the vision in Ezek 1 is apocalyptic is indicated by M. Stone, *Scriptures, Sects, and Visions* (Philadelphia: Fortress, 1980), 85. W. Zimmerli, *Ezekiel* (Hermeneia; trans. R. Clements; 2 vols.; Philadelphia: Fortress, 1979), 116, links its language to the first century CE Jewish apocalypse 2 Baruch, particularly 22:1; some of the testamental literature (for example, the deathbed prophecies of the Twelve Patriarchs of Israel) put forth in the early centuries of the Christian era, especially the Testament of Levi and the Testament of Judah, the book of Daniel, and the Christian book of Revelation. The battle against Gog from Magog (Ezek 38-39) is clearly in line with Jewish apocalypticism, but is regarded by many scholars as a later addition; see Paul Hanson, *The Dawn of Apocalyptic* (Philadelphia: Fortress Press, 1979), 234. Hanson argues that the vision of the Temple in Ezek 40-48 is not proto-apocalyptic by virtue of its hierarchical and pragmatic orientation, one that

runs counter to the visionary, democratic, and ahistorical or future orientation of "true" proto-apocalyptic (*Ibid.*, 235-38). This position seems to draw a narrow line based on class distinctions and not some aspect of the text that runs counter to the form, content, or function of other apocalyptic literature. Additionally, Stone suggests that Ezek 40-48 and the heavenly tour in 1 Enoch are structurally very similar (Stone, *Scriptures, Sects, and Visions*, 44.

General questions concerning the unity of the book of Ezekiel's authorship, its redactive history, and the relationship of these to the book's message are quite complex and as yet unresolved. Some scholars prefer to speak of a "school" of participants in the scribal transmission, edition, and composition of such texts; foremost among them is Zimmerli, *Ezekiel*, 70-71. Most, however, still write as if there is a single prophetic author behind this text, one who relates to a considerable degree his authentic experience; see especially commentaries by Moshe Greenberg, *Ezekiel 1-20* (AB 22; Garden City: Doubleday, 1983); and Bruce Vawter and L. Hoppe, *A New Heart: A Commentary on the Book of Ezekiel* (Grand Rapids: Eerdmans, 1991).

[15]Here I use the translation of Greenberg, *Ezekiel 1-20*, 61, who underscores the range of meanings for *mašmîm* ["desolate"] as discussed by N. Lohfink in "Enthielten die im Alten Testament bezeugten Klageriten eine Phase des Schweigens?" *Vetus Testamentum* 12 (1962): 267-69. Greenberg, *Ibid.*, 72, suggests that the word "adds to aloneness the notion of numbing wretchedness, unnerving shock." Ralph Klein, *Ezekiel: The Prophet and His Message* (Columbia: University of South Carolina Press, 1988), 9, compares this period of silent sitting with that of Job's friends at Job 2:13, claiming it is neither unusual nor "evidence of ill-health." The comparison is more enlightening and apt than Klein indicates. Like Ezekiel, Job, too, has lost all the good things in his life; but unlike the prophet, he has not lost the historical proof that God still resides in the land. His friends hear about his condition and go to comfort him. But they do not merely go and sit compassionately by Job's side until he decides to speak; rather, when they see him, "they did not recognize him, and they raised their voices and wept aloud; they tore their robes and threw dust in the air upon their heads. Then they sat with him on the ground seven days and seven nights, and no one spoke a word to him, for they saw that his suffering was very great" (Job 2:12-13). I cannot agree with Klein that anything about this scenario smacks of the ordinary. The friends come to comfort Job, but find him so unlike himself as to be unrecognizable. They proceed to weep and wail and perform mourning rites as if he were already dead. Then they, for all intents and purposes, sit *shiva* with him—in part for his familial losses, to be sure, but in part, one might surmise from their reaction to him, for what appears to be Job's own living death.

[16]God's forceful coaxing in feeding Ezekiel the scroll likely indicates some conflict or resistance on the prophet's part, underscoring the result of ego suppression in this act. Similar ambivalence is expressed when Ezekiel resists the command to cook on

human dung in 4:14; even more so when God subsequently commands the prophet to speak to the Exiles, only to harden their faces against him and later strike him dumb except when commanded to speak. See Daniel Merkur, "Prophetic Initiation in Israel and Judah," *The Psychoanalytic Study of Society* 12 (1988): 63; Ellen F. *Davis, Swallowing the Scroll: Textuality and the Dynamics of Discourse in Ezekiel's Prophecy* (Decatur, GA: The Almond Press, 1989), 51-53; Greenberg, *Ezekiel 1- 20*, 78. Robert Wilson, *Prophecy and Society in Ancient Israel* (Philadelphia: Fortress, 1980), 62-64, indicates that this kind of a performance is cross-culturally stereotypical for a prophet in his social position, yet seemingly uncontrollable behavior is part of a larger pattern, one appropriate to the concerns on the periphery of society that the prophet is working out. Additionally, we may compare Wilson's exposition on prophecy and spirit possession to Ezekiel's call and the subsuming of his personality to the will of God: "According to the theory of possession, the individual loses his personal identity and becomes the embodiment of the possessing spirit, which totally controls him. The two become one, so that the speech and actions of the individual are actually the speech and actions of the spirit" (*Ibid.*, 65).

[17]These psychic defenses arise in the course of defending the ego's integrity against the recognition of traumatic material. *Projection* is the unconscious displacement of painful emotion on to a non-threatening substitute. *Externalization* takes projection a step further, attributing an independent object reality to the projection. *Introjection* is the act of identifying so fully with the externalization that it is adopted by the psyche as an unconscious model of ego development and structure. The classic Freudian example of these defenses at work is found in the "myth" of the primal horde in *Civilization and Its Discontents*, in which the young men of the loose tribe that predated "civilization" per se, upset with their father's monopolization of the sexual resources of the available women, kill the father. Subsequently they feel unremitting guilt, fear, and vulnerability. To protect themselves from the recognition of their patricide, they project their feelings into the cosmos, externalize them as a fantasy of their father as an omnipotent and wrathful deity, then introject their fear and guilt of the father as a religious belief in a set of moral laws—an event recapitulated in the resolution of the Oedipal conflict (*Civilization and Its Discontents, SE* 21 [1930]: 131-33).

[18]An even more thorough psychoanalytic reading would recognize the affective split, whereby the perfectly good Yahweh acts as critical agency over and against the perfectly base House of Israel, both halves representing idealized aspects of the prophet's identity and the ambivalence he must have felt towards a God who allowed such tragedy to occur. See Merkur, "Prophetic Initiation," 53-59; Daschke, "Desolate Among Them," 112-20.

[19]The true work of mourning, however, seems to begin with the sign acts of Ezek 3:22-6:14. Relying on Freud's description of the "distinguishing mental features of melancholia," in these acts we see vividly: painful dejection, cessation of interest in

the outside world—3:24-25 (confinement to house); inhibition of all activity—3:24-26; 4:4f (dumbness, confinement to house, lying on side); lowering of self-regarding feelings, self-revilings— 4:12 (food to be cooked on human excrement); and expectation of punishment – 4:4-6; 5:1-4 (lying on side, burning and cutting of hair). One can clearly see that the rage against the House of Israel is directed at the prophet in reality, with Israel receiving punishment only symbolically. In fact, Ezek 4:4-6 explicitly states that the prophet bears the punishment of the houses of Israel and Judah.

[20]Compare Freud and Ezekiel: "It is possible for the process in the unconscious to come to an end, either after the fury has spent itself or after the object has been abandoned as valueless" (Freud, "Mourning and Melancholia," 257); "My anger shall spend itself, and I will vent my fury on them and satisfy myself; and they shall know that I, the LORD, have spoken in my jealousy, when I spend my fury on them." (Ezek 5:13).

[21]With an apparent reference to the Flavian emperors of Rome, 4 Ezra is believed to reflect the situation in Palestine around 100 CE. Referring specifically to Daniel's four kingdom structure, 4 Ezra 12:11 states categorically: "The eagle that you saw coming up from the sea is the fourth kingdom that appeared in a vision to your brother Daniel." The twelve kings of the interpretation are invariably understood to be Roman emperors, and the three heads, it is generally agreed, are the Flavians. Though 4 Ezra (2 Esdras 3-14 in the Apocrypha) has been preserved in a variety of languages and church canons, most importantly in the Latin Vulgate, and though in most collections it is followed by additional Christian material known as 5 and 6 Ezra, a Hebrew original is generally assumed. Hence the certain centerpiece of concern in this text is the fate of a Judea still under Roman control almost a generation after the sack of Jerusalem and the destruction of the Temple.

A number of treatments of 4 Ezra have already picked up on its movement from grief to consolation and the relationship of its structure, function, and meaning. E. Brandenburger, "Die Verborgenheit Gottes im Weltgeschehen," in *Abhandlungen zur Theologie des Alten und Neuen Testaments* 68 (Zurich: Theolgischer Verlag, 1981); and W. Harnisch, "Der Prophet als Widerpart und Zeuge der Offenbarung: Erwägungen zur Interdependenz von Form und Sache im IV Buch Ezra," in *Apocalypticism in the Mediterranean World and the Near East* (2nd ed.; ed. D. Hellholm; Tübingen: Mohr, 1989), 478-80, emphasize the central transformative significance of Vision Four, the Vision of the Weeping Woman, that moves the seer from opposition to support, from skepticism to wisdom. Michael Stone, *Fourth Ezra: A Commentary on the Book of Fourth Ezra* (Minneapolis: Fortress, 1990), 336, on the same vision, notes that mourning for Zion up to that point "has been the central motive of the book so far; that mourning finds its consolation in the present chapter."

Not to press the point too far, but consistent with the theme of revelation and concealment that runs through both apocalypticism and psychoanalysis, we may note with interest that 4 Ezra is an apocalypse, or revelation, which is apocryphal, or secret. All of the texts that are generally considered apocalypses, with the exception of the book of Daniel and the New Testament's book of Revelation, share this nominal paradox, which could stem, according to rabbinic tradition, from the fact that most of the apocalypses appeared after the end of the age of prophecy after the conquests of Alexander the Great, when new texts were no longer considered inspired or authoritative. See Lawrence Schiffman, *From Text to Tradition: A History of Second Temple and Rabbinic Judaism* (Hoboken: Ktav, 1991), 57-58. A more sociological theory would observe that the communities that produced and kept these texts existed, generally speaking, on the fringes of society.

[22]References to 4 Ezra are from "The Fourth Book of Ezra," Bruce. M. Metzger, trans., in *The Old Testament Pseudepigrapha: Volume One, Apocalyptic Literature and Testaments* (ed. J. Charlesworth; New York: Doubleday, 1983), 525-79.

[23]Job, too, has lost all the good things in his life, but unlike Ezra and Ezekiel, he has not lost the historical proof that God still resides in the land. Job also engages in a dialogue to understand his predicament, first with his friends and then with God himself, but unlike Ezra, Job struggles mightily not to blame God for his misfortune. Ezra seems to have no such compunction, especially in the initial complaint in chapter 3.

[24]A. L. Thompson, *Responsibility for Evil in the Theodicy of IV Ezra* (SBLDS 29; Missoula: Scholars Press, 1977), 143, terms the divine response in the first three visions "inadequate"; it is either evasive or simply reflective of the inability of Judaism on the whole to address the issues Ezra raises. A. P. Hayman, "The Problem of Pseudonymity in the Ezra Apocalypse," *Journal for the Study of Judaism* 6 (1975): 55, relates Ezra's failure to pronounce himself satisfied by the angel's answers to the author's and others' experiences in the latter half of the first century. Michael P. Knowles, "Moses, the Law, and the Unity of 4 Ezra," *Novum Testamentum* 31 (1989): 259, 267-74, calls the fact that the angel answers almost none of Ezra's questions "remarkable": "They simply flare up into a final bitter exchange...and then are left hanging somewhere between heaven and earth." Yet, he adds, "somehow Ezra is comforted."

[25]In general, when God is said to hate, his enmity is directed at sin, especially idolatry (Deut 16:22; Ps 31:5-6), or toward sinful human attributes (for example, pride in Amos 6:8, or the "six things the Lord hates" of Prov 6:16). Ben Sira does state outright, "God hates sinners" (Sir 12:6). But for one of Yahweh's people to believe his God hates him is extremely rare. In fact, the only significant parallel to Ezra is found, not surprisingly, in Job, when Job cries out that God "has torn me in his wrath, and hated me" (Job 16:9a). But a blanket statement that God hates his people, and is not simply punishing a wayward nation out of a sense of betrayal of love, seems unprecedented.

[26]This emotional display is often termed "separation anxiety" in children and adolescents, who have not individuated sufficiently from the care giver to preserve

ego integrity on their own. Hatred for the abandoning parent comes bound together with the expression of love; a shifting back between the two demonstrates the core ambivalence. See John Bowlby, *Attachment and Loss, Volume II: Separation* (New York: Basic Books, 1973), 245-57; Henry Hansberg, *Adolescent Separation Anxiety* (Springfield: Charles C. Thomas, 1972), 66-73. Related is "negative attention": any regard, positive or negative, from the loved one is still experienced as valuable and affirming. In this example from 4 Ezra, one may also still perceive the displacement of the seer's critical agency in which, as with Ezekiel above, one half of the seer's ego is set against the other half, redirecting the seer's hatred of God's abandonment to himself.

[27]See 4 Ezra 7:62-63, 11:6-17; parallels in wording and sentiment occur in other responses to such a crisis, as at Jer 15:10 and 1 Macc 2:7. Interestingly, some of Ezra's nihilistic plaints reflect what might today be termed survivor guilt, as he seems to link his inability to understand the decimation of his people with an unworthiness of his continued existence.

[28]Such a claim could be made against the apostle Paul, one of the most famous converts in all literature and a notoriously staunch (some would say intolerant) moral crusader in his epistles. The sense of an awakening to truth and clear understanding of the world (and its evils) is shared by those who experience religious transformation, as in conversion or mysticism (see the descriptions and examples from William James, *The Varieties of Religious Experience* [New York: Collier, 1961], 163-65, 299-336). These experiences clearly separate those who have been through them from those who have not. Conversion, however, often involves a reassessment of the moral direction of one's own life that engenders an explicit rejection of one's previous life—the "old self"—and all that it entailed. Hence all elements of the old life in any form are anathema to the convert, who may feel obliged to awaken others to the same truths, that is, to rescue others from the convert's former path of self-destruction. Often this is done with the attitude described commonly as "holier than thou." See Benjamin Beit-Hallahmi and Michael Argyle, *The Psychology of Religious Behaviors, Belief, and Experience* (London & New York: Routledge, 1997), 116.

Clearly conversion is similar to addiction recovery in this regard. The recovering addict often must live in complete abstention from the abused substance, but then expect or demand the same from family, friends, even co-workers, causing friction between them. The connection between rigid religious intolerance and addiction recovery in its most extreme form is made by Stephen Arterburn and Jack Felton in *Toxic Faith: Understanding and Overcoming Religious Addiction* (Nashville: Oliver-Nelson Books, 1991), 42-43. Those convinced of their own moral superiority, they say, "will sacrifice relationships with family and friends to uphold a standard or ideal of their own faith."

[29]Collins, *Apocalyptic Imagination*, 28.

A Borrowed Apocalypse:
Reading the Book of Revelation
in New Religious Movements

Eugene V. Gallagher

In the 1990s several groups often identified as "cults" or new religious movements used the biblical book of Revelation to give vividness, depth, and gravity to their own apocalyptic scenarios. Extensive references to Revelation appear, for example, in Chen Tao's account of the imminent salvation of the faithful by the descent of flying saucers, Heaven's Gate's proclamation of the imminent "spading under" of earth's present civilization, and Aum Shinrikyo's predictions of the coming catastrophe that will end human life as we know it. The book of Revelation plays a prominent role in the self-understanding of these groups even though they make only limited claims on the rest of the Christian tradition. Their borrowing of a Christian apocalypse signals the complex cultural mix that goes into many new religious movements, suggests the energizing potential of the biblical tradition well beyond the bounds of traditional orthodoxy, and reveals some crucial strategies by which new religions strive to claim and maintain legitimacy in the eyes of an often hostile public.[1]

Chen Tao attempted to unmask Revelation as a deceptive and inaccurate account of the end of the world and use it as a foil for the group's own account of what will really happen when God's judgment is exercised. For Heaven's Gate, Revelation offered an array of roles, such as the Lamb of God (Rev 5), the two witnesses (Rev 11), and the Antichrist (Rev 13:11-18), that could be assigned to participants in an anticipated end-times drama as a way of imposing narrative coherence on a chaotic situation and also as a way of claiming a deeply rooted authority. For Aum Shinrikyo, images from Revelation, like the battle of Armageddon (see Rev 16:12-16), became part of a synthetic account of the end of time that borrowed from many sources.

Precisely because they are new and different from their established rivals, new religious movements devote substantial effort to establishing and defending their legitimacy.[2] One prominent way of doing this is to graft themselves onto a pre-existing religious history. Rarely will a new religious movement present itself as completely cut off from the past.[3] It will instead attempt to offer a new understanding of a familiar past, restore to their rightful prominence long-ignored dimensions of a common history, provide a necessary supplement to an incomplete rendering of the past, or otherwise strive to assert both continuity and novelty. Since most religions enshrine their significant pasts in authoritative collections of texts or stories, new religious movements are often driven to establish their legitimacy through encounters with the scriptural heritages of dominant religious traditions. In this sense, establishing legitimacy becomes an interpretive task; it is not simply a matter of making claims but of advancing new understandings of familiar texts, figures, events, and themes.[4]

Various strategies of scriptural appropriation, application, and interpretation that are integral parts of mainstream religious traditions are also frequently employed by new religious movements. Their quest to establish themselves as worthy of attention, respect, and even affiliation frequently takes a primarily exegetical form. The strategies by which they attempt to wring distinctive new meaning from already authoritative texts often differ little from those used by mainstream religions, even when the results are thoroughly innovative.

The readings of the book of Revelation developed by some millennialist new religious movements in the 1990s thus offer a way to chart their distinctive patterns of similarities and differences with mainstream religions. A look at the interpretation of Revelation in some contemporary Christian apocalyptic writings will establish a baseline against which other readings can be compared. My attention focuses on the ways readers of Revelation choose and justify their focus of interpretation, develop and implement an interpretive scheme that will produce the desired results, and establish their legitimacy as interpreters in order to proclaim a distinctive message.

CONTEMPORARY CHRISTIAN MILLENNIALISM

Since he published *The Late Great Planet Earth* in 1970, Hal Lindsey has probably been the most popular and influential representative of the "premillennialist" strand of contemporary Christian millennialism.[5] Although he ranges nimbly throughout the Bible for sources that support his version of the apocalyptic scenario, Lindsey has always paid particular attention to the book of Revelation. In his characteristically folksy style, he has described it as "the 'Grand Central Station' of the whole Bible" because "nearly every symbol in it is used somewhere else in the Bible, but finds its ultimate fulfillment and explanation in this final prophetic book of the Bible."[6] In Lindsey's view, the biblical message is wholly transparent; as an interpreter, his task is simply "to step aside and let the prophets speak."[7] As his various interpretations of Revelation unfold, however, they reveal a more complex approach.

Whenever he turns to the Bible, Lindsey encounters passages of stunning contemporary relevance.[8] He observes, for example, that "what John the Apostle foresaw nearly 2000 years ago has more to do with this generation's immediate future than tomorrow's breaking news on CNN."[9] For Lindsey, the Bible constitutes "the greatest sourcebook of current events in the world."[10] He even offers a striking account of how the author of Revelation acquired his accurate knowledge of the present day, claiming that John "like a time traveler . . . was physically transported 2000 years into the future and was commanded to write an accurate eyewitness account."[11] In another passage Lindsey assimilates his notion of John and other prophets as time travelers to the more traditional motif of the heavenly ascent, describing Revelation as "John's firsthand account of what he saw and experienced when he was taken up to heaven."[12] Lindsey's interpretation of Revelation is founded on his conviction that John is describing events in our present within the limitations of his first century vocabulary.

Lindsey thus abandons a strict literalism for a modernizing translation of symbols. He replaces the notion that the text means precisely what it says with this idea, that the text means what it would have said had the proper vocabulary been available. He cannot "step aside and let the prophets speak" until he teaches his audience how to listen properly. Lindsey's treatment of the rider on the pale horse in Rev 6:2 provides a typical example. He points out that:

> this conqueror carries with him a warrior's bow. Why did John use the symbol of a "bow" instead of the usual code word for war—a "sword"? It could be that a sword was used for close-in hand-to-hand combat. But the bow was a long-range weapon that could hurl a missile a long way. This is code for long-range weapons like ICBMs.[13]

Although Lindsey claims that there is a "code" that enables him to decipher Revelation, in practice he is less precise than this image implies. His exposition is peppered with qualifiers like "could" and "might be" and admissions that his interpretation amounts to personal opinion. His treatment of the locusts mentioned in Rev 9 suggests the looseness of his exegesis. In the course of an argument spanning two pages Lindsey wavers between a biological and a mechanistic interpretation of the locusts. He observes first that "these locusts are actually some kind of attack helicopters with a tail-mounted sprayer for chemical/biological weapons," next that "the more widely accepted view" is "that these locusts are some sort of a demon-possessed insect," and finally that "I personally am convinced that these are literal helicopters with chemical weapons."[14] Passages like this show Lindsey's reading of Revelation to be a personal and impressionistic collection of observations whose persuasiveness is founded on readers' prior acceptance of Lindsey as an authoritative interpreter, their own predisposition to seek contemporary meaning from the Bible, and their conviction that the world is indeed in a dire situation.

Although Lindsey claims to read the Bible literally,[15] he does not let his literalism stand in the way of a desire to explain the Bible's contemporary relevance, particularly as the world edges ever closer to the time of the end.[16] Consequently, much of Lindsey's analytical work is given over to aligning biblical apocalyptic scenarios with contemporary phenomena and events. He displays virtually no interest in investigating the historical situation in which the text was formed, the audience to which it was originally directed, or any other feature of its first century context. Lindsey's focus on Revelation's contemporary relevance has, of course, led to some necessary adjustments to his message over the course of his thirty-year writing career,[17] but he has proved remarkably adept at incorporating new events, such as the dissolution of the former Soviet Union, the rise of militant Islam, and the burgeoning power of China, into his prophetic scheme.

Lindsey finds in Revelation a master plot for the end of time, the proclamation of which is made all the more urgent because time itself is running out. He brings to the text a contemporizing interpretative scheme that allows him to translate symbols from the first century into what he believes are their exact modern counterparts. He bases the need for that translation on an imaginative understanding of John's religious experience. In all of his books, Lindsey's interpretation of Revelation is in the service of a simple goal, the salvation of his readers.[18] If book sales are any indication, he has at least developed an extensive following.[19]

Although they might dispute Lindsey's interpretations of the biblical texts, few observers would locate him outside of the boundaries of the Christian tradition. This was not the case with David Koresh, the prophet of the Branch Davidian sect that was attacked by officers of the Bureau of Alcohol, Tobacco and Firearms on February 28, 1993, and almost completely destroyed in a conflagration on April 19, 1993. Koresh was widely represented to the general public as a dangerous "cult leader," and little attention was paid to what he and his followers saw as their central preoccupation: the interpretation of the Bible and particularly the book of Revelation.[20] But like Lindsey, Koresh saw Revelation as the pinnacle of the Bible's message, claiming that "every book of the Bible meets and ends in the book of Revelation."[21] Although he was less specific than Lindsey in discussing the mechanisms by which the author of Revelation developed his detailed knowledge of the contemporary world, Koresh, too, was convinced that Revelation spoke to his own time. Toward the end of the 1993 negotiations that spanned the fifty-one day siege of the Branch Davidians' Mount Carmel Center outside of Waco, Texas, one of the FBI agents asked Koresh, "Do you feel we're in the last days?" He replied, "I know we are in the last days."[22]

Koresh was convinced of the imminence of the end not because he could align current events with biblical prophecies, but because he had an unshakeable sense that he had been chosen by God precisely to proclaim the coming judgment. Like Lindsey, Koresh believed that it had only recently become possible to understand the true message of Revelation. In 1989, Koresh proclaimed, "What I teach is the true interpretation of the Bible. It's so true that people for the first time in their life can understand the complexity of scripture. That's my work and that's my mission."[23] In stark contrast to Lindsey's relatively modest claim that he is simply re-presenting the message of the ancient prophets, Koresh claimed the same type of authority that Lindsey attributed to the author of Revelation, including the experience of an ascent into heaven. On March 5, 1993, Koresh told an FBI negotiator in a somewhat indirect fashion that during a heavenly visit he had been commissioned as a prophet and even adopted as a son of God:

It says right there in Psalms 2—and this is where I'm coming from. I will declare the decree—I mean this is the law of God. The Lord said unto me, thou art my Son; this day I have begotten thee [see Ps 2:7; Luke 3:22].

Ask of me, Son, and that's what happened to me in heaven, my friend. You may not believe it. But God says ask of me, and I will give thee the heathen . . . for thine inheritance.[24]

Koresh's specific mission was to reveal to the world the contents of the book sealed with seven seals in Rev 4-5. He spent little time reading the signs of the times and much more time developing a complex mosaic of biblical texts in support of his interpretation.[25] Although Lindsey claimed simply to be letting the prophets speak, he frequently indulged in catalogues of the world's current dire straits, cobbled together from a variety of presumably authoritative secular sources. More than Lindsey, Koresh focused on the biblical text itself.

When he turned to the text of Revelation, Koresh found something there that no one else had ever found: David Koresh. He saw himself as the Lamb described in Rev 5, the only one able to open the scroll sealed with seven seals. He thus became not only an interpreter of the biblical text, but also an actor in the events it foretold. Koresh was convinced that his mission was not simply to explain the meaning of the seven seals, but actually to bring about the events that they prophesied.[26]

The events that most concerned Koresh were not the establishment of the modern state of Israel, the integration of the European Union, the dissolution of the former Soviet Union, or other aspects of contemporary geopolitics. He was more narrowly focused on the imminent salvation of the small group of the faithful and the terrible fate that awaited those who rejected the message of the seven seals. Although Koresh, like Lindsey, expected the climactic battle of Armageddon to be fought soon in Israel, he was much less interested in developing a detailed scenario of how that battle would unfold. While Koresh sometimes shares Lindsey's flare for contemporizing interpretations, as when he turns biblical chariots into modern tanks,[27] he is much more concerned with harmonizing the messages of the ancient prophets so that they form a single coherent biblical picture of the times of the end.[28] In Koresh's view, the primary actors in the end-time drama are those who accept the message of the seven seals and those who reject it. The precise mechanisms by which the unbelievers come to their terrible end are of less interest to him than his effort to bring the saving message of the seven seals to as many of them as possible.

Like Lindsey, Koresh was convinced that Revelation has a message of direct relevance and utmost importance for the present time. He viewed the text as the centerpiece of a biblical mosaic and expended considerable ingenuity in demonstrating how the message of Revelation was supported by every other book of the Bible. Koresh, however, generally avoided Lindsey's contemporizing interpretations that turned bows into missiles and locusts into helicopters. He preferred instead a blanket assertion that located the contemporary relevance of the text within the hearts and minds of individuals as they struggled to accept or reject the message of the seven seals in light of the imminent judgment.

Much more than Lindsey, Koresh established a religious community through his reading of Revelation. Through his missionary activity, Koresh's understanding of Revelation led him first to assume the leadership and then to reconstitute the nature of the community of students of the seven seals who gathered at the Mount Carmel Center.[29] Revelation became the pivot around which all their discourse and all of their lives revolved. Koresh's reading of Revelation established for the Branch Davidians their individual identities, their sense of membership in a group, their understanding of the past, and their hopes and fears for the future. As one of those at Mount Carmel said during the siege, "the reason they came here, all that they are and what they want to be revolves around what they see him [Koresh] showing from that book."[30] Koresh's reading of Revelation created the Mount Carmel community by holding the allegiance of the members whom he inherited from his predecessor, Lois Roden,[31] and by attracting new members; he maintained the community by continually reinforcing the message of the seven seals of Revelation in his marathon Bible Studies; and he gave his fellow students of the seven seals a sense of purpose, dignity, and importance by portraying them as the vanguard of the unfortunately small group that would be saved in the coming judgment.

CHEN TAO

The small group known as Chen Tao or God's Salvation Church lived in obscurity until March, 1998, when its leader, Hon-Ming Chen, announced that God would physically descend to earth in Garland, Texas, at the end of the month.[32] Teacher Chen's prophecy excited representatives of the news media, who then themselves descended on Garland. Along with a few academicians interested in millennialism and some local law enforcement representatives, they began to try to understand the surprising prophecy within the context of Chen Tao's eclectic mix of Chinese folk religion, Buddhism, Christianity, Taoism, UFO beliefs, and (pseudo-) science and to assess what might happen to the group when its prophecy, as was likely, failed. Chen Tao's expectation of the imminent arrival of God was part of a larger apocalyptic scenario that Teacher Chen had developed in his privately published writings. In them he devoted particular attention to interpreting the millennial message of the book of Revelation.

In 1992 Teacher Chen experienced a revelation that commissioned him to proclaim the coming "tribulation" that would destroy at least eighty per cent of the earth's population. Making implicit reference to the promise in Mal 4:5 that Elijah would return from heaven before the apocalyptic "day of the Lord" and to the allusions to that passage in the Gospels' depictions of John the Baptizer, Teacher Chen's interpreter Richard Liu observed: "It is stated in the Bible that one should be sent by God to prepare the way for the Lord, and actually . . . Teacher Chen assume[s] himself to be the one sent by God to prepare the way for God's coming."[33]

Chen believed that all who heeded his preaching would be qualified for an extraordinary experience:

> After the great tribulation, He shall invite the Embodied God's Kingdom to the world, and God shall descend in clouds of heaven (flying saucers) with other Buddhas, Christs, and angels unto the earth to save people from the dying of freezing cold and starvation caused by the nuclear fallout in the few years of the tribulation.[34]

As this passage indicates, Chen Tao's apocalyptic scenario draws on the biblical tradition, but is not limited to it. Although Teacher Chen does not offer a full commentary on the text of Revelation, it is crucial to him as a false account of what God will accomplish at the time of the end. Chen was convinced that "the year of 1999 will be the last year of people's community of life on earth, the year of self-destruction of human life on earth."[35]

But, unlike Lindsey and Koresh, he does not see the end as a time when God will exercise judgment against a predominantly sinful humanity. In fact, the most distinctive difference in Teacher Chen's millennial theology is his redefinition of the nature of God. Chen posits that "God won't give people judgments; nor will He be enraged or kill people. In religion, people have to believe in the real God, and the real nature of God won't be so violent."[36] On the contrary, "God is the great love of mercy; He only saves people's life."[37] If, in Teacher Chen's view, God cannot be the author of apocalyptic violence, then the texts that portray God in that fashion have to be explained. His general interpretive guideline rests on a basic theological proposition and is very clearly expressed: "If you can understand the real divine character of God, you can avoid being misguided by some fragments in the contents of the Bible which are actually heavenly devil kings' words."[38]

In reading Revelation, Chen adopts several overlapping and complementary interpretive strategies. On the basis of internal comparisons within the canon, Chen concludes: "If the Revelation were

God's message, it should have also appeared in Jesus Christ's descriptions of the end of the world, and should have been told by Jesus Christ."[39] In a more complicated but more central move, Chen appeals to the story of the fallen angels in Gen 6.[40] He envisages a heaven filled with Satan and other devils who strive to exert their control over human beings. As the end nears, they have made more progress towards their goal.[41]

One way that those "heavenly devil kings" have led humans astray is through their corruption of God's teachings in Scripture. Consequently, in order to bring the true message of salvation, Teacher Chen has had to provide a guide to reading the Bible, in particular "to clarify what parts of the Bible are 'devil's words.'"[42] In addition to stressing Revelation's discontinuities with the teachings of Jesus and its mixture of God's words and the fabrications of the devil kings, Chen also attempts to undermine the authoritative status of Revelation by disputing the source from which John gained his knowledge. He claims that "the descriptions in the Revelation were given by the heavenly devil king to John; they weren't the revelation from Jesus Christ."[43] Chen, however, attempts to preserve at least some of the book from the taint of its source by proposing that "some parts of the Revelation are true prophecies, but they were learned from God by heavenly devil kings when they were still cultivating in the human world and hadn't fallen yet."[44]

One of the sections of Revelation that Chen preserved was the narrative of the seven seals. Like Lindsey and Koresh, Chen found the sequence of the seals to be a helpful device for arranging the events that lead up to the final tribulation. Chen, however, identifies the starting point of the opening of the seals as 1911; the first seal is roughly aligned with the events that culminated in World War I. Much less enamored than Lindsey with aligning the symbols of Revelation with specific geopolitical events, Chen is content to note, for example, that "the first seal implies the Western countries of imperial power, and the wars waged by the white races of imperialism, including World War I and World War II."[45] Only with the sixth and seventh seals does Chen slow down and attempt to predict specific events that were to unfold in the year of tribulation, 1999.[46] Like Lindsey, Koresh, and so many others, Chen would subscribe to the millennialist motto that "if we could learn to read life rightly, almost everything is a sign."[47]

Chen's overarching interpretive task is to isolate what in Revelation represents God's word. The criterion on which all his decisions rest is whether the biblical statements can be seen to support his conception of a purely beneficent God. Because Teacher Chen goes through such interpretive contortions in his reading of Revelation, it becomes important to determine why he feels compelled to address the text at all. From statements scattered through his writings, it appears that Chen sees God's Salvation Church as the truest expression of human religion. Although he concentrates on the Bible, Chen implies that other religious texts have also been contaminated by the influence of the heavenly devil kings. Chen Tao has thus salvaged from existing religious traditions that which reflects the true nature of God, jettisoned the misleading additions of the heavenly devil kings, and synthesized the remnants into the only teaching that offers the truth about the coming tribulation and human prospects for salvation. The imminent appearance of God will ensure that "the twenty-first century is the century of God's religion,"[48] a religion entirely without the malign influences of the heavenly devil kings.

Revelation thus serves both as a resource and a foil for Teacher Chen. It provides a familiar bridge by which a segment of his audience may cross over to his more esoteric teachings drawn from eastern and occult traditions; it supports his sense of urgency about the coming tribulation even as it gives an inaccurate account of it; and it gives him a sequential framework in which to arrange his observations on the apocalyptic significance of current and recent events. While not as central as it is to the millennial messages of Lindsey and Koresh, Revelation nonetheless plays a pivotal role in Chen Tao's apocalyptic scenario, even after the 1999 failed prophecy.[49]

HEAVEN'S GATE

Like Hon-Ming Chen, Marshall Applewhite, who was known to the "crew" of Heaven's Gate as "Do," became convinced that our present civilization was one in a series of worlds and that, like the others, it was on the verge of completing the cycle from birth to destruction to rebirth.[50] Applewhite also shared with Chen the conviction that powerful alien creatures, in his case called "Luciferians," had successfully conspired to keep most of humanity in ignorance for at least the past 2,000 years.[51] Also like Chen, Applewhite believed that the world was on the verge of a new beginning and only a fortunate few would be saved from the imminent catastrophe to which most of humankind would be subjected.[52] Applewhite shared with Chen not only the common millennial conviction that his own teaching held the key to human salvation, but also the specific notion that the means of escape for the faithful would be a flying saucer.

While Applewhite always expressed his message with an eye to its biblical background, he never undertook a sustained interpretation of any specific biblical books or passages, although the Bible remained the substructure of his millennial message. Applewhite's approach to biblical interpretation, though never direct, shares Lindsey's concern to render the Bible relevant to the contemporary situation, Koresh's desire to harmonize the Bible's many voices into a single, coherent message, and Teacher Chen's interest in separating what is worthwhile in the Bible from the corruptions and interpolations that have been visited upon it.

Do wanted to hold fast to the Bible because "though many people think of these records as religious, they are for the most part, in spite of their many inaccuracies, the only historical record we have of periods when the Next Level was relating to man."[53] For Applewhite, Jesus' career provides the paradigm for understanding the present mission of Do and his partner "Ti" (who passed away in 1985) and specifically for grasping their authority as teachers. As one of the crew, "Glnody," observed, "If you really knew the Bible, you would recognize Ti and Do for who they are."[54]

Precisely who Do and Ti were was most often defined in functional terms. The first public statement that "the Two" issued in March, 1975, described the mission of Applewhite and Bonnie Lu Nettles:

They are "sent" from that kingdom by the "Father" to bear the same truth that was Jesus'. This is like a repeat performance, except this time by two (a man and a woman) to restate the truth Jesus bore, restore its accurate meaning, and again show that any individual who seeks that kingdom will find it through the same process.[55]

This functional identification of the mission of Jesus with that undertaken by Do and Ti could, however, shade over towards the assertion of a substantive identification of Do and Ti with the previous "Rep" from the Next Level. In a videotape series that he filmed in late 1991 and early 1992, for example, Applewhite claimed: "We're not saying that we're Jesus. We're not trying to get you to buy that we are. We have nothing to gain—it is you who might have something to gain by that belief. However, all the evidence points to the fact that we are that 'return' of the Next Level's presence."[56]

In short, it appears that Do and Ti wanted to associate their mission as closely as possible with that of Jesus without unduly raising suspicions of personal aggrandizement in the eyes of those familiar with the Christian tradition. Like David Koresh in his assertion that he was a Christ, an anointed servant of God,[57] they attempted to draw fine theological distinctions that were largely lost on their audiences. The reasons behind some of their diffidence about claiming biblical authority may stem from an event that occurred when they were convinced that, like Koresh, they could see themselves in the text of the Bible, specifically in the book of Revelation.

Soon after Applewhite and Nettles began their mission in the mid-70s, they went underground for more than a decade. They surfaced briefly in 1988 and produced a short pamphlet, "'88 Update: The UFO Two (Two Witnesses) and their Crew (Followers): a Brief Synopsis," that briskly recounted the history of the group from an insider's perspective. The pamphlet contains some of Do and Ti's strongest statements about their relationship to the biblical tradition and, perhaps, the reasons for their later ambivalence. The "88 Update" reports that from the beginning Applewhite and Nettles "consciously recognized that they were sent from space to do a task that had something to do with the Bible, an update in understanding and prophesy [sic] fulfillment."[58] Applewhite and Nettles began their career by embedding their message about the imminent arrival of spacecraft from "The Evolutionary Level Above Human" deeply into the text of the book of Revelation. Revelation was used to legitimize the prophetic authority that "the Two" claimed, to specify the duration of their mission, and to intimate the dramatic changes that would soon be forthcoming. As the "88 Update" notes: "They traveled into Canada and all over the U. S. again, leaving little calling cards on pulpits saying, 'The Two Witnesses are here.'"[59] Applewhite and Nettles also adopted imagery from Revelation to describe the false teachings which their followers should avoid; in particular, "they also came to know that the true antichrist is now here and has taken several faces, one of which is the New Age 'Ye are Gods' concept."[60]

Most importantly, Revelation offered "the Two" an opportunity to see themselves, as Koresh did, in the biblical text, particularly in Rev 11:3, where the heavenly voice tells John that "I will grant my two witnesses power to prophesy for one thousand two hundred and sixty days, clothed in sackcloth."[61] In fact, Rev 11:3-13 gave Applewhite and Nettles a complete scenario for understanding their task on earth, even as it drew strong parallels between the activity of the two witnesses and the career of Jesus himself. It showed, for example, that their mission would be of limited duration (11:3), that they would have to give their own lives for their cause (11:7), and that they could expect ultimate vindication when they were raised from the dead after three and a half days and installed in heaven (11:11-12).

Had their teaching remained within the context provided by Rev 11, "the Two" might also have been led, like Lindsey, to adopt a contemporizing interpretation of the Bible in order to incorporate their fascination with the salvation that would be delivered by UFOs. That never transpired, however, because Applewhite and Nettles quickly abandoned the paradigm of biblical millennialism in Rev 11 when they encountered opposition. The "88 Update" tells the story succinctly:

> At a New Age awareness center, they felt led to share that they were the Two Witnesses, only to find out that the leaders of the center claimed the same title! After this incident, they struggled significantly with whether to continue with this "modus operandi."[62]

"The Two's" reconsideration of their mode of self-representation apparently led them to retreat to generalized references to the message of Jesus that would minimize the opportunities for direct conflict over the precise identity of Applewhite and Nettles, while still anchoring their message in an authoritative past. This retreat from seeing themselves in the biblical text also fit well with "the Two's" reserved personalities and their early diffidence about exercising any organizational control over their followers. Applewhite and Nettles proved unwilling to face the conflict that would be produced by portraying themselves as the fulfillment of biblical prophecy. Their refusal to continue to identify themselves as Revelation's two witnesses shaped the way their message would be articulated thereafter and reinforced the weak control that they intended to exercise over their followers in the early days.

Rather than becoming a dogmatic necessity, like Koresh's identification of himself as the lamb from Rev 5, "the Two's" identity as the two witnesses from Rev 11 remained a submerged possibility in the teaching of Heaven's Gate. It was explicitly mentioned in the authoritative account of the early days contained in the "88 Update" and it remained there to be taken up by any follower who found it meaningful, but it never became a decisive element in "the Two's" self-presentation or in the later teachings of Heaven's Gate. Factors external to the movement, such as conflict with others identifying themselves as the two witnesses, and internal to the group, such as Applewhite and Nettles' early unwillingness to impose their authority on their followers, led Do and Ti to suppress, if not wholly abandon, the specific paradigm of millennial leadership expressed in Rev 11.

AUM SHINRIKYO

Well before Aum Shinrikyo achieved international notoriety with its March 20, 1995, release of sarin gas in the Tokyo subway, its leader, Shoko Asahara, had become fascinated by the account of the end of the world in the book of Revelation. Several observers have noted that speculation about the end of this present civilization in Aum Shinrikyo grew more pessimistic as Asahara became more familiar with the message of Revelation in 1988 and 1989.[63] In some of his sermons Asahara seems inclined to follow Lindsey in aligning the prophecies of Revelation with current events. For example, in 1990 Asahara proclaimed:

> We are heading for Armageddon. It becomes very clear if you analyze the situation in the Middle East. Also the coming of Haley's comet, the frequent appearances of UFOs, the Soviet Union's democratization and its introduction of the presidential system, the unification of Europe, and so forth—what are all these incidents telling us? They are telling us that the world is getting ready for Armageddon. And what will happen after Armageddon? After Armageddon the beings will be divided into two extreme types: the ones who will go to the Heaven of Light and Sound, and the ones who go to Hell.[64]

The book of Revelation appealed to Asahara because it provided a scenario of the end. Although Asahara acknowledges the interpretive difficulties involved in understanding Revelation's message for today, he stresses that "the prophecies concerning the period after the capitalist economy are written in detail in the book of Revelation."[65]

The accuracy of Asahara's reading of Revelation depends on his unparalleled religious status. Echoing David Koresh but choosing a different passage in which to find himself, Asahara claims:

> Here [in John 15:18-27] Jesus says, "He who will testify about me" is "the Spirit of truth who goes out from the Father." This refers to no one else but me because there has been nobody who could disclose the correct meaning of Jesus' teaching to this day.[66]

As in the cases of Koresh and Teacher Chen, Asahara's unprecedented insight into the Scriptures is founded on his religious experience. The enlightenment that Asahara experienced in the Himalayas in 1986 was followed on October 23, 1991, by an experience of complete comprehension of the message of the New Testament.[67] As a result, Asahara became convinced that Jesus' teaching and that of "original Buddhism" were identical.[68] In addition, he came to believe that the prophecies of

Nostradamus also harmonized perfectly with the prophecies of Revelation.[69]

What held together Asahara's eclectic collection of prophetic sources was his status as an inspired and authoritative interpreter of religious traditions and the world in general. Buttressing his special insight was what he claimed to be his extraordinary track record; Asahara confidently proclaimed that "almost everything that I have prophesied has come true" and answered the question of whether there was any other religious figure who could make the same claim with a resounding "no."[70]

What Asahara saw so clearly was only generally connected to the text of Revelation. Despite occasional forays into specific contemporizing interpretations,[71] he was most concerned to predict the imminent arrival of Armageddon. Over the course of his public preaching, Asahara relentlessly moved the date of the end closer to his present—from 2005, to 2000, to 1999, to 1997, to 1995.[72] Revelation gave Asahara a vivid language to describe the death throes of our current civilization, but it did not occupy the center of his preaching or much exercise whatever interpretive ingenuity he had. As did the seven seals for Teacher Chen, Revelation provided Asahara with a ready-made template that could impose narrative coherence on the chaotic world events that would both signal and accomplish the end of the world as we know it.

As Asahara's vision of the end left behind the idyllic Buddhist paradise of Shambala and as he and his followers perceived themselves to be victims of growing government and social oppression, the dark imagery of the battle of Armageddon became progressively more attractive to him. In fact, it seems likely that from 1993 on, Asahara and his followers crossed the line from passively expecting Armageddon to actively attempting to bring it about. As Ian Reader reports, the court case against some of those involved in the attack on the Tokyo subways alleges that "one intention of manufacturing the gas was to fit in with these prophecies [about Armageddon], and another was to encourage the destabilisation required to bring about Armageddon."[73] Revelation thus provided Asahara with a generalized portrait of the imminent violent overthrow of the current world order. Its drama and comprehensiveness rather than any specific details, such as the opening of the seven seals, suited the situation in which he and his followers became more deeply involved, as they put themselves on a "war-footing" against the rest of Japanese society.[74]

CONCLUSION

The use of the book of Revelation by some new religious movements to express their millennial visions is only a part of a much more complicated story of the complex symbiotic relationship between those groups and the broad biblical tradition.[75] It is striking that the interpretive strategies that new religions bring to the biblical text can in no way be identified as idiosyncratically "cultic,"as opposed to the interpretive strategies of "mainstream" religions. The means by which individuals establish themselves as authoritative interpreters of the textual tradition, the actual texts that they choose to interpret, the exegetical schemes that they employ in the act of interpretation, and the specific results that are produced by their readings of the texts all have multiple parallels and predecessors within the mainstream religions that locate themselves within the biblical tradition. Although many new religious movements are widely seen to be illegitimate in some way, the exegetical work that they do differs so little, in both theory and practice, from what religious groups, granted broad legitimacy by their host societies, actually do that the entire relationship between new religions and the mainstream needs to be rethought in a way that emphasizes the similarities, as well as the differences, between newer and more established religions.[76]

Specifically within the millennial tradition, new religions not only borrow the notion of an imminent apocalypse, but they also appeal to a time honored descriptive scenario of the last days, traditionally sanctioned roles that will be fulfilled in the end-times drama, classic sources of interpretive authority, such as the heavenly ascent, and well-worn exegetical devices for deriving contemporary meaning from ancient texts. They use a millennial vernacular that flows easily across religious, cultural, and social boundaries. When new religious movements like Chen Tao, Heaven's Gate, and Aum Shinrikyo borrow elements of the apocalypse from the book of Revelation, they are striving also to borrow the power and authority inherent in the text and turn them to their own advantage. As prophetic interpreters, Teacher Chen, Do, and Shoko Asahara each conceived and elaborated a vision of the imminent end; in order for their visions to become something more than personal fantasies, they had to promulgate them in such a way that they made sense to and could be acted upon by potential believers. Each developed a thoroughly eclectic and idiosyncratic system, but ties to the biblical apocalyptic tradition played an important role in each. Their experience lends support to the suspicion that for any millennial movement to succeed in a world influenced by the biblical tradition, it must develop a way of making that tradition distinctively its own.

NOTES

[1]There are relatively few systematic treatments of this topic in the literature about new religious movements, in part because much of it has been written by sociologists of religion. See, however, Stephen J. Stein, "America's Bibles: Canon, Commentary, and Community," *Church History* 64 (1995):169-84. See also Eugene V. Gallagher, "'Not Yours, Ours': Transformations of the Hebrew Bible in New Religious Movements," in *Sacred Text, Secular Times: The Hebrew Bible in the Modern World* (L. Greenspoon and B. LeBeau, eds.; Omaha: Creighton University Press, 2000), 87-102.

[2]On "cults" and new religions in general, see Timothy Miller, ed., *America's Alternative Religions* (Albany: SUNY Press, 1995) and Rodney Stark and William Sims Bainbridge, *The Future of Religion: Secularization, Revival, and Cult Formation* (Berkeley: University of California Press, 1985).

[3]See Jan Shipps, *Mormonism: The Story of a New Religious Tradition* (Urbana: University of Illinois Press, 1985), 53: "The past is a matter of fundamental importance to new religious movements. The assertions on which they rest inevitably alter the prevailing understanding of what has gone before, creating situations in which past and future must both be made new."

[4]In *What is Scripture? A Comparative Approach* (Minneapolis: Fortress, 1993), W. C. Smith observes that the study of scriptures and scriptural interpretation in new religious movements is an interesting topic, but one that he can not take up (210). See also Frederick M. Denny and Rodney Taylor, eds., *The Holy Book in Comparative Perspective* (Columbia: University of South Carolina Press, 1985); William A. Graham, *Beyond the Written Word: Oral Aspects of Scripture in the History of Religion* (Cambridge: Cambridge University Press, 1987); Miriam Levering, ed., *Rethinking Scripture: Essays from a Comparative Perspective* (Albany: SUNY Press, 1989).

[5]For a discussion of terms like "premillennialism" and "postmillennialism" and the suggestion of some cogent alternatives to them, see Catherine Wessinger, "Millennialism With and Without the Mayhem," in *Millennium, Messiahs, and Mayhem: Contemporary Apocalyptic Movements* (Thomas Robbins & Susan J. Palmer, eds.; New York: Routledge, 1997), 47-59. Wessinger observes that "premillennialism is used by scholars to denote a pessimistic expectation of universal catastrophe caused by divine intervention to destroy the world as we know it and then subsequently to establish the millennial salvation" (49). See also Wessinger, *How the Millennium Comes Violently* (New York: Seven Bridges, 2000).

[6]Hal Lindsey, *There's a New World Coming* (Eugene: Harvest House, 1984, updated edition), 7; see 13. The paperback's front cover notes that over two million

copies of the book are in print.

[7]Hal Lindsey, *The Late Great Planet Earth* (Grand Rapids: Zondervan, 1970), 8.

[8]Representing the contemporary scholarly reading of Revelation, Adela Yarbro Collins has observed: "The most fundamental problem with the premillennial interpretation of Revelation as represented by Lindsey . . . is its failure to appreciate the historical character of the Bible." See Adela Yarbro Collins, "Reading the Book of Revelation in the Twentieth Century" *Interpretation* 40 (1986): 229-42, quotation from 233. See also her *Crisis and Catharsis: The Power of the Apocalypse* (Philadelphia: Westminster, 1984). Although Lindsey might well counter that his reading is preeminently historical since Revelation was designed to recount contemporary history, he does pay little attention to the original historical setting of the first century document. He is joined in this ahistorical reading of Revelation by many millennialists outside the Christian tradition who use Revelation as a source.

[9]Hal Lindsey, *The Apocalypse Code* (Eugene: Harvest House, 1997), 30.

[10]Lindsey, *There's a New World Coming*, 6. See Lindsey, *The Late Great Planet Earth*, 20.

[11]Lindsey, *The Apocalypse Code*, 67; see 31, 36, 233; see also Lindsey, *There's a New World Coming*, 12-13.

[12]Lindsey, *The Apocalypse Code*, 136. On the motif of heavenly ascent in Greco-Roman antiquity see James D. Tabor, *Things Unutterable: Paul's Ascent to Paradise in its Greco-Roman, Judaic, and Early Christian Contexts* (Lanham: University Press of America, 1986).

[13]Lindsey, *The Apocalypse Code*, 72.

[14]Lindsey, *The Apocalypse Code*, 167-68.

[15]See Lindsey, *The Apocalypse Code*, 126, 263, and, especially, Lindsey, *The Late Great Planet Earth*, 50.

[16]See Stephen D. O'Leary, *Arguing the Apocalypse: A Theory of Millennial Rhetoric* (New York: Oxford University Press, 1994), 156; Lindsey, *The Apocalypse Code*, 283.

[17]One prominent adjustment is Lindsey's backing away from specifying a date for the end. In *The Late Great Planet Earth* (1970), he confidently predicted that "within forty years or so of 1948, all these things could take place" (54). In *The Apocalypse Code* (1997), written some years after 1988, Lindsey avoids any specific references to dates, while still trying to maintain apocalyptic expectations. He states, for example, that "this generation of believers has an opportunity to be blessed even more. For we are the generation that is going to see the sudden rending of the clouds and hear the Son of God shout, 'Come up here'" (283).

[18]See Lindsey, *The Apocalypse Code*, 279; Lindsey, *The Late Great Planet Earth*, 186-8.

[19]Toward the end of 1999, there were over 35 million copies of Lindsey's *The Late Great Planet Earth* in print; see Chris Hall, "What Hal Lindsey Taught Me About the Second Coming," *Christianity Today* (October 25, 1999): 82.

[20]On Koresh in general and on the "Waco" incident, see James D. Tabor and Eugene V. Gallagher, *Why Waco? Cults and the Battle for Religious Freedom in America* (Berkeley: University of California Press, 1995).

[21]For David Koresh's unfinished manuscript on the seven seals of the book of Revelation see Tabor and Gallagher, *Why Waco*,189-211; quotation from 197.

[22]Negotiation tape 231, April 15, 1993: 25.

[23]Howell, "Vernon's Dream," 1989. Transcripts of several of Koresh's oral Bible Studies and other communications are available from Mark Swett's electronic archive at http://home.maine.rr.com/waco. All Bible Studies referred to in this essay have been taken from that source. In August, 1990, Vernon Wayne Howell petitioned the court in Pomona, California, for a legal change of his name to David Koresh. He took his new first name from the ancient king of Israel and his new surname from the Hebrew form of the name of the Persian King Cyrus, who was hailed by the prophet Isa as a "messiah" for releasing the Jews from the Babylonian captivity (see Isaiah 45). Writings before August, 1990, will be attributed to Howell and those after will be attributed to Koresh.

[24]Tape 57, March 5, 1993: 30.

[25]See Vernon W. Howell (David Koresh), "Study on Joel and Daniel 11" (1987). See also negotiation tape 26, March 3, 1993: "We will serve and believe God and contend on a foundation of doctrine, in the fear of God, as light opens and as doctrine is properly weighed and measured, being systematically harmonized with scripture, text, chapter, took, then we develop an infallible, conclusive picture of what God's will is. Not just a little verse here, not just a little verse there. No. The content must be complete" (12-13).

[26]See negotiation tape 227, April 15, 1993: 37.

[27]See negotiation tape 27, March 3, 1993:25-29.

[28]See, for example, his comment on negotiation tape 218, April 13, 1993: "There's 150 psalms and every psalm is connected 100 percent to that vision of Revelation 4 and 5" (29).

[29]The Branch Davidians' home and church took its name from the story in 1 Kgs 18:1-46, wherein the prophet Elijah demonstrates the reality and power of God and the truth of his prophecy in a contest with the prophets of Baal. For the residents of Mount Carmel, the persistence of their community demonstrated the truth of David Koresh's prophecy.

[30]Steve Schneider on negotiation tape 129, March 15, 1993: 43.

[31]On the history of the Davidian and Branch Davidian communities, see Tabor and Gallagher, *Why Waco?*, 33-43.

[32]For background on Chen Tao, see Charles Houston Prather, "God's Salvation Church: Past Present and Future," *Marburg Journal of Religion* 4 (July 1999), available at http://www.uni-marburg.de/fb11/religionswissenschaft/journal/mjr/prather.html. See also Wessinger, *How the Millennium*, 253-63.

[33]"Transcript of Chen Tao's March 12, 1998, Press Conference in Garland, TX," 4; available at http://www.watchman.org/chentranscript.htm. Sentence and verb

form slightly altered to improve intelligibility of the English.

[34]God–The Supreme Being (Hon-Ming Chen), *God's Descending in Clouds (Flying Saucers) on Earth to Save People* (Garland: privately published, 1997), 10. The text explicitly names God as its author on ii, although it becomes clear that Teacher Chen is the vehicle through which God is communicating. I will list the text as Chen, *God's Descending,* hereafter and retain its peculiarities of English style.

[35]Chen, *God's Descending,* 60.

[36]*Ibid.,* 125.

[37]*Ibid.,* 123.

[38]*Ibid.,* 128.

[39]*Ibid.,* 125.

[40]*Ibid.,* 68.

[41]*Ibid.,* 70; see also 63, 64, and 71.

[42]*Ibid.,* 123. The interpretive strategy of excising ideologically incompatible sections from the Bible goes back at least to Marcion, in the second century CE, who attempted to purge the text of perceived Jewish interpolations. On Marcion, see R. Joseph Hoffman, *Marcion: On the Restitution of Christianity: An Essay on the Development of Radical Paulinist Theology in the Second Century* (Chico, CA: Scholars Press, 1984). For a glimpse into similar interpretive strategies in Gnostic exegesis in the early Christian period, see Elaine Pagels, *The Gnostic Paul: Gnostic Exegesis of the Pauline Letters* (Philadelphia: Fortress, 1975); Pagels, *The Gnostic Gospels* (New York: Random House, 1979); and Pagels, *Adam, Eve, and the Serpent* (New York: Vintage, 1988).

[43]Chen, *God's Descending,* 122. I have altered the obvious typographical error of "form" to "from" for ease of reading.

[44]*Ibid.*

[45]*Ibid.,* 131.

[46]For example, see *ibid.,* 133: "the first plague done by heavenly devil kings in 1999—the opening of the seventh seal. After the floods of 'Noah's Arc' in June and July of 1999, one third of the world will be involved in the turbulence of wars and battles in August."

[47]Ray Stedman, as quoted in Paul Boyer, *When Time Shall Be No More: Prophecy Belief in Modern American Culture* (Cambridge: Harvard University Press, 1992), 238.

[48]*Ibid.,* 48.

[49]The failure of Teacher Chen's prophecies led many of his followers to abandon him; a handful remain with him in Lockport, New York, where they moved in May 1998. A group later moved to Brooklyn, New York, to set up a "counseling center," which operates in Central Park. For updates, see the "Chen Tao Watch Page" on CESNUR's web site: www.cesnur.org.

[50]See Representatives from the Kingdom of Heaven, eds., *How and When "Heaven's Gate" (The Door to the Physical Kingdom Level Above Human) May Be Entered* (New Mexico Republic: privately published, 1996), Addendum 1-2, 8, 9. Pages within

the individual sections of the anthology are numbered consecutively; references will be given to the section and page. Hereafter the text will be abbreviated as *"Heaven's Gate."* See also Wessinger, *How the Millennium,*229-52; John R. Hall, with Philip D. Schuyler and Sylvaine Trinh, *Apocalypse Observed: Religious Movements and Violence in North America, Europe, and Japan* (New York: Routledge, 2000),149-82.

[51]See *"Heaven's Gate,"*1-7, 4-8, 4-85, 6-13, 1-14, 1-29, Addendum 1-10.

[52]*Ibid.*, iv, 4-6.

[53]*Ibid.*, B-1.

[54]*Ibid.*, x. "Students" in the Heaven's Gate "classroom" all took new names ending in "-ody."

[55]*Ibid.*, 3-6.

[56]*Ibid.*, 4-9.

[57]See Tabor and Gallagher, *Why Waco*, 55-7.

[58]*Ibid.*, 3-3.

[59]*Ibid.*, 3-4f.

[60]*Ibid.*, 3-4.

[61]*Ibid.*

[62]*Ibid.*, 3-5.

[63]See Ian Reader, *A Poisonous Cocktail? Aum Shinrikyo's Path to Violence* (Copenhagen: Nordic Institute of Asian Studies, 1996),43, 46: D. W. Brackett, *Holy Terror: Armageddon in Tokyo* (New York: Weatherhill, 1996),75, 95, 98.

[64]Shoko Asahara, "Heading for Catastrophe" (1990), as quoted in David E. Kaplan & Andrew Marshall, *The Cult at the End of the World: The Terrifying Story of the Aum Doomsday Cult, from the Subways of Tokyo to the Nuclear Arsenals of Russia* (New York: Crown, 1996),48f.

[65]Asahara, "Buddhism Encompasses Christianity: Transcend Yourself and Become a God!" (October 3, 1991), available at http://www.aum-shinrikyo.com/english/teaching/buddhism.htm.

[66]Asahara, *Declaring Myself the Christ: Disclosing the True Meanings of Jesus Christ's Gospel* (Shizuoka, Japan: Aum Publishing, 1992), 16.

[67]*Ibid.*, vii.

[68]*Ibid.*, 141. See also Asahara, "Buddhism Encompasses Christianity" (October, 1991); see also Wessinger, *How the Millennium,*120-57; Hall, et al., *Apocalypse Observed*, 76-110.

[69]See Asahara, "In Order to Overcome Catastrophy" (1992?), available at http://www.aum-shinrikyo.com/english/teaching/catastrophy.htm.

[70]See Asahara, "World War III is Coming Soon! The Control of Plasma" (April 10, 1993), available at http://www.aum-shinrikyo.com/english/teaching/plasma.htm.

[71]See Asahara, *Shoko Asahara's Horrifying Prediction: A Doom is Nearing the Land of the Rising Sun* (Shiauoka, Japan, AUM Publishing, 1995), 77; Kaplan & Marshall, *The Cult at the End of the World*: "'I believe that in the end a giant laser gun will be

developed.' Asahara preached in 1993. 'When the power of this laser is increased, a perfectly white belt, or sword, can be seen. This is the sword referred to in the Book of Revelations'" (207).

[72]See Reader, *Poisonous Cocktail*, 63; Brackett, *Holy Terror*, 75-76.

[73]Reader, *Poisonous Cocktail*, 72; see 89, 96. See also Reader, *Religious Violence in Contemporary Japan: The Case of Aum Shinrikyo* (Richmond, UK: Curzon Press, 2000); Robert Jay Lifton, *Destroying the World to Save It: Aum Shinrikyo, apocalyptic violence, and the New Global Terrorism* (New York: Henry Holt, 1999), both of which appeared after the work on this essay was completed.

[74]*Ibid.*, 89.

[75]For a detailed account of how one new religious movement appropriated the biblical tradition, see Jan Shipps, *Mormonism: The Story of a New Religious Tradition* (Urbana: University of Illinois Press, 1985).

[76]See Gallagher, "'Not Yours, Ours.'"

Atomic Bomb Cinema:
Judaism, the Apocalyptic Narrative Tradition, and Western Culture at the Dawn of the New Millennium

Jerome F. Shapiro

INTRODUCTION

Any successful discussion of popular films about the atomic bomb, the apocalypse, the millennium, or Judaism and other religions requires an appreciation for the mysterious power of ancient symbols and narratives in contemporary daily life. In order to illustrate this particular point, let us consider one film that is quite distant from the other films that I will be discussing. Frank Capra's 1939 film, *Mr. Smith Goes to Washington*, remains one of the most popular American films. Mr. Smith is appointed to the Senate as a dupe for a powerful business interest. Eventually Mr. Smith becomes wise to his situation and tries to expose corruption among his fellow senators, but is himself framed for corruption. The end of the film, despite its maudlin sentimentality, is particularly moving. During his defense, Mr. Smith collapses, the real villain reveals himself, everyone in the Senate chamber goes wild with joy, and the collapsed Mr. Smith is carried off the floor of the Senate in the loving arms of his admirers. What makes this finale so moving is not simply the narrative retelling of American myths about the relationship between the individual and the polity or how any American can change society, but that the hero sacrifices himself so all others can be absolved, so to speak, of their sins. In fact, that final image— Mr. Smith being carried away—is a *pietà*, a genre of painting depicting the disciples taking Christ down from his cross. In other words, ancient symbols, imagery, and narratives, continue to affect and influence us, even, or especially, when we are unaware of their presence.

Those who seriously study religion, as believers or scholars or both, know the power and importance of ancient symbols and narratives. At the

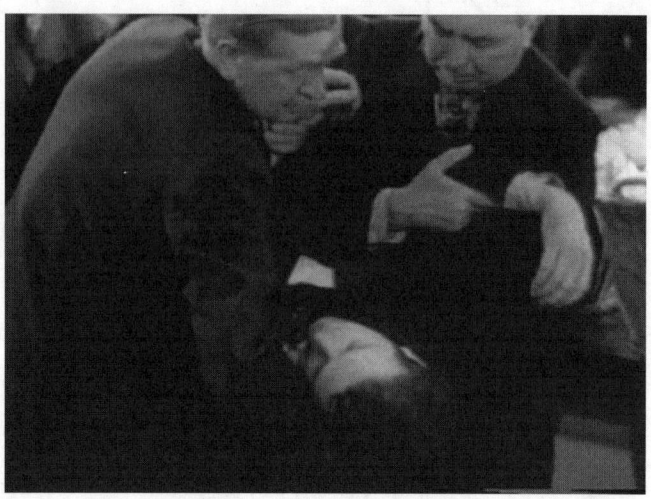

Mr. Smith Goes to Washington

same time, there is the danger that our studies of religion, Judaism in particular, inure us to the power of symbols and stories, that we begin to see symbols and stories only as petrified oddities from our past or as fugitive alien survivors in our present. These symbols and storytelling structures are especially powerful in what are often derogatorily referred to as "popular" films. As Robert Warshow so convincingly pointed out some thirty years ago, we cannot possibly hope to understand any expressive form, especially a popular art form, unless we begin by understanding our own "immediate experience."[1]

In what follows, I will briefly describe the major ideas and elements of both the apocalypse and films about the atomic bomb. Then I will describe scenes from several key films and provide brief summaries of my interpretations of them. In explaining the continuing importance of ancient symbols and narrative traditions in these popular films, I will highlight four points: first, and most important, Judaism is a vital and influential force in contemporary society; therefore, there needs to be what Daniel Boyarin calls a "revoicing of a Jewish discourse in the discourse of the West."[2] Second, cinema is the most eloquent contemporary voice or poetry for our most ancient narrative and symbolic traditions. Third, popular films about the bomb are the most recent manifestation of the apocalyptic narrative tradition; and, in Japanese films, we find a similar tradition, what I call the restoration of harmony and balance. Fourth, popular films, or at least bomb films, are a vital, healthy part our cultures and societies.

ATOMIC BOMB CINEMA: AN OVERVIEW

Countless films merely mention the bomb. In Atomic Bomb Cinema, the bomb becomes an explicit part of its visual setting, theme, context, or narrative. "The bomb" includes nuclear-related weapons, fallout, toxic poisoning, terrorism, and the anxieties these induce.[3] Between 1945 and 1998 more than seven hundred bomb films were released in the United States. On average, that works out to about thirteen each year. The first film depicting a nuclear technology is the 1914 film, *By Radium Rays.* The earliest film that is still widely circulated is a 1935 serial that was compiled into a feature-length film, *The Phantom Empire* (or *Radio Ranch*). Starring Gene Autry, it is nothing less than a Sci-Fi-Western.

Most bomb films are popular, profitable, and often critical successes. Nevertheless, they have been all but ignored by scholars, and when not ignored, grossly mischaracterized. Bomb films are bound together by not one but many recurring mythological, historical, and contemporary themes, and by many narrative or storytelling traditions. In my opinion, the single most important theme in the American Atomic Bomb Cinema is what John J. Collins calls "the Apocalyptic Imagination, the Jewish Matrix of Christianity."[4]

The apocalypse holds out the promise of what Melvin Lasky calls a "revolution" or return to a prior and pristine state.[5] At the same time, this state is new and different, the locus of spiritual rebirth. In Greek, the word *apokalypsis* means "revelation." As interpreted by David Miller, the word suggests disclosing or uncovering something, "especially as in a dream or vision."[6] In this concept, humans are bound to a world for which the forces of good and evil struggle, and are caught up in a preordained history that concludes with eschatological judgment. Collins states that the "genre is not constituted by one or more distinctive themes but by a distinctive combination of elements, all of which are also found elsewhere."[7] These elements are woven into recognizable narrative patterns in which the central character takes a spatial or temporal journey, history is recounted and foretold, a cosmological plan is revealed to the character and interpreted, and the character returns to exhort others to live in accordance with the revealed plan.[8] To this list of elements, I would add the Jewish tradition of *Tikkun Olam,* a commitment to repairing or restoring a fractured world— no matter how impossible the task.

Apocalyptic narratives use the language and symbolic imagery of poetry to encourage survival and self-actualization, evoke mystical knowledge, or criticize social conditions. As Collins shows, once we understand the formal framework of the genre, we can begin to explore its sociological, literary, or psychological contexts and functions.[9] Thus, it is wrong to think of bomb films as representations of some nuclear reality or to criticize them for their lack of verisimilitude either to a strategic reality or our fantasies about the aftermath of a nuclear war. Rather, these films must be acknowledged for what they are, a fictional form that attempts to give voice through symbol and metaphor to feelings and experiences. While other scholars see these films as evidence of psychopathology, psychic numbing, nuclearism, or bi-polar cycles of paranoia,[10] I see them rather as fulfilling the vital and healthy role of all apocalyptic literature. They are expressions of a culture struggling to find a way to make troubling events meaningful, exhort the viewer to survive and self-actualize under oppressive conditions, and criticize contemporary social conditions.

Let us now consider several key films that exemplify the narrative and visual potentials of the apocalypse and the millennium in Atomic Bomb Cinema.

KEY FILMS

The Beginning or the End (Norman Taurog, 1947) is the first film to explore the cosmological importance of the atomic bomb. While Matthew Cochran is preparing the Little Boy nuclear weapon, he dies from accidental radiation poisoning. In the final scene, he reappears as a supernatural being while his pregnant wife is reading his last letter, in which he recounts history and interprets a revelation about the future. This film is not, however, a true apocalypse: the crisis has passed and humanity has survived its most difficult test. A glorious heaven on earth is within grasp.

Them! (Gordon Douglas, 1954) is one of the most important films from the period when the Soviet Union first acquired the bomb. America lost its imagined nuclear monopoly, a new crisis appeared on the horizon, and Atomic Bomb Cinema went into high gear.[11] At the film's conclusion, Dr. Harold Medford predicts with an air of fear, or at least uncertainty, that with the atomic bomb humanity has entered "a new age." This new age includes rapid socio-cultural, technological, and even biological changes. For example, the film clearly supports Dr. Patricia Medford's insistence that as a scientist she should be treated as a professional, and not a "woman." *Them!* is also loaded with religious symbolism. The film begins, for example, with the image of Joshua Trees. The name Joshua is of obvious importance to both Judaism and Christianity. The Joshua Tree is also the Tree of Life.[12] Standing next to the carcass of a ten foot long ant, an elderly

The Beginning or the End, 1947

Them! 1947

The Incredible Shrinking Man, 1957

· *On the Beach*, 1959

Dr. Harold Medford later says, "We may be witness to a biblical prophecy come true: 'And there shall be destruction and darkness come upon creation and the Beasts shall reign over the Earth.'" While this prophecy does not come from a specific biblical passage, the general apocalyptic tone suggests the books of Daniel and Revelation.

The Bible is a real and living part of many Americans' lives. Nonetheless, most critics and scholars who write on *Them!* are openly contemptuous of the film's religiosity. This is, as Peter Clecak describes it in *America's Quest for the Ideal Self*, part of a general pattern of antagonism toward religion, particularly evangelical and neo-Pentecostal religions.[13] Initially, at least, we must put aside our own prejudices and try to make sense of the narrative and symbolism within the context of the film itself. Like the Sword of Saint Michael driving Adam and Eve out of Eden, the bomb drives humanity out of its innocence and into a new and frightening world of rapid biological and social change. *Them!* is important because it creatively reworks many elements into a visual apocalyptic text that is meaningful to modern, secular audiences. *Them!* clearly warns us that science has engendered a future crisis.

Jack Arnold's most famous film, *The Incredible Shrinking Man*, appeared in 1957. The film's hero, Robert Scott Carey, begins to shrink after being exposed to insecticide and radiation. Carey takes an otherworldly journey during which, like Odysseus, he is almost drawn into Charybdis (the whirlpool) and nearly drowned. Later, Carey battles a spider for his very survival. The journey ends when he passes through a screen that creates cross-like shadows in the background, after which he sees the moon. These images are religious, alchemical, and mythological symbols of psychic transformation.[14] Physicists Niels Bohr and J. Robert Oppenheimer asserted that the bomb is an essential part of humanity's development and that the bomb has a "complementary" nature that will either destroy or save the world.[15] In *The Incredible Shrinking Man*, the bomb sends an ordinary person on an otherworldly journey for mystical knowledge of self, human nature, and the cosmos. In apocalyptic texts, mystical knowledge empowers the powerless by teaching how to transcend oppressive conditions and prevail over evil.

On the Beach, Stanley Kramer's 1959 film, is oxymoronically praised as an apocalyptic bomb film about the annihilation of humanity, which is antithetical to the apocalyptic imagination. The film takes place after a brief nuclear war and before radiation has swept the globe killing everything. Most of the narrative takes place in Australia, where an American submarine captain falls in love with a local woman, Moria. Leaving Moria behind, the Captain elects to return home with his crew, to die along side his already dead wife and children. The narrative suggests that everyone dies. But, where there is a camera, there is a camera operator and a narrative that continues. In the final scene the camera records Moira's gaze, showing that she, at least, survives to repent and pine her unrequited love. Through clever editing techniques, the camera moves as though following Moira's gaze, going beneath the water as the submarine dives, only to resurface in a lifeless Australian city and focus on a sign that warns: "THERE IS STILL TIME BROTHER." Time for what? *On the Beach* has all the elements common to the genre of 1940s women's films known as "weepies," including what Mary Ann Doane describes as women who desire to desire.[16] Redemption, or at least some sense of satisfaction in life, is beyond Moira's grasp; for, as she notes, she missed her opportunity for happiness through marriage and family.

Whether one identifies with Moira's gaze or the camera itself, the spectators experience continuance because moral exempla beg for rejuvenation (like catharsis in Greek tragedy). That is to say, from a narrative that ends in universal annihilation, the cinematic structure of *On the Beach* recovers the apocalyptic promise of continuance beyond the nuclear holocaust. Although *On the Beach* does not describe an otherworldly journey or revelation, in accordance with the apocalyptic imagination the film does fulfill the audience's need or desire for the experience of having survived nuclear annihilation. The film also exhorts the audience to righteousness through its treatment of Moira. Like Horatio at the end of *Hamlet*, the camera survives to carry the warning message. The cinematic structure reassures the audience that surviving a nuclear war is possible. This suggests that the apocalyptic imagination shapes formal cinematic structures as well as narrative.

The Time Machine (George Pal, 1960) is one of the seminal apocalyptic bomb films. Peter Clecak, in *America's Quest for the Ideal Self*, shows that America is driven by three themes, what he names the quests for social justice, a community of like-minded others, and personal fulfillment.[17] In *The Time Machine*, H. G. Wells travels to a future where he witnesses a nuclear war, the volcanic purging of the earth, and the rebirth of humanity. Following a nuclear war, some survivors, the Morlocks, go underground where they degenerate into cannibals and raise and feed on the Eloi, the blonde-haired, blue-eyed descendants of those survivors who remained above ground. The docile Eloi now live in a veritable Garden of Eden. Wells takes

The Time Machine, 1960

it upon himself to destroy the Morlocks and, in effect, drive the Eloi out of their Edenic lifestyle. Wells returns to his own time and reveals his journey to his own people, but, like Cassandra, no one believes him. He then returns to the future to rebuild a utopian society based on the principles of his time. In his own time, moreover, Wells cannot enter his married friend's home, but he does enter the Eloi's communal hall. In *The Time Machine*, nuclear war creates an apocalyptic rebirth of the world and fulfills Wells' three quests. The hall represents not merely social justice and community, but also personal fulfillment. The shape of the hall, the graphic designs on the floor, and the arrangement of the tables and chairs, (plus the rich harvest of fruit on the tables), create a mandala, the symbol of psychic completion.

Very few bomb films end with complete nuclear annihilation. In David Greene's 1982 television-movie *World War III*, the narrative ends just as people are looking up at incoming ICBMs. Such endings are only slightly more common in Japan. The closest equivalent to the apocalyptic imagination in Japan is the obscure *masse* tradition. *Masse*, however, describes the complete end of the world and the beginning of an entirely new world.[18] Muneyoshi Matsubayashi's 1961 film *Sekai Dai Senso* is a linear narrative. The film ends with a nuclear war that reduces peace-loving Japan to a molten rock and annihilates the world. A very different scenario concludes the American release of this film, *The Last War*. Since complete narrative closure is anathema to Western consciousness and the apocalyptic imagination, the American release was reedited into a feature-length flashback with voice-over narration. Like *On the Beach*, since the narrator has survived to recount the story to an audience, the spectator is reassured that humanity can survive nuclear war.

Non-Japanese scholars of Japanese bomb films, including the very perceptive Chon Noriega, generally err by imposing western interpretations on Japanese symbols. Inoshiro Honda's seminal 1954 film, *Gojira* (*Godzilla, King of the Monsters*, re-edited by Terry Morse in 1956) establishes that nuclear weapons tests in the Pacific Ocean awaken the prehistoric creature and give him atomic powers. In Honda's 1964 film *Mosura tai Gojira* (*Godzilla vs. the Thing*, or *Godzilla vs. Mothra*), both scheming entrepreneurs and Godzilla threaten one of Mothra's eggs. A woman reporter, two tiny women from Mothra Island, and Mothra herself lead the effort to rescue the egg. Eventually, two *yochu* or larvae hatch from the egg and encase Godzilla in a chrysalis. Godzilla then falls back into the sea from which he came.

Gojira, 1956

Noriega has argued that the Mothra films indicate latent Christianity in Japanese culture.[19] But how could there be latent Christianity with no Jews, almost no Christians, and no concept of sin?[20] In cultures throughout the world both deep water and the womb-like chrysalis are symbols of psychic transformation. In ancient Japanese legal and mythological texts, moreover, women are intimately linked with the silkworm (even today the

Japanese empress is the head of the silk culture). Balance and harmony are also extremely important concepts in Asian cultures. In these films, men have become too strong, and society is out of balance with nature. So nature retaliates: the feminine element asserts itself and transforms the masculine element in order to restore balance and harmony. These themes structure most of Japan's bomb films. And this restoration of balance and harmony mirrors the Jewish tradition of *Tikkun Olam*, repairing or restoring a fractured world.

A great deal has been written about *Dr. Strangelove, or: How I Learned To Stop Worrying and Love the Bomb* (Stanley Kubrick, 1964), and it is so well known that I will not summarize it here. I will simply note that in *The Apocalyptic Imagination*, Collins points out that the ironic or subversive use of a genre is a predictable phase in its development. *Dr. Strangelove* has many of the familiar elements of the apocalyptic genre: an otherworldly journey, the recounting and foretelling of history, revelations, revelations interpreted, and final judgments. The difference is that rather than the good Eloi, in *The Time Machine*, it is the Morlocks who survive the nuclear holocaust and inherit the earth. A twisted version of *Tikkun Olam* if ever there was one! In short, *Dr. Strangelove* is brilliant in its ironic and subversive use of the apocalyptic genre.

Humor, of course, is not uniquely Jewish, but "Jewish" humor is distinctive. Steve Lipman, in *Laughter in Hell: The Use of Humor during the Holocaust*, points out that the Old Testament, the Talmud, and the writings of Jewish sages are "seasoned with dashes of irony." And, in a 1941 Nazi camp, Rabbi Erich Weiner observed that Jews' subversive humor "strengthened their will to survive as well as infused their power to resist."[21] Jewish humor, in other words, is filled with the spirit of *Tikkun Olam,* for the will to resist and survive is ultimately the will to restore one's world. There is a strong connection between Jewish subversive humor, *Tikkun Olam*, and the apocalyptic imagination—at least in its ironic mode. *Dr. Strangelove* does not simply parody the social situation, but parodies our own desires for apocalypse as well. Thus, through subversive humor and self-reflexive use of the apocalyptic genre, *Dr. Strangelove* provides us with a fictional moment in which transcendence, mystical wisdom if you will, is possible. *Dr. Strangelove*, in other words, tapped a vein of brilliant subversive humor that has invigorated Atomic Bomb Cinema.

Scholars have frequently argued that films about the bomb disappeared in the 1970s.[22] This is clearly erroneous, for bomb films declined by only about thirty-three per cent, with a number of films from the 1970s that are worthy of discussion. One such film is *A Boy and His Dog*, (L. Q. Jones, 1975), based on a story by the award winning writer Harlan Ellison. The film takes place in the early twenty-first century, after World War IV, a nuclear war described as the solution to urban blight. The central characters are the "boy," Vic, and his partner, "Blood," a highly intelligent dog with telepathic abilities but no ability to hunt. A woman, Quilla June Holmes, lures the boy to a community beneath the planet's surface—an inverted vision of Disneyland's "Main Street USA," but with its authoritarian underbelly now ironically quite obvious. Living beneath the surface, sheltered from the sun, the males eventually become sterile, and the community periodically needs an infusion of fresh blood, so to speak. In fact, the community needs the boy's seed, which they take from him in a most unmanly way: they gag and bind him to a hospital table, connect him to a semen pump, and, just to ensure propriety, ceremonially marry him to all the eligible women. And, it seems obvious to the spectator that the boy is to be killed after all the women have been impregnated so the women can remarry other more eligible men from the community.

Rather than submit to marriage and pregnancy, the politically ambitious, self-serving, and very duplicitous Quilla helps the boy escape, and together they flee to the surface. Once on the surface, the boy discovers that the dog is near death from dehydration and starvation. The boy then sacrifices the girl in order to save the dog: he kills, cooks, and feeds her to the dog, then binds its wounds with her wedding dress. The apocalyptic elements in this film include an otherworldly journey, history recounted, the future foretold, a revelation and a revelation revealed ("down under" the boy learns what happens to those who fail to follow the proper path), final judgment, and an exhortation to righteousness. Ironic and even twisted though it may be, this is a film in which the bomb purifies the world of emasculating civilization and allows men to recover their true manhood through rugged individualism.

The sleeper, low budget hit of 1984 was *The Terminator* (James Cameron, 1984). The film at first appears to be a rather predictable science fiction story about a future in which a computer becomes self aware, then starts a nuclear war in an attempt to destroy all of humanity. *The Terminator* evokes a sense of the millennium by placing the story both in the present, 1984, and in the future, 2029, just after a new millennium has begun. More importantly, *The Terminator* takes us back to the heart of the apocalyptic imagination. The story uses many of the familiar elements of the apocalyptic genre. The heroine, Sarah J. Conner, takes an otherworldly journey. The future (her own future, in fact) is revealed to her, and Kyle Reese, who travels through time to protect her, interprets the revelation. Although Reese is not a supernatural being in the biblical sense, in our day his time travel accords him and his interpretation of the revelation a supernatural status. Sarah acquires mystical wisdom and strength from this revelation. She also gains the will to survive and self-actualize under oppressive conditions, and she makes a commitment to *Tikkun Olam*, repairing or restoring her fractured world. Disbelieving that she is the "mother of the future," she even pokes fun at her own inability to balance her checkbook— funny because, while balancing a checkbook is a basic "survival skill" in our time, in the future revealed to her, other skills will become even more important, such as destroying killer cyborgs—which she learns to do quite handily. *The Terminator* seems to incorporate other ancient narrative patterns as well, such as the *Sibylline Oracles*. The sibyls were powerful female prophets who influenced the politics of the their day; by the end of the film Sarah is clearly a powerful woman, and she is recording her own prophecies of events that will dramatically alter the course of global history.

Curiously, *The Terminator* divided the ranks of feminist film scholars and sparked a minor sub-genre of scholarly literature. Some argue that *The Terminator* is a mainstream film, others that it is at the very least a protofeminist film, and still others that it is actually quite reactionary and hostile to women.[23] What is intriguing about this debate is how some of these scholars use the Bible to support their arguments, yet limit their comparisons to the New Testament. Sarah's future son, who is destined to lead the humans in a successful rebellion against the genocidal supercomputer, is named John Conner. His initials, "J.C.," match those of Jesus Christ. In the critical literature it is assumed that Sarah is the "new Virgin Mary," the mother of the New Testament's Messiah.[24] However, no one has taken the time to consider Sarah J. Conner's relationship to her biblical namesake, the wife of Abraham and mother of Isaac, with whom God makes his covenant (Gen 17:19-21). Further, Jesus encouraged passive resistance, while John Connor leads a violent rebellion; John does not sacrifice himself in order to redeem the world; and, though Reese's time travel accords him a supernatural status, his love scene with Sarah entails no virgin birth. It is, therefore, difficult to maintain that John's mother is the "new Virgin Mary." The Old Testament's Sarah is the defender of her genealogy and "a mother of Nations" (17:16). Because God gave her a child at a very late age, Sarah complains to God that "everyone that heareth will laugh on account of me" (21:6). Likewise, in *The Terminator* Sarah is a mother of nations; she is laughed at for having been taken in by what others believe to be Reese's lunatic story of time travel. In the sequel, *Terminator 2: Judgment Day* (1991), she is not only laughed at but imprisoned for what others think is an insane belief in her child's extraordinary (not virgin) birth. In short, *The Terminator* is another brilliant example of how Atomic Bomb Cinema reformulates the apocalyptic narrative tradition into films that appeal to contemporary audiences.

Whenever people learn about my research, the first thing they ask is: "Have you seen *Dr. Strangelove* and the *Mad Max* films?" In fact, neither of the first two Mad Max or Road Warrior films, as they are called, make any narrative or visual references to nuclear technologies. However, the third film, *Mad Max Beyond Thunderdome* (1985, George Miller, George Ogilvie, Australia), does make reference to them. Having lost the vitality and energy of its initial impetus, this third film is consciously self-referential and intentionally ironic in subverting the clichés it helped establish, and uses references to cold war era slogans, fears of radioactive fallout, and Japanese ghost stories to embellish its already campy style. In *Mad Max Beyond Thunderdome*, Max, now a nomad traveling the dessert in a horse-drawn wagon, is robbed of everything he owns. He makes his way to Bartertown, where he becomes embroiled in a local power struggle. Eventually, Max is tied to a donkey and sent back into the dessert to die. Like Moses, however, he is rescued by a young woman who rafts him down a river to an oasis where her tribe of children live. The children mistake Max for their long missing benefactor who had promised to return them to the cities. The children "tell the tell" of nuclear war and last minute escape to the outback. Max, in a cynical attempt to remain cynical, tells them he is not their benefactor and refuses to help, thus setting off a chain of events that at last forces Max to fulfill his destiny. In the end, Max is not only the vehicle for the destruction of wickedness in Bartertown, but he also helps relocate the children to the promised land, the abandoned cities. Again, like Moses, Max is left behind as the tribe he leads crosses over into the land of milk and honey. But in the film's coda Max makes his way to the cities where the children now live. Unlike the Biblical story of Moses or the first two Mad Max films, *Mad Max Beyond Thunderdome* provides at least the possibility of a happy ending for the aging Max.

From its very beginning, *Mad Max Beyond Thunderdome* evokes the sense of an age having finally passed and of a new one dawning, but there is still one final, apocalyptic crisis to be overcome. The film exhorts us to survive and self-actualize during oppressive times by using an otherworldly journey, revelations, revelations interpreted, final judgment, *Tikkun Olam*, and the promise of a world reborn. Anyone who has participated in a Jewish Passover Seder should recognize Savannah's "take the tell." This "tell[ing] the tell" is a recounting of the community's past and a foretelling of the future, when they will return to their home in the city. Just as at each Seder Jews recount the Exodus and proclaim "Next year in Jerusalem," Savannah and her friends recount their history and long to go home. The Seder encourages children to see themselves as part of the Exodus. Likewise, at the end of *Mad Max Beyond Thunderdome*, Savannah asserts for the second time that her story is "the tell of us all" and that the newborn should learn their story.

Mad Max Beyond Thunderdome, 1985

One very significant film that incorporates a millennial revolution into a typical apocalyptic otherworldly journey is Terry Gilliam's highly unusual *The Adventures of Baron Munchausen* (1989). The central character, Sarah, goes on an otherworldly journey in order to save her city; she is filled with the spirit of *Tikkun Olam* and, like other Sarahs, defends her genealogy. She also defends her gender, eventually convincing her father to change the wording on his theater company's poster from "and Sons" to "and Daughter." More importantly, she is on a journey to gain mystical wisdom: the knowledge that a story is more than just a story and that the imagination can save worlds.[26] The film's crucial scene takes place on Mount Etna, during a tour of the Roman god Vulcan's munitions factory. Vulcan, as depicted here, is an arms merchant who is "willing to supply arms and equipment to anyone that's prepared to pay the price." In defense of his rather sordid vocation, he rhetorically asks: "It's not my fault if they're crazy enough to slaughter each other, is it?" Vulcan then shows his guests a weapon, calling it his "RX, ah, Intercontinental Radar Sneaky Multi-Warheaded Nuclear Missile," that simply kills "all" the enemy. When an astonished guest reproachfully asks, "Well, where's the fun in that?" Vulcan replies, in an allusion to *Dr. Strangelove*: "Oh, we cater to all sorts here. You'd be surprised." What is wonderful about this film is that Gilliam inverts all the usual narrative background and foregrounding structures. In particular, the one discussion about the bomb becomes the foreground rather than the background, thus creating a surreal critique of contemporary social conditions and helping to move the heroine toward the conclusion of her otherworldly journey and the lessons she must learn. *The Adventures of Baron Munchausen* criticizes the bomb as the perverse panicle of Enlightenment thinking, which can only be disarmed, so to speak, by rediscovering the power of imagination—especially the apocalyptic imagination.

Let us take a look at one other Japanese bomb film, *Rhapsody in August* (*Hachigatsu no Rapusodi*, Akira Kurosawa, 1991). Some critics have publicly stated that Akira Kurosawa must have been senile by the time he completed this film.[27] Such criticism completely overlooks the Japanese symbol systems used in films about age, aging, death, and the bomb. The story centers on an aged woman and her four children. Her husband was killed by the atomic bomb in Nagasaki, and she herself was exposed to radiation several days later. Now, nearly fifty years later, despite her outward displays of acceptance, she remains embittered by the experience. When at the end of the film this grandmother reconciles with her American nephew and lets go of her anger and hatred, balance and harmony appear to have been restored. However, in the final scene, the grandmother, apparently mad, rushes out into the storm. Her children and grandchildren follow her, but they stumble and fall as the elderly grandmother slowly makes her way in harmony with the winds. Suddenly her umbrella inverts. In the background we hear the voices of children singing Franz Peter Schubert's *Nobara*, or *The Wild Rose*, and the film ends as the image of the grandmother fades to black.

This last image suggests the conclusion to perhaps the most famous Kabuki play, *Shunkan*. Kabuki and other forms of Japanese theater build meaning through highly symbolic and evocative codified gestures. At the end of this particular play, the central character Shunkan is abandoned on a remote island. From a cliff, he watches his family sail away, back to the Japanese homeland. With one hand he clings to a pine tree, as he frantically waves good-bye with his other hand. Suddenly, the pine branch breaks. The pine is a symbol of life, and the breaking of the branch suggests that Shunkan's connection to life is broken and that he is making his way to the next world. Though subtle, the inverted umbrella at the end of *Rhapsody in August* evokes the gestural and symbolic end to the play *Shunkan*, and suggests that with balance and harmony restored to the world, the grandmother can at last make her way in peace to the next world.

Rhapsody in August, 1991

Waterworld (Kevin Reynolds, 1995) is the final film to which we turn our attention. It is, simply, a post-deluge story. The silent but noble hero, the Mariner, is forced on an adventure to save a young girl. This young girl has the map to salvation, called "Dryland," literally tattooed on her back. There are also the bad guys and the love story of a typical Hollywood film. *Waterworld* also openly copies and reuses scenes and narratives from many familiar films. Perhaps for these reasons it has been misunderstood and panned by critics and scholars alike. In my view, however, *Waterworld* is not a typical Hollywood film. Rather, it is a dramatic departure from almost every prior Hollywood film, and certainly any other bomb film.

Waterworld, 1995

The plot is rather simple. The Mariner visits a manmade atoll to trade. As in *A Boy and His Dog,* he is asked to impregnate a young girl in order to bring fresh blood to the community. When the Mariner declines, they discover he is a mutant and piously condemned him to be recycled as landfill. As in *The Road Warrior* (or *Mad Max II*), the atoll is attacked by a predatory horde known as the Smokers. The Smokers destroy the atoll in an attempt to capture Enola, the girl with the map of "Dryland" tattooed on her back. With the atoll under attack, Helen saves the Mariner in exchange for passage for herself and Enola. After many adventures and a final confrontation in which the Mariner destroys the Smokers, the Mariner realizes that the map is upside down. In a hot air balloon piloted by a rather scatter-brained old man, the Mariner, Helen, Enola, and Priam make their way to Dryland. A single seagull alights on their ship— this image nicely evokes the symbol of the dove with an olive branch in the story of Noah and his Ark (Gen 8:11) — announcing that land is near, the deluge is receding and there will be no more apocalypses (see God's covenant with Noah in Gen 9:11).[28] Once on land, Enola announces, "I'm home." All, needless to say, feel as though they are indeed home, except the Mariner, who must return to the sea.

Waterworld shows us a world so utterly changed that it seems to lack an environment; to a large degree the environment that remains is a limitless body of water. The very point of the film is a fictive exploration of what life would mean in an environment so completely ruined by humanity's carelessness that annihilation is all but a foregone conclusion. *Waterworld* cleverly gives almost no background to the story; it assumes that filmgoers are now so familiar with the post-nuclear survival sub-genre that we can easily fill in the details for ourselves. All we are told is that the story takes place centuries in the future and that "the ancients" (that is, us) have done something terrible that created a new deluge. Only later does the film, awkwardly, make clear the nuclear connection. Less obvious in *Waterworld* is the mosaic of social and mythological themes that makes this film such an important and intriguing example of Atomic Bomb Cinema.

As an apocalyptic text, *Waterworld* has all the essential elements: the unfolding of history, an otherworldly journey, final conflicts, judgments, an exhortation to righteousness, revelations and the interpretation of revelations, mystical knowledge gained, and the promise of rebirth beyond our present oppressive conditions. In the film we also find that the hero's resolution of his personal crisis, his anger and self-hate (at, perhaps, being a mutant), coincides with the resolution of the plot and the rebirth following the apocalypse. The bomb is of course the mechanism that brings about the desired apocalypse, but the bomb has become part of a broader concern with environmental issues. Irrespective of the reasons for the film's success or failures, *Waterworld* is a fascinating example of the apocalyptic tradition's power to communicate ideas and of the apocalyptic imagination's ability to adapt to and critically respond to changing socio-cultural conditions.

CONCLUSION

After watching hundreds of popular films about the bomb, I am convinced that bomb films are not evidence of widespread denial or global numbing to the world in which we live. I am convinced, furthermore, that Atomic Bomb Cinema contributes to the process by which people assimilate and understand the tremendous socio-cultural changes that are taking place, including how the bomb has changed our lives. In this sense, Atomic Bomb Cinema is a kind of poetry that speaks to the modern audience. Unfortunately, the cinema speaks in a poetic voice that many academics do not understand and may, in fact, denigrate. Perhaps, as Robert Sklar has pointed out, the popular cinema appeals and speaks to social groups that are in conflict with professional scholars and other elites who would impose their own cultural values on the larger society.[29]

In the fifty-five years since the first nuclear weapons were used in war, in the six years since *Waterworld* was released, and in the months since we passed into a new millennium, many more bomb films have been produced. During these decades the essentials of Atomic Bomb Cinema have not changed; nor, in the eons that have passed, have the essentials of the apocalyptic imagination and the apocalyptic genre. Despite all the current talk of modernism, postmodernism, the New Economy, and the new millennium, in the nearly six thousand years of Jewish history the world has not drastically changed either. Everywhere there is still suffering and oppression, and still a need for stories (in our time, moving pictures) that exhort us to survive, self-actualize, and repair or restore a fractured world.

ACKNOWLEDGMENTS

My colleague at Hiroshima University, Professor Michael Gorman, read a draft of this manuscript from beginning to end, and I wish to thank him for his many helpful suggestions and encouragement. I am indebted to H. Arthur Taussig, Professor of Film and Photography at Orange Coast College, Costa Mesa California, for his frequent comments and insights on film and culture. I am also indebted to Rabbi Mel Silverman, of Costa Mesa, California, for his critical reading of my writings and for his insights and suggestions, particularly regarding *Tikkun Olam*.

NOTES

Many of the images I discuss in this article, as well as others from bomb films and works of art not discussed here, are available on my website, www.atomicbombcinema.com.

[1]Robert Warshow, *The Immediate Experience: Movies, Comics, Theatre and Other Aspects of Popular Culture* (New York: Athenum, 1972).
[2]Daniel Boyarin, *Intertextuality and the Reading of Midrash* (Bloomington: Indiana University Press, 1994), xi.
[3]Two oft-cited films that mention the Bomb but are not "Bomb" films are *The Lady From Shanghai* (1948), and *Suddenly* (1954).
[4]John J. Collins, *The Apocalyptic Imagination: An Introduction to the Jewish Matrix of Christianity* (New York: Crossroad, 1989).
[5]Melvin J. Lasky, *Utopia and Revolution: On the Origins of a Metaphor, or Some Illustrations of the Problem of Political Temperament and Intellectual Climate and*

How Ideas, Ideas, and Ideologies Have Been Historically Related (Chicago: The University of Chicago Press, 1976).

[6]Collins, *The Apocalyptic Imagination*, 3. David Miller, "Chiliasm: Apocalyptic with a Thousand Faces," in *Facing Apocalypse* (ed. V. Andrews et al.; Dallas: Spring, 1987), 5.

[7]Collins, *ibid.*, 9.

[8]*Ibid.*, 1-32.

[9]*Ibid.*, 1-32, 205, 214.

[10]For example, see Donald Richie, "'*Mono No Aware*': Hiroshima in Film," in *Film: Book 2* (ed. R. Hughes; New York: Grove, 1962). Susan Sontag, "Imagination of Disaster," in *Against Interpretation* (New York: Farrar, Straus, and Giroux, 1967), 209-25. Robert J. Lifton, *Death in Life: Survivors of Hiroshima* (New York: Random House, 1967), 461-63, 570. Paul Boyer, *By the Bomb's Early Light: American Thought and Culture at the Dawn of the Atomic Age* (New York: Pantheon Books, 1985). Gar Alperovitz, *The Decision to Use the Atomic Bomb and the Architecture of an American Myth* (New York, Alfred A. Knopf, 1995). Robert J. Lifton and Greg Mitchell, *Hiroshima in America: Fifty Years of Denial* (New York: G. P. Putnam's Sons, 1995).

[11]In June 1946, according to historian Richard Rhodes (*The Making of the Atomic Bomb* [New York: Simon & Schuster, 1986], 736, 765), "The U.S. nuclear weapons stockpile consisted of only nine Fat Man bombs, of which no more than seven could be made operational for lack of initiators." By mid 1947, the number had increased to only thirteen bombs. Considering the size of the Soviet military at the end of the war (1.6 million Soviet troops were prepared to invade Japan alone!), it is unlikely that even under the most favorable conditions nuclear weapons could have decided a war with the USSR. One top-secret evaluation of the Strategic Air Offensive, dated May 11, 1949, notes that an "Atomic offensive would not, per se" win a war on Soviet territory: see Thomas H. Etzold and John Lewis Gaddis, eds., *Containment: Documents on American Policy and Strategy, 1945-1990* (New York: Columbia University Press, 1978), 362.

[12] J. E. Cirlot, *A Dictionary of Symbols* (2d ed.; ed. and trans. J. Sage; New York: Philosophical Library, 1971), 346-50.

[13]Peter Clecak, *America's Quest for the Ideal Self: Dissent and Fulfillment in the 60s and 70s* (Oxford University Press, New York, 1983), 138-39. For Clecak's fuller critique, see pages 135-44.

[14]George Ferguson, *Signs & Symbols in Christian Art* (New York: Oxford University Press, 1954), 45. Cirlot, *Dictionary of Symbols*, 214-18.

[15]Richard Rhodes, *The Making of the Atomic Bomb* (Simon & Schuster, Inc., 1986), 778, 787, 789.

[16]Mary Ann Doane, *The Desire to Desire: The Woman's Film of the 1940s* (Bloomington: Indiana University Press, 1987).

[17]Clecak, *America's Quest for the Ideal Self,* 6 -10.

[18]In Buddhist canons *masse* is an age of moral decadence, or in ancient times it also meant a retributive event that guides humanity. Today it just means the end of the world, a morally exhausted society, decadence (Shinmura Izuru, ed., *Kojiten* [3d ed; Tokyo: Iwanami Shoten, 1983], 2257). Rather than connoting rebirth and divine intervention, the battle of good and evil, *masse* simply denotes punishment for crimes rather than sin (for example, Professor Katsuhiko Takeda, of Waseda University, says Japan lacks the word and the concept for sin). *Masse* does not include a cosmological reorganization as we have come to know it; rather, the world ends and then something else takes its place. *Masse* does not appear to grip the Japanese imagination as the apocalypse does the Western imagination. It may also be that *masse* was used as an excuse for the decadence of the elite. According to Professor William R. LaFleur of the University of California, Los Angeles, at one time in history ancient nobility used the immanent end of the world to justify their extravagances (Tokyo, Japan, April 4, 1989).

[19]Chon Noriega, "Godzilla and the Japanese Nightmare: When *Them!* is U.S.," *Cinema Journal* 27:1 (Fall 1987): 63-77.

[20]Statistically, there are no Jews in Japan. According to *Nippon: The Land and Its People,* Christianity in Japan reached "its peak, in the early seventh century," was vigorously repressed during World War II, and strictly controlled during the Occupation (Tokyo: Nippon Steel Corporation, 1983, 257). Based on 1993 data, only 1.2% of the population is baptized as Christian. (Teruo Maruyama, ed., *"Shukyo"* [Religion], in *The Asahi Encyclopedia of Current Terms 1995* [Tokyo: Asahi Shimbun-Sha, 1995]: 329, 953.) Many Japanese Christians also continue to participate in Buddhist and Shinto practices. A large number of Japanese scholars argue, moreover, that Japan is a "shame" culture rather than a guilt or sin culture and that there is no word or concept for sin, only for crime.

[21]Steve Lipman, *Laughter in Hell: The Use of Humor during the Holocaust* (Northvale, New Jersey: Jason Aronson, Inc., 1993), 134-35, 153. The quotation by Rabbi Weiner comes from Ulrike Migdal, *Und die Musik spielt dazu: Chansons and Satiren aus dem KZ Theriesinstadt* (Munich: Piper, 1986), 24; cited by Lipman, 153.

[22]Boyer, *By the Bomb's Early Light,* 355, 356.

[23]See Constance Penley, "Time Travel, Primal Scene and the Critical Dystopia," *Fantasy and the Cinema,* ed., James Donald (London: British Film Institute, 1989), 196-212, first published in *Camera Obscura* 15 (1988). Margaret Goscilo, "Deconstructing *The Terminator,*" *Film Criticism* 22:2 (Winter 1987-88): 37-51. Lillian Necakov, "*The Terminator*: Beyond Classical Hollywood Narrative," *CineAction* 8 (March 1987): 84-87.

[24]Necakov, "*The Terminator*: Beyond Classical Hollywood Narrative," 86. Also see Goscilo, "Deconstructing *The Terminator,*" 48.

[25]As the Marxist critics Herbert Marcuse and Eric Fromm have pointed out, fantasy is an important part of social criticism. See, Peter Clecak, *Radical Paradoxes:*

Dilemmas of the American Left: 1945-1970 (New York: Harper and Row, 1973), 197. For an overview of Fromm, see Christopher F. Monte, *Beneath the Mask: An Introduction to Theories of Personality*, Second Edition (New York: Holt, Rinehart and Winston, 1980), 484-509.

[26]See, for example, David Desser, "*Madadayo*: No, Not Yet, for the Japanese Cinema," *Post Script* 18:1 (Fall 1998): 52-58.

[27]I am indebted to my student Caleb Bendix, in my class on Atomic Bomb Cinema, for pointing out this symbolic parallel to me (July 19, 2000).

[28]Robert Sklar, *Movie-Made America: A Cultural History of American Movies* (New York: Random House, 1975); and, "*Oh! Althusser!*: Historiography and the Rise of Cinema Studies," in *Resisting Images: Essays on Cinema and History* (ed. R. Sklar and C. Musser; Philadelphia: Temple University Press, 1990), 20-21.

The End of the World and *The X-Files*: The Dismemberment of Christian Millennialism in American Mass-Mediated Entertainment

Brenda E. Brasher

In Christian tradition, millennialism—the transformation of the world into a just and peaceful society—is a central component of the main story told about the end of time. In its definitive form, the story, which includes millennialism in its sweep, stretches throughout the biblical book of Revelation.[1] There it appears as the mystical vision of a prophet named John of Patmos (Rev 1:9). Against an assumed backdrop of Jewish apocalypticism, John describes a vision: a divine plan is at work in human history that includes a future time when a transcendent God will judge all (Rev 22:8-12). Where contemporary sociologists of religion employ "millennialism" to describe any belief in earthly redemption, for some Christians the term refers to an interval of universal peace and justice usually associated with this plan, during which Earth becomes the "Kingdom of God."[2] When used in this context, millennialism embraces a theological claim that history conforms to a transcendent design, even though that design is largely beyond human knowledge.

While millennialism is one element in the Revelation narrative about the cessation of time, in evangelical Christian theology the overarching story to which it contributes neither begins nor ends with a returning Jesus; rather millennialism is the penultimate element in a multi-faceted story of cosmological transfiguration. According to some evangelical theologians, when the millennium ends the denouement of Earth begins.[3] It includes an abbreviated re-entry of evil into the world, followed by its rapid defeat. This final defeat of evil unleashes a "reincursion of God's primal creative power,"[4] which, in turn, yields the ultimate conclusion of history: the transformation of all existence into a "new heaven and a new earth" (Rev

1:3).

Setting the history of earth in parallel with that of its Christian savior, Revelation indicates that there will be a resurrection of existence after the crucifixion of time, where finitude will be radically overwhelmed and ultimately subsumed into a new reality. After what Revelation describes as the second death by the lake of fire (Rev 20:14), death will be no more. A new heaven and a new earth will appear. The holy city, "the new Jerusalem," will descend (Rev 21:1-2). All things will be made new (Rev 21:5b). In the realm of contemporary literary theory, millennialism could be constructed as a divine postcolonial tale.[5] It depicts a period when humanity, whose actions occupy the center of biblical narratives from the introduction of Eve and Adam in Genesis 1, is finally marginalized and the divine Yahweh regains the center.

Terrifying images of destruction fly out of John's metaphoric vortex to create a destabilized landscape, yet one with a holy purpose. The fragile structure that holds this landscape together is a reoccurrence of sevens. They include seven trumpets, seven letters, seven plagues, three scrolls including one with seven seals, seven bowls, and a harlot seated on seven hills. Beastly and angelic beings alike inhabit Revelation's landscape of numbers: a celestial woman descended from heaven, a dragon that attacks her, woman, a beast, a lamb, Satan, and a warrior Messiah. Their battle on the plains of Armageddon, the last conflict on earth, precipitates the final judgment of all dead and the arrival of a new Jerusalem on earth. Taken together, landscape, entities, and events constitute the resilient, textual danse macabre of Revelation. It has inspired an enduring literary tradition of learned millennialism among Christian clergy, exemplified by pastors such as Jonathan Edwards and Pablo Richard.[6] It has helped instill, as well, a grass roots passion for millennial ideas that persists into the present, as pointedly revealed in the enormous popularity of the Left Behind millennial fiction series of the late twentieth century.[7]

The three major institutional manifestations of Christianity— Orthodoxy, Roman Catholicism, and Protestantism—acknowledge different collections of biblical texts as canonical, yet each includes Revelation in the canon it recognizes. As a consequence, the primary biblical text associated with millennialism is part of the collection of authoritative texts of the entire Christian tradition.[8] Nonetheless, church leaders rarely advocated millennial belief. In fact, an anti-millennial stance was far more common among them. In his monumental tome, *City of God*, Augustine decisively deflated millennial expectations by insisting that

God's final judgment happens every day and that the millennium referred to the entire Christian era.[9] What scant endorsement early Church fathers were inclined to extend to millennialism vanished after the third century.[10] According to historian Richard Landes, medieval church leaders of the Latin West were so intent upon discouraging millennial expectations that they altered the common calendar multiple times to defuse recurrent waves of popular millennial enthusiasm.[11] Like a parent putting an item her children are not to touch on a high shelf, dates that had become associated with the end of time in popular imagination were moved out of reach each time Christian clerics altered the year.

During the 1500s, Protestant leaders, who stressed the centrality of biblical authority, furthered their movement by taking advantage of an expanding printing press technology to disseminate their teachings. This same technology was also put to use increasing the availability of biblical writings, often translated into accessible, colloquial languages by Protestant scholars in an attempt to increase lay access to biblical texts.[12] This constellation of factors produced a situation in which greater numbers of Christians had direct access to the textual base of millennial belief and thus the potential to bypass ecclesiastical impediments to it, though this was no guarantee that any would do so.

In spite of this dearth of authoritative institutional support, millennialism has been a popular religious belief throughout Christian tradition.[13] From the earliest followers of Jesus to the Millerites, from the Cult of Mary to the Calvary Chapel movement, a persistent steam of Christian believers have embraced the second coming of Jesus and his millennial rule as a pivotal tenet of their faith.[14] As persistent as millennial beliefs have proven to be, those holding them have never achieved a consensus on either the manner of Jesus' return or the relationship it has to the millennium. The dominant interpretive currents are post-millennialism and pre-millennialism. Post-millennialists believe that the divine plan for humanity will eventually transform the world into a kingdom of heavenly peace and justice. In addition, some believe that this heavenly society will be one over which the Christian church, as the social embodiment of Jesus, will rule for a thousand years. Pre-millennialists expect Jesus to return bodily to earth and to rule over it for a thousand years of earthly peace and justice.[15] Biblical literalists, they interpret Mark 13:26, in which Jesus refers to a "Son of Man coming in clouds," to mean that Jesus—their interpretation of the "Son of Man"—literally will return to earth on a cloud. Practically the only thing pre- and post-millennialists agree upon is that the epoch of peace and justice that Jesus will either occasion or sustain will endure for a thousand years; hence each commonly uses the term "millennium" to refer to it.

Because destruction and judgment are integrally linked to the final transformation of the cosmos in Revelation, millennialism elicits a peculiar combination of fear and hope in pre-millennialists who appropriate Revelation as literal biblical prophecy. These millennium "true believers" fear the battles and judgment they expect to accompany the world's end, but also hope for the rapture of the faithful and the divine transformation of the earth that they believe ultimately will follow.[16] Bernard McGinn refers to reading Revelation as "the obsession" for Christians, a response made intelligible by the realization that those pre-millennialists who deem Revelation biblical prophecy consider its passages a Rosetta Stone to the ultimate intentions of the divine.[17]

In the closing years of the twentieth century—the time immediately preceding the onset of a new thousand-year period according to the common calendar--millennialism attracted considerable interest from many sources. The post-millennial stream found expression in congregational spirituality and health programs, White House millennium conferences, and other irenic efforts to imagine and construct a more just society. The pre-millennial stream found its articulation in end-of the-century prayer vigils and pilgrimages to Jerusalem. In a development that reflected the commercialism of the age, millennialism was also transformed into a commercial product. Or, at least, the word "millennium" was. There were millennium films, television shows, books, clocks, computers. There was even, for a while, a millennium fashion line. Advertising programs designed to promote millennium artifacts gave the term "millennium" wide cultural exposure. But end-of-the-millennium marketing of the millennium largely excised "millennium" from its root in biblical texts, thereby diluting its significance to Christian traditions. Hence, while discourse about the millennium was an oppressively prevalent feature of 1998-1999 American culture, the teachings of John the Divine did not experience a comparable cultural eminence. Millennialism went up, way up; but, Revelation, to which it had been wedded for centuries, scarcely went anywhere.

As a consequence, excitement about the year 2000 and the new millennium was neither tightly connected to Revelation-based millennialism nor limited to the population of Christian congregations. Certain sociological changes furthered this trend. According to numerous studies, the highly mobile, media-dependent lifestyles favored by late twentieth century Americans serve to diminish the theological relevance of traditional religious group boundaries.[18] This development enabled millennial expectations to surface in alternate social groups including militias, some environmentalists, and the third wave of the feminist movement.[19] Thus, while Revelation's imagery adorns the millennial sermons of Christian fundamentalist pastors, non-Christian activist groups advocating quite similar scenarios flesh out their millennial vision with imagery unique to the group's cause.

One place where millennial visions with significant non-religious content regularly appear is in mass-mediated entertainment, with the television series *The X-Files* a paramount example.[20] Broadcast on Sunday nights at 9:00 p.m. EST on the Fox Television Network, The *X-Files* premiered on September 10, 1993. In its opening episode, titled "Pilot" and set vaguely in the present, the series introduced its two principal protagonists: FBI agents Fox Mulder, played by David Duchovny, and Dana Scully, played by Gillian Anderson. Mulder is an Oxford graduate recruited to work for the FBI, whose career at the bureau has taken a strange, mystic path. Scully, an M.D. with a specialty in forensics, is assigned to the Bureau's training facilities. *The X-Files* series opens on the day Scully is assigned by a high ranking FBI official to work with Mulder. Her assignment is to work with Mulder as his partner, while surreptitiously reporting on his activities to agency executives.

As Mulder is introduced in the early episodes of the first season, Scully's in-house espionage assignment does not seem completely unwarranted. Mulder is pensive, inwardly directed, driven by very personal demons. He is embarked upon a quixotic quest for "the truth" that alienates him from others in his institution and, as the audience gradually learns, almost everyone else he encounters. In keeping with a fashionable, if dubious, therapeutic trend, Mulder's truth quest is fueled by memories he recovered in regression therapy. As a result of his treatment, Mulder became convinced that aliens abducted his sister, Samantha, missing since the two were young children. At bureau headquarters, Mulder learns that starting in 1946, on the instructions of FBI Director J. Edgar Hoover, the FBI files its reports on inexplicable events under the letter *X*. Mulder attaches himself to these X-files and shapes his career within the FBI as the agent summoned when paranormal-seeming things occur. His grand obsession in *The X-Files* is to discover the truth about the role of aliens in his sister's disappearance.

Scully, by contrast, is a logical positivist. She is a skeptical scientist who has been assigned by bureau officials to observe Mulder and report back on his behavior. As Scully watches and slowly comes to sympathize with Mulder, the two become a team that specializes in investigating paranormal incidents reported to the FBI. Through their regular interaction, Scully comes to respect, although not share, Mulder's worldview as something that opens her eyes to new possibilities. Mulder, in turn, develops respect for Scully's thoroughness and level-headedness as traits that keep him human.

Countless examples of boundary-crossing give *The X-Files* an intriguingly postmodern aura. Presented in a docu-drama format, the series' graphic design includes white info-script that scrolls across the bottom of the screen at the start of each new scene. Accompanied by the sound of typing, it informs viewers about what they are about to be shown, thus mimicking location shots on a nightly newscast. *The X-Files* is blatantly and intentionally ambiguous regarding the relationship of its weekly plots to real life events. Its tone, format, and timely topics teasingly suggest that the series addresses real events; in many episodes, however, Mulder and Scully mug at the camera as if to insist that each show is firmly planted in the realm of fantasy. This ambiguity was introduced in the series pilot, which opened with the phrase, "The following is inspired by actual documented events." Although Chris Carter, *The X-Files* creator, ceased using the phrase after the first episode, subsequent episodes retained a docu-drama ethos. Fans question whether *The X-Files* frames entertainment as reality to startle, delight, and amuse, or presents reality as entertainment to disseminate government-censured information to a deluded public.[21] Through the regular use of topical events in its narratives, the show produces a postmodern relationship to reality among its audience. *The X-Files* elicits a suspension of disbelief toward its own narratives and, to the contrary, an engagement of disbelief toward official accounts of public life.

The reality-confusion it encourages is rather different from that in Shakespeare's day, when author and actor on occasion combined to make a story's plot and characters so compelling that audience members were pulled into the story. Instead, it comes through an irregular erasure of the wall between story details and daily news events such that it is unclear where fictionalization begins. In contrast to docu-dramas such as *America's Most Wanted*, which tailor factual events to produce a fictional story, *The X-Files* fictions teem with thick, empirical details that provoke some fans to wonder whether its stories are, at least in part, factual, as well as whether such distinctions are worthwhile or relevant to make.[22]

In *The X-Files*, the cohesion of time, plot, and narrative vary tremendously from week to week. Disregarding the Aristotelian unities, *The X-Files* is both a regularly progressing, open-ended serial and episodic. Some episodes move a continuing plot forward (for example, Mulder's search for Samantha, leading to his obsession with finding the truth "out there" about aliens, as in "Deep Throat", "Fallen Angel," "E.B.E.," "The Erlenmeyer Flask," and "Little Green Men"); others, like "Chinese Box" and "Slime," stand alone, allowing Scully and Mulder to explore unique events. Some episodes deal with the occurrences of a single day in the present. Others go back in time to establish the rationale for aspects of the main story line's development.[23]

Fragments of millennialism are scattered throughout the fictive landscape of *The X-Files*. That these fragments are aspects of millennialism as grounded in Revelation is suggested by the series' recurrent biblical and Christian subtexts. That they are pieces of millennialism is made evident by the series' preoccupation with signs of the times, as expressed covertly through the meanings and implications attributed to aliens. In the following, I address each of these issues and then discuss how the pieces of millennialism that appear in *The X-Files* in some ways resemble and in other ways dramatically differ from Revelation-based millennialism. Finally, I assess the implications of these continuities and differences for the public understanding of millennialism in particular, as well as its implications for viability of biblical religion in general.

The biblical and Christian subtexts of *The X-Files* are established in both direct and subtle ways. Many episode titles reflect an explicit Christian heritage, although rarely do the contents of episodes make this explicit. In the first year of the series (1993-1994), in an episode titled "Eve," a group of scientists clone human beings, all of whom develop severe psychotic symptoms. Only one Eve manages to control those symptoms through the use of psychopharmaceuticals. To people familiar with biblical writings, Eve connotes the first female created by God in Gen 1. When viewed against this Genesis subtext, the episode calls into question the ability of humans to create life and suggests that the creation of humans should remain the province of God. For those who viewed "Eve" with no knowledge of its biblical context, the story worked as well—most likely as a reprisal of the cloning controversy in contemporary bioethics.[24]

A subtle Christian subtext is implicitly maintained through the small cross necklace that Scully constantly wears, almost always visible regardless of her dress. In the second year of the series, a sub-theme was introduced that explored Scully's religious background and the role her cross plays in it. In the episode titled "Ascension," viewers learn that Dana Scully received the cross necklace as a gift from her mother, Margaret Scully, on Dana's fifteenth birthday.[25] Throughout the first season of the show, the adult Scully is shown incapable of either believing in or discarding her religious roots. Scully's attitude toward her cross reflects this ambivalence. She can neither set it aside nor fully claim its religious meaning. When Mulder queries Scully about the significance of the cross she wears, Scully claims that it holds only family meanings. But is this the case? The camera lingers on the cross as Scully issues her denial, inviting viewers to speculate on how credible Scully's claim is.

In the second episode of the story, titled "3," Scully is kidnaped. Mulder realizes Scully is in desperate straits when he finds her cross in a car trunk. He and the viewers know that Scully would never voluntarily take off her cross. Treating the cross as a fetishized substitute for Scully, Mulder picks it up and keeps it with him while he searches for her. The concluding episode has the title "One Breath." In it, Scully is finally found, but is seriously injured. She is taken to a hospital, where doctors say she may not live. When it becomes obvious that Scully will recover, Mulder places the cross necklace back in her hands, poignantly establishing the cross as a symbol firmly tied to Scully's identity.

The foreshadowing of Scully's struggle with faith is realized in the series' fifth season. Scully is no longer ambiguous about her Roman Catholicism heritage. While not a conventional Catholic believer, she does operate within Catholic tradition. In "All Souls," an episode that initially aired near the end of the series' fifth year, Scully makes her confession to a Roman Catholic priest. She also encounters an otherworldly creature that she later describes to a priest, who explains to her that what she saw was a seraph, a member of the highest rank of angels depicted in biblical texts. Scully's deepening relationship to Roman Catholic tradition is not generated by her acceptance of its official ideas or beliefs or by her participation in its social life, but as a response to the increasing enchantment of her reality. Confronted with evidence that a world beyond science exists, Scully tentatively embraces the possibility that traditional religion may contain valuable truths as well. Thus, hers is a very postmodern religiosity, well in keeping with the series' overall ethos.

Although these intertwined biblical and Christian subtexts undergird the symbolic world of the series, it would be a mistake to consider *The X-*

Files as part of the American evangelical church's efforts to use contemporary culture (for instance, with Christian rock music) as a missionary strategy. However, the persistent use of Christian symbols, figures, and myths in *The X-Files* indicates that the millennialism of the series should not be compared to Karl Lagerfeld's apparently ignorant use of parts of the Quran in a Chanel fashion line (subsequently withdrawn in response to Muslim protests). In *The X-Files*, Christian symbols, stories, and ideas are a central source of the meaning debris that spills across the landscape of Mulder and Scully's world. It is debris neither readily understands.

While differing from it in important ways, Scully and Mulder's situation is reminiscent of the concluding scene of *Planet of the Apes*, the 1968 film version of Pierre Boulle's *La Planete des Singes*. In the film's dramatic close, Taylor and Nova, two people walking down a beach, find the top third of Statue of Liberty lying askew in the sand. Taylor, an astronaut returned to earth after 700 years, understood what the statue had symbolized and what its broken abandonment implied. Upon seeing it, he fell to his knees and howled in despair. Nova (the "new" woman) had been born after the destruction of America. Because the statue held no meaning for her; she stared blankly at it. Like Taylor and Nova, Mulder and Scully encounter symbols in almost every episode. When they do, neither Mulder nor Scully exhibits Taylor-like despair, but they are too well educated to respond with Nova-like oblivion. Instead, they exhibit an interested ambivalence toward the artifacts of meaning they encounter.

Overall, it is ambiguity rather than belief or disbelief that characterizes the series' attitude toward the transcendent. For example, in the first year of the series (1993-94), in an episode titled "Miracle Man," Samuel, the 18-year-old adopted son of Christian evangelist Reverend Calvin Hartley, is presented as an authentic faith healer. In keeping with the ambiguity that characterizes almost all action in *The X-Files*, Samuel's ability to miraculously heal is a dubious gift. For example, Samuel brings Leonard Vance back from the dead; Vance later murders the people Samuel touches in order to discredit his ministry. Vance does this, he says, because his post-healing life was miserable. Samuel's sacred touch enabled Vance to survive the fire that would have ended his life, but his restored life was not a blessing but a curse.

According to the pre-millennial interpretation of Revelation, widespread and intense societal decay is a chief sign of the onset of the millennium.[26] Such intense decay exactly depicts the state of the world in

The X-Files. The government is corrupt. Individuals are corrupt. Water is corrupt. Families are corrupt. Sex is corrupt. Mulder and Scully wander through a universe in which everyone and everything cries out for change, for redemption.[27] Conditions are so bad in *The X-Files* universe that degenerate life forms, akin to Revelation's beasts, habitually emerge. In what would become a prototypical example of the impact of Earth's imminent degradation, the second year of the series (1994-1995) featured Flukeman. In an episode titled "The Host," Flukeman first came on the screen in the slop of a pit toilet. A bizarre hybrid, part human being and part worm, Flukeman was born of planetary pollution, his existence a symptom of earth's desperate plight.

In *The X-Files*, aliens are the paramount means by which distorted fragments of millennialism are introduced into the series. Episodes contributing to the ongoing narrative repeatedly suggest that a full-scale arrival of aliens on earth will end of human life as we now know it. This is not because aliens will introduce humanity to novel technologies or ideas that will transform earthly life into a post-millennial paradise, but because their full-scale arrival will entail a pre-millennial final judgment on all humankind, albeit a biological one. Human beings will be replaced by alien/human clones. Through a regular showcasing of alien/human cloning experiments, the series writers intimate that aliens' interest in earth is also derived from millennialism. Similar to the goal of the end-times story in Revelation, aliens come to earth to achieve nothing less than "a new creation." But the new being they wish to create is not suffused with justice; instead, it is derived from the intermesh of alien and human genetic materials—a socio-biological millennialism of the galaxy.

Heightening the effect of these millennial motifs are the important millennial patterns that help structure the series. Like Revelation, *The X-Files* exhibits a penchant for combining familiar and eclectic symbols. Much as the author of Revelation used images from the Hebrew Bible that were familiar in his day while introducing new ones that were considerably more opaque, *The X-Files* includes numerous traditional Christian symbols supplemented by symbols that are strange and novel.[28] The series' avid fans, known as X-philes, maintain several web sites where the symbolism of the series is analyzed and discussed. Like those who ruminate over Revelation, X-philes endlessly debate what these symbols and events portend. In addition, the way *The X-Files* episodes are shown is much like the circular patterns of Revelation. Just as Revelation repeats its important themes such as the end or the salvation of the just with no apparent logic to their order,[29]

The X-Files episodes are frequently and randomly repeated in a non-linear manner.

Strengthening the impact of these discrete millennial elements and patterns is an underlying organizational premise that is itself millennial. In every episode, Mulder is on a millennial search, looking for evidence not merely of alien life but of anything mysterious enough to shatter what he understands as the illusion of conventional reality. In Mulder's mental world, the central idea of millennialism, that there is import and purpose to life, comes out in a fractured way, through the nebulous hope that "the truth is out there." His millennial motivation is given concrete expression in a poster that adorns his spartan office. Beneath a photo depicting a UFO in mid-flight is the phrase, "I want to believe."

Given the postmodern tendency of audiences to appropriate the meaning they want from the products of mass mediated culture, there is, in my opinion, no one right way to interpret *The X-Files* (i.e., as fragmented millennialism). The series changes focus, intent, and perspective so frequently that an insistence upon interpretive consistency would contradict the series' essential diversity. Also, in keeping with its postmodern character, the manner in which fans appropriate meaning from the series does not necessarily entail erotic surrender to a singular meaning; rather, *The X-Files* encourages viewers to interpret the series in a myriad of ways. Fan mail attests to its success in this regard. In *The Chronicle of Higher Education*, one scholar wrote about her passion for *The X-Files* as something she shared with her students. She stated that while aliens are a major element of the series, they did not interest her. What attracted her to *The X-Files* and what made it "profoundly" American, she claimed, was its "disbelief and distrust—especially of centralized government."[30]

In spite of this interpretive variability, the regular occurrence of millennial themes and patterns in *The X-Files* does make a few overarching assessments possible. One is that the millennial motifs and patterns integral to *The X-Files* occur in a perverse form. Revelation-based millennialism has an outward orientation and a twin link to fear and hope. *The X-Files* millennialism is absent any connection to wider meaning or divine plans; hence, the millennialism of *The X-Files* offers no hope. To the extent that millennial themes and patterns appear in *The X-Files*, their assimilation into this vehicle of mass-mediated entertainment erases millennialism's historic universal and social aspects. Because their theological meaning has been terminated, I describe them as dead and my analysis of them an autopsy. The consequences are telling.

Where Revelation-based millennialism is necessarily social, the imploded millennialism of *The X-Files* is a frightening future that ensnares individuals into meaning webs whose transcendence has been exhausted and pressures them into accepting finite resolutions that bring them little hope. When "the day of judgment" comes in Revelation, humanity learns the meaning of human history, experiences ultimate judgment, and sees the face of God. If the millennialism of *The X-Files* ever takes place, humanity will be gone and alien/human clones will occupy the earth. The millennialism of Revelation confronts all of humanity with a singular, comprehensive meaning of life. The possibility that "the truth is out there" drives Mulder, as the poster in his office hints, but, in *The X-Files*, "out there" is never where the truth is found (on the infrequent occasions when writers attempt to portray something as true). Instead, truth and meaning in *The X-Files* comes from working out childhood repressions (so Mulder), or in the ability to reject faulty, albeit culturally respected paradigms of knowledge in favor of contradictory marginalia (as with Scully). Most frequently, it is deemed, the truth cannot be ascertained at all. "Believe the lie" is Mulder's latest slogan.

Revelation-based millennialism overtly draws upon Revelation and contextualizes its narrative in relationship to the life of Jesus, the history of Christian tradition, or both. In the millennialism of *The X-Files*, any explicit link between millennialism and a historic religious tradition has vanished. Instead, glimpses of Revelation, the bits of a shattered traditional narrative, glitter like fool's gold falsely promising meaning that is never delivered. Revelation-based millennialism has had a decisive impact on those whose imaginations it aroused to prepare themselves and the earth for heavenly transformation. People who avidly embrace Revelation-millennialism as a theological ideal have been inclined either to invest themselves in building a more just world through post-millennial social justice activism[31] or to curtail normal life activities in pre-millennial anticipation of a better world. This is quite a contrast to the millennial world of *The X-Files*, where the possibility of another world is more a nightmare than a dream and where a genuine encounter with someone or something wholly other does not augur transcendent judgment, but biological replacement. And, in the final analysis, even these fragmented millennial imaginings are possible only if they draw an audience with advertiser-desirable demographics and can fit between 1-1/2 minutes of commercials every 12 minutes.

The truncated emotions that *The X-Files* millennialism seeks to evoke the type of human desire shaped by the spread of global consumer capitalism are eerily compatible. Our reigning socio-economic paradigm depends upon the proliferation of people whose desires are directed toward the tangible goods of the present; moreover, these desires should be endless, capable of temporary relief, but never finally sated. For desire to be this resilient, it must be joined to the material, finite things of the world, to that which breaks down, decays, and must be replaced. What is the probable fate of millennialism in such a society? Based on the cultural success of *The X-Files,* the post-millennialism tradition is of little use, but pre-millennialism can be tolerated. In fact, it can even be celebrated as long as it is separated from the hope for a positive earthly transformation and harnessed to the business of maintaining and expanding consumer desire—as the pre-millennialism of The X-Files clearly demonstrates.

CONCLUSION

The idea that human life possesses a transcendent meaning that will eventually become clear to all is the central religious claim of Revelation-based millennialism. Similar claims can be found in the sacred texts of most world religions. However, for the immanent, materialistic value paradigm that sustains our global consumer economy, this idea is extremely problematic. Not surprisingly, the rational secular culture that enables capitalism to thrive provides little scope for traditional religious millennial energies, while efforts to assimilate millennialism find ready outlet.

The painful paradox of *The X-Files* is that, as an amalgam of New Age, New Thought, and noirish 50s paranoia embedded in a Christian subtext, it does function for many of its fans as a kind of popular culture "book" of Revelation. It is a material object through which they take stock of the span of their end-of-the-world anxieties and fears. But as entertainment, *The X-Files* assimilates viewers' millennial interest into amusement and mines their millennial energies for profit. To the extent it is successful in this regard, it also strengthens the plausibility of rational civil life necessary for the smooth functioning of our global consumer economy.

It is critical to note that the assimilation of millennialism that occurs in *The X-Files* raises issues well beyond intra-Christian argument. Amid cultural fragmentation, a competition for the imagination is under way over whether and how humanity will envision its ultimate future. In this competition, millennialism as a Judeo-Christian religious idea grounded in the biblical text of Revelation must contend with commodified fragments of itself like *The X-Files*. From the Heaven's Gate tragedy, it is sadly obvious that mass-mediated entertainment and millennialism can be fashioned into a popular culture religion capable of motivating people to end their own lives. With its imploded configuration and absence of constructive vision, *The X-Files* millennialism neither facilitates hope nor animates people to engage in social justice. But it does encourage people to be frightened, suspicious, and conservative. For the millennial message of *The X-Files* is that, as awful as the status quo may be, any dramatic change that transpires will almost certainly make life worse.

NOTES

[1] Though significant extra-biblical literature on millennialism exists, the only explicit biblical reference to the millennium outside Revelation is located in 1 Cor 15:23-28.

[2] In contemporary academic literature, scholars regularly categorize all date-driven, end-times beliefs as "millennialist" regardless of their religious genealogy; however, in this article I use "millennialism" in the more restrictive sense of end-times beliefs grounded in Christian tradition linked to the biblical book of Revelation that anticipate the return of Jesus to Earth.

[3] See, for example, Joel A. Carpenter, *Revive Us Again: The Reawakening of American Fundamentalism* (New York: Oxford University Press, 1997), 247-49.

[4] Rosemary Radford Ruether, "Healing the World: The Sacramental Tradition," in *Feminist Ethics and the Catholic Moral Tradition: Readings in Moral Theology* 9 (ed. C. E. Curran et al.; New York: Paulist Press, 1996), 564.

[5] For a good introduction to postcolonial theory, see Diana Bryndon, ed., *Postcolonialism: Critical Concepts in Literary and Cultural Studies* (New Jersey: Routledge, 2000).

[6] See, for example, Jonathan Edwards, *Works* (4 vols.; ed. Worcester; Boston: Leavitt & Allen, 1843); Pablo Richard, *Apocalypse: A People's Commentary on the Book of Revelation* (Maryknoll: Orbis, 1995).

[7] Tim LaHaye and Jerry Jenkins, *Left Behind: A Novel of the Earth's Last Days* (Wheaton: Tyndale House, 1995).

[8] In addition, the canons of all three contain the foundational texts of Jewish apocalypticism such as Daniel, and the four gospels contain eschatological sayings attributed to Jesus, such as: "Then they will see 'the Son of Man coming in clouds' with great power and glory" (Mark 13:26).

[9] Augustine, *City of God*, 20:3-29.

[10] Ruether, "Healing the World," 567.

[11] Richard Landes, "Lest the Millennium be Fulfilled: Apocalyptic Expectations and the Pattern of Western Chronography 100-800 CE," in *The Use and Abuse of*

Eschatology in the Middle Ages (ed. W. Berbeke et al.; The Netherlands: Leuven University Press, 1988), 203-4.

[12]Mark U. Edwards, *Printing, Propaganda, and Martin Luther* (Berkeley: University of California Press, 1994),109-30.

[13]David L. Barr, "The Apocalypse of John as Oral Enactment," *Interpretation* 40 (1986):243-56; Aron Gurevich, *Medieval Popular Culture: Problems of Belief and Perception* (Cambridge: Cambridge University Press, 1988); Stephen O'Leary, *Arguing the Apocalypse: A Theory of Millennial Rhetoric* (New York: Oxford University Press, 1995).

[14]See, for example, Norman Cohn, *The Pursuit of the Millennium: Revolutionary Messianism in Medieval and Reformation Europe and Its Bearing on Modern Totalitarian Movements* (New York: Essential Books, 1957); Robert Fuller, *Naming the Antichrist: The History of an American Obsession* (New York: Oxford University Press, 1995); David Katz and Richard Popkin, *Messianic Revolution: Radical Religious Politics to the End of the Second Millennium* (New York: Hill & Wang, 1998).

[15]George J. Marsden, *Fundamentalism and American Culture: The Shaping of Twentieth-Century Evangelicalism 1870-1925* (Oxford: Oxford University Press, 1980), 55-62.

[16]"Rapture" describes the belief of faithful Christians that they will be bodily assumed into heaven at some point in the unfolding of end-times events. For a concise summation of the differing interpretations regarding when this would occur, see Timothy P. Weber, *Living in the Shadow of the Second Coming: American Premillennialism 1875-1925*, (New York: Oxford University Press, 1979).

[17]Bernard McGinn, "Revelation," in *The Literary Guide to the Bible* (ed. R. Alter and F. Kermode; Cambridge: Harvard University Press, 1987), 548. For a firsthand demonstration of how pre-millennialists organize their end times ideas around Revelation passages, see Hal Lindsey and C. C. Carlson, *The Late Great Planet Earth* (Grand Rapids: Zondervan, 1977).

[18]Robert Wuthnow, *The Restructuring of American Religion: Society and Faith Since World War II* (Princeton: Princeton University Press, 1988).

[19]Tom Robbins and Susan Palmer, *Millennialism, Messiahs and Mayhem: Contemporary Apocalyptic Movements* (New York: Routledge 1997).

[20]The presence of millennial motifs in *The X-Files* should not be attributed to an interest on the part of commercial broadcasters in furthering religious ideas. As a new broadcast network, Fox needed to attract viewers. It has attempted to do this by developing a distinct identity for itself; thus, Fox introduced *The X-Files* as part of a counter programming effort against the established broadcast networks to create a viable, distinct identity. *The X-Files* helped Fox further its corporate aim because the series offered a novel delving into horror, a genre that the three major television broadcasters—ABC, NBC, and CBS—rarely broach. Like the Fox Network's decision to back the prime-time adult cartoon "The Simpsons," *The X-*

Files helped Fox create a commercial identity in the television media market. Thus, *The X-Files* is a striking example of one media company's attempt to survive amid the diverse meaning systems that are a critical characteristic of postmodern culture.

[21] Fan reactions are a regular feature of numerous X-Files web sites. A good clearing house for fan sites can be found at http://bedlam.rutgers.edu/x-files/.

[22] One of the most straightforward displays of the show's postmodern world view occurred near the end of the series third season, in an episode titled "Jose Chung From Outer Space." In this episode, the possible abduction of two teenagers—Chrissy Giorgia and Harold Lamb—is enacted and re-enacted according to the details supplied by a competing series of narrators, each of whom claims to know what happened, but none of whom agree, in certain cases even with themselves. See Eileen Meehan, "Not Your Parents' FBI: The *X-Files* and Jose Chung's *From Outer Space*," in *The Postmodern Presence: Readings on Postmodernism in American Culture and Society* (ed. A. Berger; Walnut Creek: AltaMira, 1998), 125-56.

[23] For a provocative academic cross section of X-Files studies, see David Lavery and Angela Hague, eds., *Deny All Knowledge: Reading the X-Files* (Syracuse: Syracuse University Press, 1996). Also see Jan Delasara, *Poplit, Popcult and the X-Files : A Critical Explanation* (North Carolina: McFarland, 2000).

[24] While people familiar with biblical texts can find it difficult to imagine that there are others who might be unaware of a connection between the name Eve and the biblical story of Adam and Eve, I regularly encounter such a lack of basic biblical knowledge in undergraduate classrooms at the small liberal arts college where I currently teach. In one introductory class in which most students were freshman, during a mid-semester discussion of Elie Wiesel's poignant semi-autobiographical book *Night*, not one of twenty students could identify or understand Wiesel's reference to Job or Job's suffering.

[25] This story of Scully's abduction was introduced as a plot device to cover for Gillian Anderson's absence during the latter stages of a pregnancy.

[26] See Cohn, *Pursuit of the Millennium*.

[27] Dan Noel argues, quite convincingly in my opinion, that relief from what I portray as the oppressively pre-millennial state of *The X-Files* world is provided by the wry attitude of Mulder and Scully toward the bizarre, oppressive circumstances they regularly encounter, as well as by the friendship the two share (public conversation at the 1997 Annual Meeting of the American Academy of Religion Annual Meeting during a Religion, Arts and Literature Session where an earlier generation of this chapter was presented.)

[28] For a thorough introduction to the relevance and familiarity of Revelation symbols to ancient Near Eastern peoples, see John J. Collins, *The Apocalyptic Imagination: An Introduction to the Jewish Matrix of Christianity* (New York: Crossroad, 1984).

[29] Adela Yanbro Collins, *The Apocalypse* (New Testament Message 22; Collegeville: Liturgical Press, 1979).

[30]Ruth Rosen, "The Sinister Images of 'The X-Files,'" *Chronicle of Higher Education* 43:4 (1997): B7.

[31]Lois W. Banner, "Religious Benevolence as Social Control: A Critique of an Interpretation," *Journal of American History* 60:1 (1973): 3-41.